# Political Parties in Local Areas

# Political Parties
# in Local Areas

*Edited by William Crotty*

*William Crotty*
*Samuel J. Eldersveld*
*Anne H. Hopkins*
*Dwaine Marvick*
*Richard W. Murray*
*Kent L. Tedin*

The University of Tennessee Press
Knoxville

Library of Congress Cataloging-in-Publication Data

Political parties in local areas.

   Bibliography: p.
   Includes index.
   Contents: An agenda for comparatively studying local
parties / William Crotty—The emergence of two-party
competition in the Sunbelt / Richard W. Murray and Kent
L. Tedin—Campaign activities and local party organization / Anne H. Hopkins . . . [etc.]
   1. Local elections—United States.   2. Political
parties—United States.   I. Crotty, William J.
JS395.P65   1986      324.273       86-7093
ISBN 0-87049-511-9

# Contents

# Illustrations

## Figures

## Tables

# Acknowledgment

We are particularly grateful to Mavis Bryant, former acquisitions editor of the University of Tennessee Press and copyeditor for this volume, for her excellent work. We would also like to thank Cynthia Maude-Gembler and Katherine Holloway, both of the University of Tennessee Press, for their considerable efforts in bringing this volume to publication. A number of our colleagues were especially helpful with their advice and guidance. Among these, we particularly appreciate the efforts of Cornelius P. Cotter, L. Sandy Maisel, Samuel C. Patterson, and Francis E. Rourke. We would also like to thank the anonymous readers of the manuscript whose comments were helpful and whose work was appreciated.

# Political Parties in Local Areas

CHAPTER 1

# An Agenda for Studying
# Local Parties Comparatively

*William Crotty*

## Introduction: A Party System in Dispute

Political parties are believed to be a significant contributor to a democratic polity. They perform group and issue aggregation, voter mobilization,
coalition-building, policy linkage, policy making, officeholder recruitment,
and accountability functions that other agencies either cannot perform with
any degree of efficiency or are too unrepresentative to perform in a manner beneficial to the society. Giovanni Sartori asserts that political parties
". . . are an instrument . . . for *representing* the people by *expressing* their
demands. As parties developed, they did not develop . . . to convey to the
people the wishes of the authorities, but far more to convey to the authorities
the wishes of the people."[1]

Robert Michels, one of the founders of the party organizational school of
analysis, agreed in his 1911 work *Political Parties* that "democracy is in-
conceivable without organization."[2] It "is the weapon of the weak in their
struggle with the strong . . . It is only by combination to form a structural
aggregate that the proletarians can acquire the faculty of political resistance
and attain to a social dignity."[3] As a consequence of these beliefs, and the
development of political parties to fill a void in representative systems not

*My thanks to Cornelius P. Cotter, David H. Everson, Anne H. Hopkins, Charles H. Longley,
and John S. Jackson III, for their comments on an earlier draft of this essay.*

anticipated by political theorists or constitution-builders, many observers and certainly most political scientists have come to feel that political parties are essential to the democratic enterprise.[4] The major students of political parties — V. O. Key, Jr.; Avery Leiserson; Frank Sorauf; Samuel J. Eldersveld; Maurice Duverger; Walter Dean Burnham; Dwaine Marvick; Charles Merriam; Harold F. Gosnell — have all, in one form or other, stressed the significance of political parties for the democratic enterprise.

The importance of political parties, then, is not in dispute. What is in question is the vitality of the party system and the quality of its contributions to contemporary governance.

The major intellectual debate among party scholars at the moment is the "party decline" thesis. Basically, the argument is not new. Political parties have never been well received,[5] and each succeeding generation seems to undergo its own critical reexamination of the health and adequacy of the party system.[6] And each generation seems to be left with the issue unresolved, yet with faith renewed that the political parties *should* remain viable for the collective good.[7]

The present debate over party decline is multifaceted. It centers around three areas. First, the evidence shows that the major parties' base in the electorate is eroding; fewer and fewer voters affiliate with the parties, and among those who do, the intensity of identification has lessened.[8] Second, the contention is that the parties have lost a great degree of control over their nominating processes, and in particular their presidential nominating process.[9] Nominations for elective office are believed to be the single most important function performed by the parties. And third, a number of groups and other government agencies now compete with the parties in performing their functions, thus weakening their position and forcing them to begin redefining their role in society. Single issue, ideological, and policy groups; political action committees (PACs); the federal funding of presidential prenomination and general election races; candidate-centered organizations; and for-hire professional consultants (pollsters, direct mail specialists, media advisors) all compete directly with the parties in performing services, mobilizing clientele groups and electorates, defining policy options, running campaigns, and even recruiting candidates.[10] Consequently, a series of recent studies, employing a variety of different approaches, have referred to the "demise," "decline," "decomposition," "dismantling," or "atrophying" of the contemporary political parties. The consequences are said to be uncertain but are presumed to be bad for the political system.[11]

Not everyone agrees. John S. Jackson III, for example, argues that despite two decades of critical assessments of the American parties, they still have shown a remarkable capacity for persistence.[12] While allowing that parties have changed, Jackson notes:

> The parties have not disappeared as viable organizations; in fact, in some ways they may be more viable than ever, particularly at the top . . . The parties have not disappeared in the minds and allegiances of the American voters . . . In fact, the two major parties may now be more sharply focused than ever in defining the issues and choices that face the voters . . . Certainly the Party in Government has not disappeared; on the contrary, it may be as strong as ever in performing its role of integrating the various fragmented parts of the structure of American government.[13]

There is evidence to support Jackson's contentions. Cornelius P. Cotter, James L. Gibson, John F. Bibby, and Robert J. Huckshorn have engaged in a systematic comparative study of state party organizations, assessing such things as organizational maturation, party and leadership professionalization, resource availability, campaign involvement, electoral mobilization, and policy initiatives and implementation. They uncovered a greater degree of state party activity than anticipated, along with indications that state party organizations, while presently classifiable as "moderate" (the modal categories were "moderately strong" for Republicans, which included 60 percent of the Republican state parties; and "moderately weak" for the Democrats, which included 57 percent of the state Democratic parties), may actually have strengthened over the period from the early 1960s to the late 1970s.[14] The authors use recall data and individual projections back into time. Based on their examination of these, they conclude "that party organizations scored substantially higher on the organizational strength measures at the close of the 1970s than in the early 1960s. In terms of the generally accepted thesis of party decline, these data have startling implications: the year in which *The American Voter* appeared (1960) marked the beginning of a decade or more of growth for party organizations. As subjective attachments weakened in the 1960s and 1970s, the level of party organizational strength increased."[15]

Cotter and his associates extended their analysis to "local parties." The sampling unit was the county party, and the respondents were asked to rate aspects of precinct party activity. The authors compared their findings with a related nationwide county study, based on a a 1964 survey by the Center for Political Studies and analytically developed by Paul A. Beck.[16] From their analyses, they concluded that while heavily personalized and less bureaucratized than the state parties, the local parties countrywide in the late 1970s were substantially more active than in 1964.[17] The local parties did sustain a fairly high level of programmatic activity; "a significant minority of such organizations conducts some party-maintenance activity in non-election periods"; and "local party organization strength is relatively independent of the strength of the state party organizations."[18]

Cotter et al. are aware, as they diplomatically put it, that their study and its results "complicate" the party demise thesis. They argue two things: that "dissimilar and maybe even compensatory change" may take place in the different component parts of the party system (electoral party, organizational party, governmental party), and that the party's organization must be given separate weight and attention in any discussion of party transformation.[19]

The party-in-decline controversy would suggest that, for better or worse, parties from local to national levels may be becoming progressively weaker, less effective contributors to democratic representation. Is this true? Or more accurately, how true, or in what situations, are such contentions valid? Are the parties changing? Most would agree that they are. But if so, in what manner, and with what consequences for governing? for the quality of public representation? for the future of the political parties themselves? Can we address such questions in relation to the local parties? What have the studies on local parties contributed to our understanding of the state of their present health?

There is evidence, then, that political parties at the state and county levels may be better organized, have command of greater resources, and be in a better state of repair—actually becoming stronger—than has been known or anticipated.[20] The explanations for this strength may be convincing, or the phenomenon may be transitory, a lag in the broader evolution of a party system in transition. American parties may also be in the process of becoming more nationalized, although such a development in itself need not refute any arguments concerning local decline or stagnation and in fact might contribute to a lessening in significance of the local party units. The Democrats have nationalized their presidential selection process.[21] The national Republican party is providing services and resources to candidates and state and local parties at a rate never previously seen in this country.[22] And public funds are being used to meet the costs of presidential prenomination and general election campaigns and national party conventions, and, through the national parties and less directly, to subsidize state and local party activities.[23] How has all of this affected the local parties (defined more specifically as the urban-based or community-based party)? Are they stronger? Are they more relevant to their constituents and to urban policy making and representation? or less? Have their duties been preempted by higher-level party organizations? or by the PACs, candidate organizations, campaign consultants, and the media?

Who is to say? We know so little about the urban, suburban, and small-town parties that we have at best a limited baseline as to past or present activities, from which to establish: what they did; to what degree and in what manner they have been, and are presently, organized; what contributions they have made or are making to governance; and how they have fared during the contemporary era in their quest for survival.

The studies in this volume, implicitly and at times explicitly, first of all address these concerns. Each one attempts to assess the vitality, organization, and operation of the urban party. The cities chosen for analysis, should be representative of broader tendencies. Detroit and Chicago provide two examples of local party adjustment to the declining economic base of the frost belt. The Los Angeles analysis focuses on a city and a region historically less sympathetic to traditional party politics and more receptive to the "new politics" of volunteerism, candidate-centered organizations, and campaign-by-media. Houston and Nashville give evidence of how local parties in historically one-party urban areas are adjusting to the economic and (especially in Houston) population changes that have led to an emerging Republican vote and a potentially more competitive politics. Each of the studies makes a contribution to an understanding of the contemporary status and operations of local parties. In addition, the studies of Detroit and Los Angeles offer longitudinal comparisons that can be used to address directly the question of the parties' demise. Such studies, it would seem, are needed in order to make any intelligent assessments of the responsiveness of the local parties to their changing political environments.

## Researching Political Parties at the Local Level

A second concern in developing the present studies was to produce a broadly collaborative effort that would begin to address questions of continuing significance in social science research—studies that might provide one baseline for future and related works. The studies would build on previous research while permitting variation of efforts in response to differing political cultures and locales (see below).

In developing an overview of the work on community-level political parties, we may begin by emphasizing the differences in context and environment encountered at the local level. It is likely that local parties are products of their immediate political and social environments and their past histories.

This is not unusual. Political parties in the United States are dependent variables, structures that evolved to serve political needs within their cultures. What might well be unusual, however, is the extent to which local communities are independent of the forces that shape state-level and national-level parties. Consequently, it may well be that the community level—more than, for example, the state level—is likely to spawn a wide variety of party operations in response to the varied influences operating in a given immediate political culture. Further, the interrelationship between local parties and those at significantly higher (state or national) levels is likely to be sporadic, circumstantial, and unimportant, of no great concern to either set of parties and of no great significance in their operations. That is to say, (a) the urban culture offers an enormous variety of contexts for the parties to operate within, with varying degrees of efficiency and bureaucratization; and (b) the contexts of local politics—the conformity and value structures; the settlement and economical industrialization patterns; the ethnic, social, and religious composition of the electorates—are likely to exert an influence on local parties powerful enough to result in agencies that bear little resemblance to and have few ties of any consequence to, party organizations at higher levels. Local parties may be just that: creatures of the local environment.

To a large extent, the literature on local parties has at least implicitly recognized this local autonomy, producing a variety of studies of given communities and perceiving a range of party environments and operations —from the classic studies of the urban machine, to those of parties, in whatever form they may be found, struggling to survive in communities with nonpartisan local elections. Taken in such a context, the literature is varied and colorful, constituting one of the oldest and most voluminous lodes in the political science repertoire.

### At the Polar Extremes: The Urban Machine and the Nonpartisan Electoral Environment

Generations of students have heard of the exploits of the legendary Boss Tweed of New York, Boston's genial James Michael Curley, or the dour but highly successful Mayor Richard J. Daley of Chicago. For some, the once-despised machine, the bête noire of the earlier Progressive Era, came to symbolize the most perfect of the party organizations, one that seemed destined never to be paralleled nationally.[24]

The literature of the machine boss is rich in romanticism and nostalgia.

For example, analyses of the most recent, and possibly the last, of the legendary urban bosses, Daley, and his machine go by such colorful labels as "Clout," "Himself," and, of course, "Boss."[25] The commentaries on the urban machine extend back at least to Bryce and Ostrogorski and provide one of the most descriptive and entertaining sets of readings in the social sciences.[26] The urban machine has been in decline for generations.[27] What do we know of the present state of the machines or the political parties that have attempted to fill in for them at the local level?

Curiously, we know less of these than we do of the operations and consequences of partyless systems at the local level. We *can* say something about the effects that the absence of political parties has on the conduct of public business. Nonpartisan elections, a residue of the Progressive Era and one attempt to restrict the power of the party in urban politics, hold sway in roughly two-thirds of the three thousand cities with population over five thousand in the United States.[28]

The effort to take the parties out of politics in American cities touched a deep chord in the American people. The movement appealed to a Jeffersonian belief in the efficacy of government as a public trust, and to a radical democratic concern with individual initiative, professionalized expertise, and personal involvement in government. Strains of nativism; an antipathy to the ethnic and religious groups that settled the cities; a middle-class conservatism and status-quoism, opposed to the evolving new politics of government (and political party) as advocate and intervenor in the distribution of economic and social rewards; the blatant dishonesty and corruption of the urban machine—all these contributed to the spread of nonpartisan politics.

The results were not those anticipated. If anything, nonpartisan elections affirm the value of political parties to a community. According to various studies, nonpartisan elections decrease involvement, interest, and turnout in elections; favor those of higher socioeconomic status; are more resistant than partisan-based electoral systems to social and political change; increase the advantages enjoyed by the incumbents; result in less serious, less policy-oriented campaigns at the local level; and are less effective in keeping office-holders accountable.[29] Nonpartisan electoral systems provide a primer in the functional relevance of political parties to democratic governance.

If this assertion is true, the neglect of continuing research on local parties is difficult to understand. Perhaps the answer lies in the fact that they are at once so close, close enough to be overlooked as subjects of serious academic concern, while at the same time they are remote, difficult to conceptualize adequately and to explore in a meaningful, comparative framework.

### Perspectives for Studying Local Parties

What is the present status—the vitality, operations, and contributions—of political parties in those urban areas that have them? What do we know of these agencies, their operations, their intraorganizational ties to state and national parties, and their relationships with their constituencies? What do we know of their role in policy making and representation? Unfortunately, our knowledge is fragmentary, and much of the evidence we do have that bears on these questions may be outdated. Concern with local political party performance has not kept pace over the last several decades with the study of political parties at the national or state levels or of behavioral developments in other related areas. Now may be a good time to rekindle the exploration of such fundamental concerns. And a good way to begin would be to return to the roots, review the promising work formerly done in the area, and assess its relevance to a new concentration on the local parties and their role in allocating rewards and linking ruler with ruled. A quick mental scan of the literature brings to mind Harold F. Gosnell's classic early study of the machine in Chicago;[30] the efforts, only partially successful, to integrate party institutions with voter decision making in Elmira and to delineate the role of the party in mobilizing voters;[31] and work on the influence structure, including the role of the local party and its leaders, in selected areas of policy making in an urban setting (Chicago).[32] None of these studies is in any sense recent. Yet one would be hard pressed to think of works of equal scope or imagination published in the last decade or so.

A comprehensive effort to assess the relevance of previous work for future explanations will not be attempted here.[33] What we will try to do is suggest the utility of three theoretical orientations, each in its own way familiar, in approaching the problems of comparative urban parties' research. The three are: organization research; a service (constituency) functional theoretical focus; and a party activists/recruitment perspective.

### The Party Organization

During the last several decades the number of studies of local party organizations, once considered a promising point of departure for the development of a social-science data base in party performance,[34] has been limited. The most influential study, one that seemingly could have shown the way for a generation of party scholars, was Samuel J. Eldersveld's analysis of political party organization and operations in Detroit.[35] Eldersveld's investigation was conceptually and thematically impressive. To explain and guide parties' research, it introduced into the working vocabulary of the urban parties' specialist the concept of "stratarchy," decentralized layers of political decision makers with different group boundaries and characteristics within the party hierarchy.[36] The survey methodology employed in the field research met the concerns of behavioral research; the data were thoroughly developed; and the resulting publication of findings constitutes the most thorough depiction of an urban party in the contemporary literature.

The field research for the project was conducted in 1956 and 1957, and the results were published in 1964. The hoped-for spur to comparative urban parties' explorations never materialized, however. For reasons that are unclear efforts to duplicate Eldersveld's work in other localities have encountered difficulty. In fact, Eldersveld's continued sampling of Detroit precincts at eight-year intervals (1956, 1964, 1972, 1980) and Dwaine Marvick's serial studies of middle-level activists in the Los Angeles parties may represent the only sustained, over-time research of consequence on local party operations.[37]

This state of affairs seems especially sad when one considers the related work in organizational structure and effectiveness by Peter H. Rossi and Phillips Cutright, among others, and the long line of demographic and political profiles of urban party activities. In an earlier age, the work of Gosnell, Sonya Forthal, Frank R. Kent, J.T. Salter, William E. Mosher, David H. Kurtzman, and Roy V. Peel is memorable.[38] The last three decades have seen broadly related themes in the research of Hugh A. Bone, James Q. Wilson, Samuel C. Patterson, Robert A. Salisbury, Robert S. Hirchfield, Bert E. Swanson, and Blanche D. Blank, Lewis Bowman and G.R. Boynton, M. Margaret Conway and Frank B. Feigert, and Lee S. Weinberg, among others.[39] Conceptually and substantively, however, little of consequence has been added to these lines of inquiry in recent years.

There are recent exceptions, of course, and related, alternative avenues could be pursued. Joseph Schlesinger's work is one example.[40] In an effort to link a theory of party organization to one of competitive democratic elections, Schlesinger takes as his point of departure the rational man–economic modeling approach. His definition of political parties is borrowed from Anthony Downs ("a team seeking to control the governing apparatus by gaining office in a duly constituted election"[41]). In such a perspective voters are posited as choosing among or, in the American context, between the candidates and policy positions put forward by the major parties. The voters are *not* seen as an intrinsic or integral part of a political party per se.

They are consumers investing in the marketplace by their response to and choice among the competing brand names and advertising appeals of the parties and candidates.

From these assumptions, Schlesinger then moves on to address questions of organizational maintenance, output, and worker/participant motivation and satisfaction. Political party behavior and organization is dominated by marketplace demands (the need to win elective office), more perhaps than that of other bureaucratic organizations. It offers collective goods (winning elections, influencing policies), but the payment to the individual is so marginal and indirect that side payments—personalized, private benefits (see Eldersveld's essay in this volume)—evolve to keep active the relatively small number involved in party work.[42] In part, this emphasis could answer one of the questions raised earlier. While the party-in-the-electorate appears to be reformulating its relationship to the parties (seen in the party decline thesis, with its emphasis on less party-line voting, weaker individual party ties, and proportionately fewer people identifying with the parties), party organizations appear to be maintaining a reasonably consistent level of party strength over time (the work of Cotter et al., Eldersveld and Marvick in this volume). The organization survives because it supplies private goods (friendship, sociability, loyalty) to its participants. According to Schlesinger, "the political party offers collective benefits, compensates its participants indirectly, yet is market-based. From this unique combination of properties flows the peculiar character of the party and its ability to adapt to a changing world."[43]

Schlesinger's contribution is clear in focus and more theoretical than that usually found in the parties' literature. But there are problems. He stresses the severity of the market-based standard ("trial by elections is a ruthless test") and the relative purity of the parties in meeting such a criteria[44]; yet in a market sense, the two major American parties are not seriously challenged by competing party organizations in any semblance of a "free enterprise"context. To fail totally, they have to be virtually completely out of touch with the major public sentiment of the day and then for lengthy periods of time (the pre–Civil War period is an example). It is a cartel arrangement, a monopolization of the market by two giants, and one sanctioned in law. Realistically speaking, the two major parties have no competitors. The voter takes what is offered by the two oligarchic giants, or abstains. The marketplace analogy here seems a crude guide. Further, the dominance of the major parties has been written into law; they are legally recognized by the state and enjoy benefits in candidate recruitment, funding, and certification not available to potential competitors.

Alternative explanations may be found for the seeming discrepancy between continuing party organizational activities and weakened mass affiliation patterns. First, the comprehensive analysis of party organizational operations is relatively new; for the most part, its measures of past party performance are not based on empirical data collected at a given point or over time. Rather, such comparisons depend on projections by today's actors concerning past party conduct. Such data can be unreliable; their validity is hard to assess. Memories can be faulty, and projections idealized or rationalized. Turnover in party organizations is notoriously fast, and party organizations are noted for their virtual absence of a collective memory.

Secondly, the gap between party organizational activity patterns and tendencies to mass disaffection may reflect a cultural lag; the organizations continue to perform in habitual response patterns, while the environment in which they operate changes. The effect of the contextual redefinitions may, on traditional organizational arrangements and operations, not be seen for another decade or more. In effect, this argument, as opposed to Schlesinger's, stresses the insularity of the political parties from ongoing market forces.

Finally, there is the simple question of analytic utility in approaching parties' research from the rational man-economic modeling perspective. The Schlesinger/Downs/Olson approach offers an overarching theoretical perspective for approaching party organizational questions, but one that (a) limits the scope of party concerns, and (b) reduces the party to a basic analytic unit that may lose as much in its economy scale as it offers in theoretical explanation. As Schlesinger himself notes:

> Nothing in the model ascertains how well the parties represent the variety of interests in the society, how good they are at articulating or moderating conflict, how well they are perceived by the electorate, how successful they are in inducing popular participation, how good they are at providing effective government, nor in how "responsible" they are in providing realistic alternatives.[45]

These are significant omissions. The analytic utility of such a market-based approach would depend on the questions on which the researcher chooses to focus.

Schlesinger concludes by arguing the lack of value bias in his approach: "Just as winning office is simply instrumental and thus neutral to other political values, this model is also neutral."[46] Is it? Every approach has its value assumptions and its weaknesses. What type of concerns can it address? To whom are these important? What does it omit? The utility of the perspective is determined by the problem being analyzed and by what the researcher hopes to accomplish. In these regards, the Schlesinger/Downs/ Olson point of departure offers an organizational perspective different from those discussed above. The choice depends on the investigator's conception of the most important questions in parties' research and of those most urgently requiring understanding.

There have been no lack of promising leads. The organizational perspective is one of the most challenging.[47] Eldersveld's study of Detroit is proof of what can be accomplished with it. His analysis provides a model—one possibly needing modification for current use—and a flexible theoretical perspective that both testifies to the relevance of the organizational focus and integrates the disparate types of data (survey-based attitudinal and opinion data with demographic and political quantitative data) and perspectives (organizational, performance-based, individually-oriented, and, implicitly at least, systemic).[48] The Eldersveld research, or some modification of it, could serve as a general manual for a modified study in the contemporary context.

### A Constituent-Based Party

There are, to be sure, other approaches. A service-based or loosely functional approach to local party activities could be a starting point for comparative research.[49]

What does (did) a local political party do for its supporters? What kinds of services does (did) it provide? What kind of linkage functions does (did) it fulfill?[50] What does (did) it get in return? How have the service and linkage functions changed over time? With what consequences for the party? for the voter? for decision making in urban areas? for the growth and importance of other groups that might have assumed some of these duties? What needs of their constituents do parties now serve? How effectively do parties perform their functions? And to what extent do the answers to these questions explain the position of parties in modern urban society?[51]

We know something of what local parties tried to do in previous eras. How these functions are translated in today's world, and the extent to which the services offered by parties today serve the needs of their present constituents, are problematical. Earlier studies indicated that a variety of services directed to an ethnic-based and lower-class constituency served as building blocks of the urban machines. Harold F. Gosnell compared the services offered by Chicago precinct captains in 1921 and 1936.[52] The focus in both years was much the same: material rewards and assimilative or adaptive functions. The brokerage functions listed by Gosnell, though changed in substance, would still appear to be of relevance now to a constituency-sensitive local party.

Richard T. Frost investigated related aspects of the service offerings of a sample of New Jersey county party leaders.[53] The leaders were selected through attributional nominations by local party activists in selected New Jersey counties, stratified by competitive patterns, geographic location, and urban-rural dimensions. The services provided by these party leaders and their organizations were not dissimilar to those provided by the Chicago ward organizations in the 1920s and 1930s.

Frost mixes categories, but the general emphasis is clear. A good deal of attention is given to material rewards, to serving as an advocate or intermediary with government, and to assimilative functions. One explanation for the demise of the machine was predicated on the belief that those functions had been assumed by the state during the New Deal period.

In Thomas M. Guterbock's case study of one Chicago ward in the early 1970s,[54] the point of departure is an examination of two exchange models, a material exchange model and an affectual exchange model. The first emphasizes personalized, segmented, and utilitarian motivations, primarily specific material incentives, for machine support. The second model is more diffuse, focusing on the cultural and social subgroup formations that bred machine loyalty. The two models are not contradictory, although they place different explanatory priorities on various types of incentives. Both "have in common the notions that the inducements [offered for local party support] are specific . . . and are made available on a regular basis in face-to-face encounters in the precincts."[55] As a consequence of his research, Guterbock offers a third, and related, explanatory position. He develops what he calls a "commitment model" that emphasizes the party's attempts to justify its relevance by "pursu[ing] a public strategy that articulates with the notions locally-attached residents have about what is best for their communities."[56] The local party attempts to develop its image in line with what its constituents believe to be the proper and legitimate role of the party in the public realm. How does a service orientation at the local level fit in with this conception of the party? Guterbock writes:

> The distribution of services is relevant to the success of ward politicians, for voters judge local leaders in part according to their performance as advocates of community improvement and monitors of city services. But these beliefs and judgements are formed on the basis of what the voter hears from acquaintances,

community leaders, the press, the pulpit, and the political candidates themselves. His or her vote is not controlled by direct linkage to party agents; it is won by the party's continuous efforts at legitimating itself. While the machine's supporters are certainly not models of informed and rational voting, they are not any less committed to democratic ideals than other mass constituencies. They give their support to a materially motivated party not because they lack political morality or knowingly act in violation of the norms of democratic citizenship, but simply because they do not perceive the party as being self-interested.[57]

It is an interesting idea. Within a city concepts of legitimacy may differ between blue-collar, ethnic neighborhoods and middle-class, business, and higher-income areas. They may also differ among areas of the county and among large, medium, and smaller cities. The extent to which the parties fit local expectations and norms of dependable or politically relevant behavior at this point can only be raised as an open question.

As for the services performed by the party for constituents, Guterbock found that while many activities were provided in the 1970s as they had been in the 1920s and 1930s, the orientation was different: "Very few voters today receive grants of material value . . . The largest proportion of the services the party provides are of the least significant types—provision of information and mediation services—or they are priority referrals which expedite routine maintenance services that have little significance for the fundamental welfare of the citizen."[58]

Yet it is likely that the services provided by the ward organizations in Chicago exceed those of local parties in other urban areas. And while the core nature of the services supplied has been in decline and material rewards to voters are less pronounced, the Chicago machine in the 1970s still was able to maintain its dominant political position. The reasons for this are not difficult to find. A survey of ward voters found that 72 percent of the respondents believed that the local Democratic party would help them out with a problem if asked to; 50 percent would seek help for local problems from a political figure within the ward; 77 percent knew that they had a Democratic precinct committeeman in their precinct; over 80 percent could name their Democratic precinct committeeman, ward committeeman, or alderman; and just under 60 percent knew their precinct captain by sight.[59] In this ward the local party was visible to its constituents, played a role of consequence in their lives, and, not incidentally, reaped the political reward. How many local parties can say as much?

Guterbock makes no attempt to integrate a service orientation with the broader organization and electoral activities of the local party or to extend his findings beyond the ward in which he did his field research. Nonetheless, the citizen-directed efforts of the party in this one area do provide, first, an insight into how an effective local party organization relates to its base and, second, one gauge of party performance at the local level, against which to measure party activities in other localities.

The number of studies of this nature is limited. We have presented representative examples in more detail than their contributions to an understanding of local parties might warrant, because they are not well known, have not been widely replicated, and provide a manageable point of departure for related comparative research. The locus of research can be narrow (precinct, ward), can differ by geographical area or size of city, and can focus on different party levels (ward, city, district, state). The research is relatively straightforward and easy to execute and does not encounter the problems implicit in the more complex organizational investigations.

A more elaborate theoretical justification for such work could be developed, if needed, by combining what are essentially highly-focused empirical investigations with a modified version of functional analysis. The resulting perspective would be broad and diffuse, conditions that indicate both its strengths and weaknesses.[60] Additionally, it would have the virtue of accommodating comparative and even cross-national studies in a variety of settings. Nonetheless, it would not appear to be a necessity for such research ventures at this juncture.

*Party Activist / Recruitment Approaches*
A third and more popular approach in political parties' research has been to focus on party activists or recruitment problems. Such research has investigated the means or institutions through which categories of political actors have entered political life and such actors' identifications, demographic characteristics, socialization backgrounds, professionalization and career advancement patterns, policy views and ideological commitments, introductory and sustaining motivational drives, and activity styles. This approach has become a staple of political research in many areas of political science and characterizes much of Marvick's and Eldersveld's work.[61]

The research is guided by several assumptions: (1) that there is an elite with identifiable group bonds that exercises authority in any given political situation, (2) that the defining characteristics (demographic, attitudinal, experiential) that distinguish the group can be identified, (3) that those background factors contribute to the thinking and behavior of those so identified, and (4) that a knowledge of such group attributes and recruitment processes contributes to an understanding of political institutions.

This perspective has had a long line of advocates. Justifications for and applications of the approach trace back to Vilfredo Pareto, Gaetano Mosca, Robert Michels, and Max Weber, among others.[62] The logic and appeal of this line of inquiry are not difficult to identify.

Mosca advanced the argument for a "ruling class" that directed social behavior, one that "performs all political functions, monopolizes power and enjoys the advantages that power brings."[63] For Mosca and his intellectual descendants, the key questions were who formed this ruling class and whose interests they represented.

One answer to this question, a partial one, is to identify the social background of the members of the political elite that exercises power. A person from one social subgroup will perceive events and act on these perceptions differently than one from another subgroup.[64] It is likely that he or she will behave differently and represent different interests. In short, we are all products of our environments. By knowing this and by developing descriptions of the specific strands that tie political actors to their social substratums, we begin to lay the groundwork for differentiating their objectives and explaining their behavior. It is a necessary beginning in any such research undertaking.

A related, and complementary, approach (in fact, the two often are not distinguished) is to focus more on the recruitment of political actors. This perspective accepts the assumptions previously developed and augments these with institution-oriented and process-oriented investigations, yielding a more dynamic picture than the former approach, which is often cross-sectional, a snapshot in time (a point to which we will return).

Moshe M. Czudnowski has put forward one justification for employing a recruitment perspective in research:[65] recruitment investigations provide a linkage between the society at large and its political sphere. There are tensions implicit in the relationship:

1. A political order requires institutional continuity, but continuity implies a turnover of personnel.
2. Policy-making aims at relevance, consistency, and effectiveness, but society displays continuous social, economic, and cultural change.
3. Government is predicated on authority, but the maintenance of authority is subject to legitimization through responsiveness or responsibility to society.[66]

Czudnowski claims that "the manner in which each of these dilemmas is resolved at any given time depends on the prevailing patterns of political recruitment and the changes occurring in these patterns."[67] Recruitment studies can make a signal contribution, first, by developing the linkage between the polity and the broader social system and, second, by providing insight into the relationship between political change and the maintenance of social order, as a basis for illuminating theoretical and research concerns of significance to the political scientist. Political parties are frequently viewed as linkage agencies and contributors to the societal patterns of stability and change. In addition, parties themselves have their own internal dynamics of growth, homeostasis, and decline. Consequently, this perspective can have particular relevance for parties' research.

To the extent they can be realized, these benefits alone would justify such investigations. Czudnowski goes on to argue that recruitment studies also help to indicate the relevance of politics for achieving nonpolitical goals, one criterion in comparatively assessing the nature and performance of competing political systems.

Moreover, research on recruitment could also add a degree of understanding to several theoretical concerns basic to the discipline: the split between macro- and micro-level analyses; the "what is" versus "what should be" orientations of political thinkers; the difference between institutional and legal as against individual and behavioral approaches; and the gulf between the staticism of time-bound research and the reality of constant political change.[68]

Whatever its ultimate merits, the recruitment approach has been widely used. The potential for comparative research of consequence is appreciable. For example, Marvick and Eldersveld recently coedited in the *International Political Science Review* a collection of research pieces, all comparative and several cross-national. They employed an activist/recruitment point of view to advance the argument that in such studies: "System differences [can] emerge . . . from comparative analysis. The relevance of political generations, and of socio-political environment changes, [can] appear in the longitudinal analysis. The factors contributing to activism [can be] . . . suggested in the causal theory utilized. [And] the consequences of party activism for parties and for the system [can be] implied, if not explicitly demonstrated, . . . [by such] studies."[69]

This then is a promising line of inquiry, and in fact the editors hoped that their journal issue might "constitute a beginning for cross-national research on party elites."[70] Much of Eldersveld's work has been in this vein. Eldersveld has tied activist/recruitment questions to broader research concerns: the linkage between environment and party role, the interrelationship between party elites and organizational adaptability, and the comparative assessment and promotion of like-minded research.[71]

In the present volume, Eldersveld combines a comparative perspective with a longitudinal one, comparing the social characteristics, political perspectives, experience levels, and policy, organizational, and motivational commitments of party activists in both Detroit and Los Angeles in 1956 and 1980. From these comparisons he devises a model to explain the differential levels of party involvement. Social concerns, loyalty, political aspirations, and ideology (liberal for Democrats, conservative for Republicans) are important influences on members of both parties. Demographic factors work somewhat differently within the two parties, with race and education having more explanatory power within the Democratic than within the Republican party. The analysis could serve as a basic exploratory piece for related studies in other urban localities.

Marvick has engaged in a series of creative analyses of attitudinal dimensions associated with party activism in Los Angeles comparatively and over time (1963, 1968, 1969, 1972, 1974, 1976, 1978, 1980).[72] He has advanced a rationale for a "developmental approach" emphasizing continuities in changes in political actors and institutions, and meant to transcend the static and time-bound limitations of most activist/recruitment research undertakings.[73] Marvick is more interested, for example, in longitudinal examinations of the role performance, within an institutional and political environment, of the cadremen, or middlemen, that he focuses on, than he is in inferring values or commitment from social background characteristics.

Much of Marvick's work has been experimental and provocative, as are his contributions to this volume—on the substance of the activists' communications, on their perceptions of the utility of issue positions and campaign strategies within their immediate political environments, and on the stability of their policy commitments and ideological self-ratings over time. Marvick also examines the relative balance in ideological perspective among rival Democratic and Republican cadremen in Los Angeles, a problem he has explored before,[74] and, for the 1980 election year, the perceptions of contrasting campaign activities engaged in by various party and other groups (candidate groups, PACs, higher-level party organizations) within the respondent's community. Marvick finds an insularity in perceptions and knowledge among activists; most focus on their own activities and have little information about or interaction with rivals. Cadremen differentiate among voters on an issue basis; give evidence of being more receptive to the value of "emotionalizing, personalizing, negativizing, and counter-smearing"[75] in campaigning; and become more pragmatic and skeptical in adjusting to the pressures of political life. A knowledge of the personal values and strategic decision making of such middlemen helps to understand the manner in which campaigns are formed and policy and candidate choices presented in a democratic society. The activists shape the boundaries and alternative choices to which most of us respond; this area of investigation has been much neglected. Marvick's work is innovative and, beyond its substantive contributions, frames a research agenda others might borrow from in related research efforts.

*Where Does This Leave Us?*
Each of our three perspectives makes its own contribution. Each has enjoyed success and is relatively easy to apply. Still, the systemic execution of recent rigorous comparative social science investigations of the urban party is rare.[76] The problem appears to center on the scarcity of available resources (funding for such studies is difficult to come by) and a lack of will and/or interest, rather than on the availability of role models for research, the originality and conceptual value of previous pilot studies, or the adaptability or applicability of research methods used in related undertakings. There are exceptions, of course; some of these have been mentioned. Overall, however, contemporary research on the urban political party has made only a limited contribution to the ongoing debate concerning political parties and their place in democratic governance.

## Researching Local Parties

Perhaps it would be profitable at this point to outline the types of data needed in order to assess the operations, relevance, and contributions of local parties. Such a list would include:

1. The social characteristics of the party activists and their civic representatives, i.e., the extent to which their demographic profiles correspond to those of the citizens of the areas in which they are active, their roots in the community (length of residence in neighborhood and area); and their ties to the community through involvement in civic groups and local associations.
2. The political background and experience of the party activists, expected to range from those with minimal investments of time and effort—the equivalent of volunteers for a library drive or United Fund canvass—to those whose extensive political experience and ambitions give them almost a "politics is a way of life" approach to party work.
3. Party activists' career pathways in government and politics, incentives and motives for involvement, resocialization during careers, and ambitions for the future.
4. The motivations of party activists, why they do what they do. These explanations can be expected to include a stress on ideological motivations (a feature of the "new politics" and a reflection of the changing political climate), as well as community service-connected reasons.

5. Linkage relations between local party personnel and other organizational levels—how frequently there are contacts upward, lateral, or downward within the party, and, also, with other politically relevant groups in the community; how well the party is linked to the public it attempts to mobilize and represent.

6. Perceptions and evaluations of the "environment" within which the party must work, and the manner in which that environment has been changing. Characteristics of the population, of voter support groups, of problems and conflicts in the community, of party competition and strength—all are relevant in this regard.

7. The party workers' orientations towards politics—their trust, efficacy, cynicism, inclinations toward split-ticket voting, and strength of party loyalty. Their participation in electoral and party activities and their evaluations of such institutions as the primary, the convention, the campaign process, and the parties themselves—institutions with which they are intimately familiar and within which they work—are important.

8. Party activists' views concerning how campaigns are and should be conducted and concerning campaign tactics and ethics.

9. Group affiliations, perceptions, and contacts of party workers (whom they see themselves representing).

10. The activists' issue positions, ideological self-ratings, and rankings on a liberalism-conservatism scale, especially in relation to the populations they represent.

11. The extent of organizational activity of the party at the local level and its effect, especially in relation to campaign activities and election- and non-election-year contacts with voters.

12. Intraorganizational processes—democracy; decision-making, communication, and mobility patterns; and reward systems—within the parties.

13. The political culture and the political and demographic environment in which the parties contest: the degree of competition and participation in elections, the broader state and region political cultures, the demographic characteristics of voters, and the past history of political development in the city.

These represent only a partial listing of the types of information needed for a fuller understanding of local party operations and effectiveness. Limited it may be, but such reports are not now available and may not be for some time to come.[77]

Eldersveld has noted in another context that "local parties in a democratic society such as ours, if they are to maximize their power and role, are inclined to be nonhierarchical, open, voluntaristic, nonideological, and inefficient given the conditions of American society and political culture."[78] He goes on to add, however, that due to community variations there is "the possibility, indeed the capability, of local parties to move in other direc-

**Table 1.1. Dimensions for Evaluating Local Parties**

| *Dimensions* | *Party Types* | |
|---|---|---|
| Organization | Hierarchical | Decentralized |
| Decision making | Authoritarian | Democratic |
| Membership | Closed | Open |
| Careerism | Professional | Voluntaristic |
| Motivation | Economic, materialistic | Altruistic, social |
| Policy orientation | Nonideological, particularistic | Ideological, programmatic |
| Activities | Year-round, wide range of activities (campaign-oriented, social, fundraising, advocacy) | Limited to election period |
| Campaign period | Intense electioneering | Sporadic electioneering |
| Inter-campaign period | Service-oriented, constituent-based | Quiescent |
| Political support | Loyal, consistent core vote | Fluctuating, unpredictable |
| Constituent base | Heterogenous, mixed, competing subgroup populations | Homogeneous subgroup population |

tions."[79] With this as a starting point, and allowing for a range of forms and combinations of forms, it should be possible to diagram the comparative placement of local parties on a series of dimensions. The potential variations can be bewildering.[80]

There are examples of polar extremes in such a schema, as well as a variety of intermediate positions on each of the dimensions. The Chicago machine, particularly during the Daley era (1955–1976), comes close to epitomizing the closed, hierarchical, authoritarian party organization with a clearly identifiable membership, base of support, career lines, professionalized cadremen, and materialistic, parochial, and often job-related incentive systems; much of this structure remains intact today.[81] And although the constraints on party development differ in each as do the demands put forth by their respective political environments, the Los Angeles, Houston, and possibly Nashville parties come close to representing the voluntaristic, open-membership, weakly-centralized type of organization with programmatic and social appeals operating in a fluid and changeable political environment. These motivational patterns clearly contrast with the Chicago model.[82] The Detroit party system, allowing for different placements on many of the dimensions, would come closer to the Chicago pattern than to the one represented by Los Angeles.[83] The "open" party category, with nonhierarchical organizations and soft political support, may well represent the most common model of the local party system. The contention seems realistic, although the evidence in support of it would be primarily impressionistic.

The agenda for research is ambitious. It should be adequate to engage the energies of interested academicians.

## The Present Studies

The collaborative approaches in this volume were initiated to begin to fill some of these research lacunae. Specifically, the intentions were:

1. To assess the value and relevance of political parties in urban America at a critical time in the nation's and the parties' evolution.
2. To empirically evaluate the contributions and activities of political parties at the local level, in order to determine the extent and importance of their contributions to a representative democratic system.
3. To provide a baseline for future research into political party effectiveness.
4. To test and place in perspective the current argument, prevalent in academic circles, that parties are in a state of "decline" of such magnitude that their traditional roles in the society are being transformed.

The hope was to make a beginning, by employing the same unit of analysis in investigating related dimensions of party operation in five localities during the 1980 election year. The focus was on interviewing ward or precinct committee members or their functional equivalents (party workers in state assembly districts in Los Angeles, for example). The questionnaires used were similar to each other (see Appendix) and borrowed heavily from the previous work of Marvick in Los Angeles and Eldersveld in Detroit. Some adaptation to local circumstances was necessary and encouraged. It was felt the studies should relate to, and describe, the differences to be found in the individual political environments. A general effort was made to keep the research as broadly comparative and as conceptually and substantively related as feasible. The cities identified for treatment were meant to include several of the largest and most significant in the country. It was not possible to find researchers willing to expend the time and resources necessary to execute the study in a wide range of major urban areas, such as New York, Atlanta, Minneapolis, Miami, San Francisco, Boston, Phila-

Table 1.2. Profiles of Five Cities in Local Parties Study

| | Los Angeles | Chicago | Detroit | Nashville | Houston |
|---|---|---|---|---|---|
| Population | 2,966,850 | 3,005,072 | 1,203,339 | 455,651 | 1,595,138 |
| Population rank | 3 | 2 | 6 | 25 | 5 |
| Percent population change 1970–1980 | + 5.5 | −10.8 | −20.5 | + 7.0 | +29.3 |
| Percent Black | 17.0 | 39.8 | 63.3 | 23.2 | 27.6 |
| Percent Hispanic | 27.5 | 14.1 | 2.4 | 0.7 | 17.6 |
| Percent of workforce in | | | | | |
| Manufacturing | 23.0 | 26.6 | 28.6 | 16.7 | 16.9 |
| Wholesale and retail trade | 19.9 | 18.6 | 16.4 | 21.6 | 21.8 |
| Professional and related services | 20.1 | 20.1 | 23.2 | 23.1 | 18.4 |
| Unemployment rate | 10.4 | 11.7 | 20.3 | 7.1* | 7.0 |
| Median family income (in dollars) | 19,467 | 18,776 | 17,033 | 19,366 | 21,881 |
| Per capita income (in dollars) | 8,408 | 6,933 | 6,215 | 7,276 | 8,793 |
| Political environment | Competitive | Democratic | Democratic | Democratic | Republican |
| Social and cultural base | Far West, Sunbelt | Midwest, industrial | Midwest, industrial | Mid-South, traditional | Sunbelt, oil, gas, Southwest |

*Data are for Davidson County; data for city are not available.
Source: Data in table are from the 1980 U.S. Census.

delphia, St. Louis, Seattle, and Phoenix. What we were able to do was to investigate within a compatible conceptual framework five major cities that offered the promise of a range of party types. This more limited objective was realized.

The five cities chosen for study—Los Angeles, Chicago, Detroit, Nashville, and Houston—included four of the nation's six largest cities. Two (Detroit, Chicago) were representative of the frostbelt, with its declining industrial base, high unemployment, relatively low income levels, varied ethnic populations, high concentrations of blacks (63 percent of the population in Detroit, 40 percent in Chicago), and traditional party politics (Table 1.2). Nashville offered the chance to observe party patterns in a mid-South city with a traditional old-line style of politics just beginning to experience the effects of the region's current economic, population, and political shifts. Los Angeles has come to represent the "new politics" of candidate-centered coalitions, weak party ties, and media-oriented campaigns.[84] Houston, the prototypical boom city of the 1970s and early 1980s, perhaps more than any other urban area, symbolizes the emerging politics of the Sunbelt. Given its population explosion (in 1980, up 29 percent from a decade before); low rate of unemployment; economy based on oil, gas, and services, in contrast to the manufacturing and industrial base of the Midwest and North; high income level (highest of the five cities studied); and large Hispanic population (among the five, second only to Los Angeles), Houston may suggest what to expect from the developing politics of the Southwest. The five urban areas also tap into the political cultures of differing regions and varying political environments, from the heavily Democratic politics of the older cities to the emerging Republican strength of the South and West.

Within this context, the analyses of the data, while containing common threads, focus on questions of particular concern to the researchers. In Houston, Richard W. Murray and Kent L. Tedin (Chapter 2) were concerned with the levels of competing party activity and the motivations of the two parties' activists. They found, for example, that the Republican party shows impressive organizational and cohesive qualities and can call on a core of ideologically committed partisans. Potentially less beneficial to the party's success at the local level, Republican activists identify with national-level policy issues and campaigns and relate less to local political concerns.

Anne H. Hopkins (Chapter 3) found that in the Nashville/Davidson County Republican party, operations were minimal and that the Republican party had yet to organize with any degree of thoroughness at the local level. In fact, Hopkins suggests that the traditional dominance of one party in an area (the case in much of the South) may lead to an across-the-board depression of party organization and activity. The Republican party vote is concentrated in higher-level contests and does not do well in local-level races (in fact, in most of these it fails to field candidates). The Democrats, in turn, are less organized and active than reasonably might be expected. There are reasons for this, of course.[85] To assess the extent and activity levels of the Democratic party and candidate organizations, Hopkins devises two sets of measure, one an index of campaign activity for each political unit and the other a campaign activity intensity score. Cross-matching these with levels of two-party competition, she finds that both the Democratic party organizations and candidate organizations were least active in areas of Democratic dominance and most active in areas where the Democrats faced some form of Republican challenge. Activity and organizational levels should increase for both parties if the Republicans can convert their state-level successes into a local-level political presence.

Eldersveld (Chapter 4) explores his data from comparable Detroit precincts over a generation and Marvick's longitudinal data for Los Angeles, to trace changes in personnel, incentive structures, and operational levels and assess the political parties' adaptiveness to changing political and social environments. He argues that the incentive systems and activity levels of the parties in the 1980s are comparable to those in earlier eras, as measured by the data at hand, and that the parties have managed to retain their distinctive appeals.

Marvick (Chapter 5) develops the complexion of competing party teams —their personal views, preferred campaign strategies, ideological commitments, policy beliefs, voter perceptions, and estimates of comparative organizational efforts. His findings begin to shape an understanding of the competing teams—their priorities, qualifying features, and range of perceptions—at the local level in Los Angeles. It is a subtle portrait. Party activists are concerned with the substance of politics, yet pragmatic in tailoring policy positions to the campaign environment and in their skepticism regarding the voters' interest in, and capacity to respond to, an issue-based politics. Many activists were motivated by a strong sense of commitment—strong enough, in fact, for many to concentrate their attention only on what their party and its candidates were doing, with little feel or concern for what the opposition was attempting or for the effectiveness of such efforts. The picture that emerges of the party worker is more highly differentiated than that usually encountered; it might outline the contours for similar probes in other areas.

The major finding in the Chicago study (Chapter 6) was the high level of organizational development and the heavy investment in campaigns: politics is serious business here. The major organizational forces were the Chicago Democrats and, on another plane and operating in a different political space, the suburban Republicans. The resources, organizational emphases, and, of course, clientele of the two parties' most effective units differed significantly. The in-city Chicago Republicans and suburban Democrats serve mostly as appendages to their more assertive sister organizations. Also, the traditional image of the Chicago ward leader, derived from earlier studies of the machine, needs some revision. While the machine's activities

**Table 1.3. Comparative Dimensions (In Percent) of Five Urban Parties**

| | Chicago | | | Detroit | | | Los Angeles | | | Houston | | | Nashville[a] |
|---|---|---|---|---|---|---|---|---|---|---|---|---|---|
| | Dem. | Rep. | T | Dem. | Rep. | T | Dem. | Rep. | T | Dem. | Rep. | T | Dem. |
| *Sex* | | | | | | | | | | | | | |
| Male | 97 | 93 | 94 | 58 | 62 | 59 | 63 | 63 | 63 | 72 | 65 | 69 | 44 |
| Female | 3 | 7 | 6 | 42 | 38 | 41 | 37 | 37 | 37 | 28 | 35 | 31 | 56 |
| *Age* | | | | | | | | | | | | | |
| Under 40 | 80 | 89 | 84 | 32 | 35 | 32 | 36 | 27 | — | 16 | 20 | 11 | — |
| Over 40 | 20 | 11 | 16 | 68 | 65 | 68 | 64 | 83 | — | 84 | 80 | 54 | — |
| *Race* | | | | | | | | | | | | | |
| Black | 10 | 21 | 16 | 59 | 35 | 52 | — | — | — | 19 | 5 | 11 | 28 |
| White | 90 | 79 | 84 | 41 | 65 | 48 | — | — | — | 77 | 95 | 86 | 72 |
| *Education* | | | | | | | | | | | | | |
| High school or less | 33 | 49 | 41 | 20 | 14 | 17 | 29 | 30 | 30 | 53 | 46 | 50 | 40 |
| College | 67 | 51 | 59 | 80 | 86 | 83 | 71 | 70 | 71 | 47 | 54 | 50 | 60 |
| *Occupation* | | | | | | | | | | | | | |
| Blue collar | — | — | — | 33 | 39 | 34 | — | — | — | — | — | — | — |
| White collar | 95 | 91 | 93 | 50 | 68 | 56 | 74 | 85 | 80 | 58 | 71 | 62 | 68 |
| Other[b] | 5 | 9 | 7 | — | — | — | — | — | — | 31 | 21 | 25 | 14 |
| *Professional Experience* | | | | | | | | | | | | | |
| Years active in party work: | | | | | | | | | | | | | |
| Less than 5 | 7 | 5 | 5 | 21 | 42 | 30 | — | — | — | 8 | 9 | 9 | 24 |
| 5–10 | 4 | 2 | 4 | 17 | 6 | 15 | — | — | — | 11 | 20 | 15 | 8 |
| 11 or more | 89 | 93 | 91 | 62 | 52 | 55 | 74 | 72 | 73 | 81 | 61 | 76 | 61 |
| Hours per week spent on campaign activity: | | | | | | | | | | | | | |
| Up to 10 | 2 | 4 | 3 | 41 | 53 | 1 | 43 | 46 | — | — | — | — | 32 |
| 11–19 | 23 | 14 | 20 | 19 | 18 | — | 22 | 20 | — | — | — | — | 18 |
| 20 or more | 75 | 82 | 77 | 40 | 29 | — | 34 | 35 | — | — | — | — | 50 |

Note: Total may not add up to 100% due to rounding or missing information. Column T refers to the composite for both parties. Where there is no figure, data were unavailable.

a. The Nashville study included only Democrats.

b. Figures represent approximations. The category "other" includes not known, retired, housewife, student, etc.

appear as vital as ever, the leadership corps is as well educated and socially accomplished as that in the other cities studied. It is, however, still a product of the machine environment.

While each of the profiles of the urban parties is different, as expected, commonalities in the data also emerge. For example, the party workers fit common demographic characterizations of political elites (Table 1.3). The party leaders in all five cities were predominantly male (although less so in Detroit) and college-educated (Houston party activists were less so than the others). Most had been active in politics for long periods of time. Partisanship was weaker among many of the leaders in Houston and Detroit than among those in Chicago or Los Angeles, and the commitment of time to party work varied by city. In both Detroit and Los Angeles, a bimodal pattern was evident: party leaders engaged in campaign activities predominantly at either the low or high ends of the scale. In Nashville, one-half of the Democratic leaders made a heavy investment of time, as did three-fourths of the Chicago party workers, the mostly highly professionalized and consistently involved of those studied. Politics, it would seem, was the primary job, the major vocational pursuit, of the Democratic ward leaders in Chicago (who *averaged* better than forty hours a week in party-related work). Other professional pursuits were seemingly less significant, appendages to their political jobs. The Chicago picture is unlike the one that emerges in most studies of political party involvement.

The results suggest that party organizations respond to differing environmental cues. The implications for a broader universe of local parties will have to await further development, as will the potential range of party operational types, procedures, and organizational arrangements. Perhaps it is enough if studies of local parties in these five cities constitute modest and still fragmentary early steps towards a more comparative urban-based parties analysis.

## Conclusion

What are the implications of the data for the broader questions posed earlier concerning the consequences of party activity for democratic performance and the applicability of the party decline thesis to local parties? Are urban parties in decline? The argument over party decline has focused primarily on the national level and has employed evidence of the weakened affiliative patterns of the mass public, the increasing rejection of a party-consistent vote, and the rise of groups with independent resources to compete with the parties in areas once assumed to be the domain of the parties.[86] The thesis has not been explicitly applied to operations of the party organizations and, as indicated, independent verification exists of the increasing assertiveness of the national parties (or at least of the Republican party) and of the continued functioning at consistent levels of performances of the state and county parties.[87] The argument, one way or another, has not been investigated with regard to the local parties, and the absence of data on community political affiliation patterns and the consistency of the party vote means that principal components of the argument cannot be addressed here. We do have data on party organizational operations for the five cities, however. It could be argued that the variations in party performance and personnel from one area to the next are significant and too great to permit comfortable generalizations. It could also be argued that the local parties studied were more active than could have been expected, and that their vitality is such that the party decline thesis has limited applicability at the local level. Further, it could be argued that the distinctive nature of urban parties and their political settings mitigates the relevance of findings from party-related research at other levels. The factors that condition party behavior and those factors' relationship to the electorate at the national or state levels may be different enough for the influences and response mechanisms operating at the local level to distort the relationship and severely modify the operative assumptions. We do not know. This is speculative. What we do know, and can address in a limited manner with the data from the studies, is, first, the competition to the parties at the local level provided by non-party groups; and, second, the cross-sectional comparative extent of party organization and campaign operations and their perceived constancy over time.

First, how active are the party competitors? Regardless of how well (or poorly) organized or active (or inactive) the local parties might be, competing groups such as PACs, business and labor organizations, and candidate-centered coalitions (except for Nashville, in a state with a tradition of individually-sponsored candidate efforts) were not (or were not perceived by party workers to be) very influential or active in most of the campaigns. Two things may be noted here. First, the type of competing groups identified may concentrate on political races in broader geographical settings and of more direct consequence in national or state policy-making. As a result, little attention may be given to specific urban areas. Second, if the urban political culture is as distinct from the state and national races and concerns as the data suggest, then a different assortment of groups, not identified in the studies and with primarily parochial objectives, are the ones most directly involved in community races. It indeed may be that on

**Table 1.4. Key Activities Performed by Party Leaders (In Percent)**

|  | Activity | | |
|---|---|---|---|
|  | Voter Registration | House to House Canvassing | Election Day Get-out-the-Vote Activities |
| Los Angeles | | | |
| Democrat | 60 | 53 | 68 |
| Republican | 72 | 48 | 77 |
| Chicago | | | |
| Democrat | 96 | 87 | 93 |
| Republican | 78 | 85 | 91 |
| Detroit | | | |
| Democrat | 42 | 60 | 69 |
| Republican | 19 | 61 | 62 |
| Houston | | | |
| Democrat | 80 | 36 | 47 |
| Republican | 77 | 49 | 43 |
| Nashville* | | | |
| Democrat | 88 | 68 | 56 |

*The Nashville study included Democrats only.

the local level the urban parties do most of what needs to be done in terms of conventional campaigning.

A second major question then is, How active are the parties themselves? Even allowing for the expected variations in intensity and/or scope of concerns, the local parties in each of the five cities were influential actors in the political contests in their communities. Focusing on three critical areas of campaign activity—voter registration, door-to-door canvassing, and election-day get-out-the-vote drives—and comparing the parties across urban areas, two things stand out: all of the local parties engaged in each of the activities to a significant degree; and the intensity of effort invested in the individual activities is impressive, again higher than might have been assumed (Table 1.4). Involvement ranged from a low of one in three Houston Democrats undertaking house-to-house canvassing, to an average of better than 90 percent of the Chicago Democrats performing each of the three campaign activities. In these cities, at least, the political parties were major contributors to the campaigns in their localities.

Eldersveld's and Marvick's data allow for some comparisons on these and related dimensions over time. Changes have taken place, of course, but a fair conclusion would be that the level of party activity (as measured by the three indicators cited) has not decreased. Eldersveld, in particular, has been quite clear on this point. Based on his Detroit sample of precincts, he concludes that "these data do not really support the contention that there has been a decline in local party activities in the past twenty-five years" (1956–1980).[88]

The party decline thesis is multifaceted, and its exact relationship to the local parties (and, for that matter, their relationship to the rest of the party system) has yet to be clearly conceptualized. What it is possible to say, based on the results in these five cities, is that the local parties are active in critical areas of campaigning, that they appear to be principal actors in the electoral process, and that there is no evidence of an atrophying of party activity or organization.

The studies that follow, then, explore various aspects of urban party operations. They do so from a common perspective and with a shared set of assumptions. We hope that the research will serve to begin the process of accumulating a long-run data bank on local party activities; to provide a baseline, however limited, for future research efforts; and to demonstrate the variety of problems and analytic questions that can be addressed in such analyses. If the analyses in this volume and the questionnaires reprinted in the Appendix provide a necessary stimulus for like-minded research efforts in other localities, our work will have achieved its goal.


### Notes

1. Giovanni Sartori, *Parties and Systems: A Framework for Analysis* (New York: Oxford Univ. Press, 1976), 27.

2. Quoted in Samuel J. Eldersveld, "The Condition of Party Organization at the Local Level" (Paper prepared for Annual Meeting of the Southern Political Science Association, Savannah, Nov. 1984), 1. The quote is from Robert Michels, *Political Parties* (1915; rpt. New York: Dover Publications, 1959), 21–22.

3. Ibid.

4. The point is made in various ways in: E.E. Schattschneider, *Party Democracy* (New York: Rinehart, 1942); Samuel P. Huntington, *Political Order in Changing States* (New Haven: Yale Univ. Press, 1968); Avery Leiserson, *Parties and Politics* (New York: Knopf, 1958); and Walter Dean Burnham, "The Changing Shape of the American Political Universe," in *Controversies in American Behavior*, ed. Richard G. Niemi and Herbert F. Weisberg (San Francisco: W.H. Freeman, 1976), 431.

5. See Jack Dennis, "Changing Public Support for the American Party Sys-

tem," in *Paths to Political Reform*, ed. William Crotty (Lexington, Mass.: Lexington Books/D.C. Heath, 1980), 35–66.

6. David S. Broder, *The Party's Over* (New York: Harper and Row, 1971); Walter Dean Burnham, *The Current Crisis in American Politics* (New York: Oxford Univ. Press, 1982); Burnham, *Critical Elections and the Mainsprings of American Politics* (New York: Norton, 1970); and William Crotty, *American Parties in Decline*, 2d ed. (Boston: Little, Brown, 1984).

7. As one example of this strain, see: John S. Saloma, III, and Frederick H. Sontag, *Parties: The Real Opportunity for Effective Citizen Politics* (New York: Knopf, 1972).

8. Martin P. Wattenberg, *The Decline of American Political Parties, 1952–1980* (Cambridge: Harvard Univ. Press, 1984); and Crotty, *American Parties in Decline*.

9. Nelson W. Polsby, *Consequences of Party Reform* (New York: Oxford Univ. Press, 1983); Jeane J. Kirkpatrick, *Dismantling the Parties* (Washington D.C.: American Enterprise Institute, 1977); and William Crotty and John S. Jackson, III, *Presidential Primaries and Nominations* (Washington, D.C.: C Q Press, 1985).

10. Crotty, *American Parties in Decline*.

11. Different aspects of this theme are developed in: Burnham, *Critical Elections and the Mainsprings of American Politics*; Burnham, *The Current Crisis in American Politics*; Crotty, *American Parties in Decline*; Dennis, "Changing Public Support"; E.C. Ladd, Jr., *Where Have All the Voters Gone?* (New York: Norton, 1978); and Kirkpatrick, *Dismantling the Parties*.

12. John S. Jackson, III, "The Party's Not Over: It Has Just Moved to a New Place" (Paper prepared for Annual Meeting of the Southern Political Science Association, Savannah, Nov. 1984), 6.

13. Ibid.

14. Cornelius P. Cotter, James L. Gibson, John F. Bibby, and Robert J. Huckshorn, *Party Organizations in American Politics* (New York: Praeger, 1984), 30.

15. Ibid., 33.

16. Paul A. Beck, "Environment and Party: The Impact of Political and Demographic County Characteristics on Party Behavior," *American Political Science Review* 68 (Sept. 1974), 1229–44.

17. James L. Gibson, Cornelius P. Cotter, John F. Bibby, and Robert J. Huckshorn, "Whither the Local Parties?: A Cross-Sectional and Longitudinal Analysis of the Strength of Party Organizations," *American Journal of Political Science* 29 (Feb. 1985), 144.

18. Ibid., 155.

19. Ibid., 156.

20. John F. Bibby, James L. Gibson, Cornelius P. Cotter, and Robert J. Huckshorn, "Trends in Party Organizational Strength, 1960–1980," *International Political Science Review* 4 (1983), 21–27; Gibson, Cotter, Bibby, and Huckshorn, "Assessing Party Organizational Strength," *American Journal of Political Science* 27 (May

1983), 193-222; Cotter et al., *Party Organizations in American Politics*; and William Crotty, *The Party Game* (New York: W.H. Freeman, 1985), ch. 8.

21. William Crotty, *Decision for Democrats* (Baltimore: Johns Hopkins Univ. Press, 1978); Crotty, *Party Reform* (New York: Longman, 1983); David E. Price, *Bringing Back the Parties* (Washington, D.C.: C Q Press, 1984); James W. Ceaser, *Reforming the Reforms* (Cambridge, Mass.: Ballinger, 1982); Polsby, *Consequences of Party Reform*; Charles H. Longley, "Party Nationalization in America," in Crotty, *Paths to Political Reform*, 167-205; Longley, "National Party Renewal," in *Party Renewal in America*, ed. Gerald M. Pomper (New York: Praeger, 1980), 69-86; and Longley, "Party Reform and Party Nationalization: The Case of the Democrats," in *The Party Symbol*, ed. W. Crotty (San Francisco: W.H. Freeman, 1980), 359-78.

22. Cornelius P. Cotter and John F. Bibby, "Institutional Development of Parties and the Thesis of Party Decline," *Political Science Quarterly* 95 (Spring 1980), 1-27; John F. Bibby, "Party Renewal in the National Republican Party," in Pomper, *Party Renewal in America*, 102-115; and Robert Harmel and Kenneth Janda, *Parties and Their Environments: Limits to Reform?* (New York: Longman, 1982), 95-120.

23. Herbert E. Alexander, *Financing Politics*, 2d ed. (Washington, D.C.: C Q Press, 1980); Ruth S. Jones, "Financing State Elections," in Michael J. Malbin, ed., *Money and Politics in the United States* (Washington, D.C.: American Enterprise Institute, 1984), 172-213; and other studies in Malbin, *Money and Politics in the United States*, and in *Parties, Interest Groups, and Campaign Finance Laws*, ed. Malbin (Washington, D.C.: American Enterprise Institute, 1980).

24. See, as examples of the literature on the urban machine: Seymour J. Mandelbaum, *Boss Tweed's New York* (New York: Wiley, 1965); Leo Hershkowitz, *Tweed's New York: Another Look* (Garden City, N.Y.: Anchor Books, 1978); Lyle W. Dorsett, *The Pendergast Machine* (Cambridge: Oxford Univ. Press, 1968); Dorsett, *Franklin D. Roosevelt and the City Bosses* (Port Washington, N.Y.: Kennikat Press/National University Publications, 1977); William L. Riordan, *Plunkitt of Tammany Hall* (New York: Dutton, 1963); Zane L. Miller, *Boss Cox's Cincinnati* (Cambridge: Oxford Univ. Press, 1968); James M. Curley, *I'd Do It Again* (Englewood Cliffs, N.J.: Prentice-Hall, 1957); John M. Allswang, *Bosses, Machines, and Urban Voters* (Port Washington, N.Y.: Kennikat Press/National University Publications, 1977); Michael H. Ebner and Eugene M. Tobin, eds., *The Age of Urban Reform* (Port Washington, N.Y.: Kennikat Press/National University Publications, 1977); Milton Rakove, *Don't Make No Waves . . . Don't Back No Losers* (Bloomington: Indiana Univ. Press, 1975); Rakove, *We Don't Want Nobody Nobody Sent* (Bloomington: Indiana Univ. Press, 1979); Roger Biles, *Big City Boss* (DeKalb: Northern Illinois Univ. Press, 1984); Alex Gottfried, *Boss Cermak of Chicago* (Seattle: Univ. of Washington Press, 1962); Harold Zink, *City Bosses in the United States* (Durham, N.C.: Duke Univ. Press, 1930); Amy Bridges, *A City in the Republic* (Cambridge: Cambridge Univ. Press, 1984); and Alan Ware, *The Breakdown of Democratic Party Organization, 1940-1980* (New York: Oxford Univ. Press, 1984).

25. Rakove, *Don't Make No Waves*; Len O'Connor, *Requiem: The Decline*

*and Demise of Mayor Daley and His Era* (Chicago: Contemporary Books, 1977); O'Connor, *Clout: Mayor Daley and His City* (Chicago: Henry Regnery, 1975); Mike Royko, *Boss: Richard J. Daley of Chicago* (New York: Dutton, 1971); and Eugene E. Kennedy, *Himself: The Life and Times of Richard J. Daley* (New York: Viking, 1978). See Also: Samuel K. Gove and Louis H. Masotti, eds., *After Daley* (Urbana: Univ. of Illinois Press, 1982); and Melvin Holli and Paul Green, eds., *The Making of a Mayor* (Grand Rapids, Mich.: Eerdmans, 1984).

26. James Bryce, *The American Commonwealth* (New York: Macmillan, 1888); and M. Ostrogorski, *Democracy and the Organization of Political Parties, Volume II: The United States*, ed. S.M. Lipset (New York: Anchor Books, 1964).

27. A challenge to the conventional wisdom can be found in Raymond E. Wolfinger, "Why Political Machines Have Not Withered Away and Other Revisionist Thoughts," *Journal of Politics* 34 (May 1972), 365-98.

28. See Crotty, *The Party Game*, ch. 9.

29. See: Willis D. Hawley, *Non-Partisan Elections and the Case for Party Politics* (New York: Wiley, 1973); Charles R. Adrian, "Some General Characteristics of Nonpartisan Elections," *American Political Science Review* 46 (Sept. 1952), 766-76; Adrian, "A Typology for Nonpartisan Elections" *Western Political Quarterly* 12 (June 1959), 449-58; Phillips Cutright, "Nonpartisan Electoral Systems in American Cities," *Comparative Studies in Society and History* 5 (Jan. 1963), 212-26; Charles Gilbert, "Some Aspects of Nonpartisan Elections in Large Cities," *Midwest Journal of Political Science* 6 (Nov. 1962), 346-54; Eugene C. Lee, *The Politics of Nonpartisanship* (Berkeley: Univ. of California Press, 1960); and Robert C. Wood, *Suburbia* (Boston: Houghton Mifflin, 1953).

30. Harold F. Gosnell, *Machine Politics: Chicago Model* (Chicago: Univ. of Chicago Press, 1937).

31. Bernard R. Berelson, Paul F. Lazarsfeld, and William McPhee, *Voting* (Chicago: Univ. of Chicago Press, 1954), 153-81. This section was prepared primarily by John P. Dean and Edward Suchman.

32. Edward C. Banfield, *Political Influence* (New York: Free Press, 1961); and Banfield and James Q. Wilson, *City Politics* (Cambridge: Harvard Univ. Press, 1963). See also: Robert Dahl, *Who Governs?* (New Haven: Yale Univ. Press, 1961).

33. Useful review of the relevant literature can be found in: Eldersveld, *Political Parties in American Society* (New York: Basic, 1982), 131-91; Alan R. Gitelson, M. Margaret Conway, and Frank B. Feigert, *American Political Parties: Stability and Change* (Boston: Houghton Mifflin, 1984), 79-82, 100-125; Frank J. Sorauf, *Party Politics in America*, 5th ed. (Boston: Little, Brown, 1984), 64-113; and Robert J. Huckshorn, *Political Parties in America*, 2d ed. (Monterrey Calif.: Brooks/Cole, 1984), 84-87.

34. William Crotty, "A Perspective for the Comparative Analysis of Political Parties," *Comparative Political Studies* (Oct. 1970); Crotty, "Political Parties Research," in *Approaches to Political Science*, ed. Henry Kariel and Michael Haas (San Francisco: Chandler, 1970), 267-322; Robert T. Golembiewski, William Welsh, and

William Crotty, *A Methodological Primer for Political Scientists* (Chicago: Rand McNally, 1969), ch. 10; Bernard Hennesey, "On the Study of Party Organization," in *Approaches to the Study of Party Organization*, ed. William Crotty (Boston: Allyn and Bacon, 1968), 1–44; and William E. Wright, "Comparative Party Models: Rational-Efficient and Party Democracy," in *A Comparative Study of Party Organization*, ed. W.E. Wright (Columbus, Ohio: Merrill, 1971), 17–54.

35. Samuel J. Eldersveld, *Political Parties: A Behavioral Analysis* (Chicago: Rand McNally, 1964). See also Daniel Katz and Samuel J. Eldersveld, "The Impact of Local Party Activity Upon the Electorate," *Public Opinion Quarterly* 25 (Spring 1961), 1–24.

36. Eldersveld, *Political Parties: A Behavioral Analysis*, 9. The concept was originally developed in Harold Lasswell and Abraham Kaplan, *Power and Society* (New Haven: Yale Univ. Press, 1950), 219–20.

37. See the Eldersveld and Marvick contributions to this volume.

38. J.T. Salter, *Boss Rule* (New York: McGraw-Hill, 1935); Roy V. Peel, *The Political Clubs of New York City* (New York: Putnam's, 1935); Gosnell, *Machine Politics*; Sonya Forthal, *Cogwheels of Democracy* (New York: William-Frederick Press, 1946); Frank R. Kent, *The Great Game of Politics* (Garden City, N.Y.: Doubleday, 1928); William E. Mosher, "Party and Government Control at the Grass Roots," *National Municipal Review* 24 (Jan. 1935), 15–18; and David Kurtzman, *Methods of Controlling Votes in Philadelphia* (Philadelphia: Univ. of Pennsylvania Press, 1935).

39. Hugh A. Bone, *Grass Roots Party Leadership* (Seattle: Bureau of Governmental Research and Services, Univ. of Washington, 1952); James Q. Wilson, *The Amateur Democrat* (Chicago: Univ. of Chicago Press, 1962); Samuel C. Patterson, "Characteristics of Party Leaders," *Western Political Quarterly* 16 (June 1963), 332–52; Lewis Bowman and G.R. Boynton, "Activities and Role Definitions of Grass Roots Party Officials," *Journal of Politics* 28 (Feb. 1966), 121–43; Robert S. Hirschfield, Bert E. Swanson, and Blanche D. Blank, "A Profile of Political Activists in Manhattan," *Western Political Quarterly* 15 (Sept. 1962), 489–506; Robert H. Salisbury, "The Urban Party Organization Member," *Public Opinion Quarterly* 29 (Winter 1965–66), 550–65; M. Margaret Conway and Frank B. Feigert, "Motivation, Incentive Systems, and the Political Organization," *American Political Science Review* 62 (Dec. 1968), 1159–73; and Lee S. Weinberg, "Stability and Change Among Pittsburg Precinct Politicians, 1954–1970," *Social Science* 50 (1975), 10–16.

40. Joseph Schlesinger, "On the Theory of Party Organization," *Journal of Politics* 46 (1983), 369–400. The quotations refer to pages in Schlesinger, "On the Theory of Party Organization" (Paper prepared for Annual Meeting of the American Political Science Association, Chicago 1983).

41. Anthony Downs, *An Economic Theory of Democracy* (New York: Harper, 1957), 29. Schlesinger's approach also borrows from Joseph A. Schumpeter, *Capitalism, Socialism, and Democracy*, 3d. ed. (New York: Harper, 1950); and Mancur Olson, *The Logic of Collective Action* (Cambridge: Harvard Univ. Press, 1965, 1971).

42. This perspective is developed in Olson, *The Logic of Collective Action.*

43. Schlesinger, "On the Theory of Party Organization" (paper), 26.

44. Ibid., 29.

45. Ibid., 36.

46. Ibid.

47. See note 34 above.

48. See: Robert L. Dudley and Alan R. Gitelson, "Alternative Models of Party Organization" (Paper prepared for Annual Meeting of the Southern Political Science Association, Savannah, 1984); Elinor Ostrom, "An Agenda for the Study of Institutions" (Paper prepared for Annual Meeting of the Midwest Political Science Association, Chicago, 1984).

49. For an explanatory approach employing this perspective, see Wolfinger, "Why Political Machines Have Not Withered Away."

50. See the discussion in Kay Lawson, ed., *Linkage and Political Parties* (New Haven: Yale Univ. Press, 1979).

51. The perspective is not new. Robert K. Merton provided a justification in his influential *Social Theory and Social Structure* (New York: Free Press, 1957), 71–81.

52. Gosnell, *Machine Politics,* 69–90.

53. Richard T. Frost, "Stability and Change in Local Party Politics," *Public Opinion Quarterly* 25 (Summer 1961), 221–35. See, in particular, Table 7, p. 231. A distinction is being made here between service activities meant to sustain a party over time, and campaigning activities limited to election periods. For examples of treatments of the latter, see William Crotty, "Party Effort and its Impact upon the Vote," *American Political Science Review* 65 (June 1971), 439–50; Gerald H. Kramer, "The Effects of Precinct-Level Canvassing on Voter Behavior," *Public Opinion Quarterly* 34 (1970), 560–72; Raymond E. Wolfinger, "The Influence of Precinct Work on Voting Behavior," *Public Opinion Quarterly* 27 (Fall 1963), 387–98; and Katz and Eldersveld, "The Impact of Local Party Activity."

54. Thomas M. Guterbock, *Machine Politics in Transition* (Chicago: Univ. of Chicago Press, 1980).

55. Ibid., 9.

56. Ibid., 10.

57. Ibid., 9–10.

58. Ibid., 104–105.

59. Ibid., 96–97. Some comparisons with county-level parties can be made. See James L. Gibson, John P. Frendreis, and Laura L. Vertz, "Party Dynamics in the 1980s: Changes in County Party Organizational Strength 1980–1984" (Paper prepared for Annual Meeting of the Midwest Political Science Association, Chicago, April 1985), esp. Tables 1 and 2.

60. Gabriel A. Almond, "Introduction: A Functional Approach to Comparative Politics," in *The Politics of Developing Areas,* ed. G.A. Almond and James S. Coleman (Princeton: Princeton Univ. Press, 1960), 3–64; and G.A. Almond and G. Bingham Powell, *Comparative Politics: A Developmental Approach* (Boston: Little, Brown, 1966). For a basic discussion of the theoretical approach, see Talcott

Parsons and Edward A. Shils, eds., *Toward A General Theory of Action* (Cambridge: Harvard Univ. Press, 1952); and Parsons, "The Political Aspect of Social Structure and Process," in *Varieties of Political Theory*, ed. David Easton (Englewood Cliffs, N.J.: Prentice-Hall, 1966). For various applications to party-related research, see: Beryl L. Crowe and Charles G. Mayo, "The Structural-Functional Concept of a Political Party," in *American Political Parties: A Systemic Perspective*, ed. Mayo and Crowe (New York: Harper and Row, 1967); Talcott Parsons, "Voting and the Equilibrium of the American Political System," in *American Voting Behavior* ed. Eugene Burdick and Arthur Brodbeck (Glencoe, Ill.: Free Press, 1960), 80–120; Douglas S. Gatlin, "Toward a Functionalist Theory of Political Parties: Inter-Party Competition in North Carolina," in Crotty, *Approaches to the Study of Party Organization*, 217–46; Marvin Harder and Thomas Ungs, "Notes Toward a Functional Analysis of Local Party Organizations" (Paper prepared for Annual Meeting of the Midwest Political Science Association, Chicago, April 1963); Theodore Lowi, "Toward Functionalism in Political Science: The Case of Innovation in Party Systems," *American Political Science Review* 57 (Sept. 1963), 570–83; and Howard A. Scarrow, "The Function of Political Parties: A Critique of the Literature and the Approach," *Journal of Politics* 29 (Nov. 1967), 770–90. Giovanni Sartori treats such approaches within a broadly comparative parties' perspective in *Parties and Party Systems: A Framework for Analysis* (New York: Cambridge Univ. Press, 1976).

61. See, as examples, their contributions to this volume.

62. Vilfredo Pareto, *The Mind and Society*, ed. and trans. A. Livingston (New York: Harcourt, Brace, 1935); Gaetano Mosca, *The Ruling Class*, ed. A. Livingston and trans. H.D. Kahn (New York: McGraw-Hill, 1939); Roberto Michels, *Political Parties*, (1915; New York: Dover Publications, 1959); and Max Weber, *The Theory of Social and Economic Organization* (New York: Oxford Univ. Press, 1947).

63. Quoted in Donald R. Matthews, *The Social Background of Political Decision-Makers* (Garden City, N.Y.: Doubleday, 1954), 7.

64. Ibid., 3.

65. Moshe M. Czudnowski, "Political Recruitment," in *Handbook of Political Science, Volume 2: Micropolitical Theory* ed. Fred I. Greenstein and Nelson W. Polsby (Reading, Mass.: Addison-Wesley, 1975), 155–242.

66. Ibid., 156.

67. Ibid.

68. Ibid., 157–59

69. Samuel J. Eldersveld and Dwaine Marvick, "Work on the Origins, Activities, and Attitudes of Party Activists," *International Political Science Review* 4 (1983), 12. Emphasis omitted.

70. Ibid. See also the summary materials contained in *European Elections Study: European Political Parties' Middle-Level Elites Project*, ed. Karlheinz Reif and Roland Cayrol (Mannheim: Institut fur Sozialwissenshaften und Europa-Institut of the Universitat Mannheim, Aug. 1981).

71. See, as examples of his work, Eldersveld, *Political Parties*; Katz and Eldersveld, "The Impact of Local Party Activity"; Eldersveld and B. Ahmed, *Citizens and Politics: Mass Political Behavior in India* (Chicago: Univ. of Chicago Press, 1978); Eldersveld, "Motivations for Party Activism: Multi-National Uniformities and Differences," *International Political Science Review* 4:1 (1983), 57–70; and Eldersveld's contribution to this volume.

72. For examples of his work, see Dwaine Marvick and Charles Nixon, "Recruitment Contrasts in Rival Campaign Groups," in *Political Decision-Makers*, ed. Marvick (New York: Free Press, 1961), 193–217; Marvick, "Party Organizational Personnel and Electoral Democracy in Los Angeles 1963–1972," in Crotty, *The Party Symbol*, 63–86; Marvick, "Political Linkage Functions of Rival Party Activists in the United States: Los Angeles, 1969–1974," in Lawson, *Linkage and Political Parties*, 100–128; Marvick, "Recruitment Patterns of Campaign Activists in India: Legislative Candidates, Public Notables, and the Organizational Personnel of Rival Parties," in *Elite Recruitment in Democratic Polities*, ed. Heinz Eulau and Moshe M. Czudnowski, 133–62 (Beverly Hills: Sage, 1976); Marvick, "Ideological Thinking Among Party Activists: Findings from India, Germany and America," *International Political Science Review* 4:1 (1983), 94–107; and Marvick's contribution to this volume.

73. Dwaine Marvick, "Continuities in Recruitment Theory and Research: Toward A New Model," in Eulau and Czudnowski, *Elite Recruitment in Democratic Politics*, 29–44; and Marvick, "Introduction: Political Decision-Makers in Contrasting Milieus," in Marvick, *Political Decision-Makers*, 13–28. See also Marvick, "Political Recruitment and Careers," in *International Encyclopedia of the Social Sciences* (New York: Macmillan, 1968), 12:273–282.

74. Marvick, "Party Organizational Personnel"; and Marvick's contribution to this volume.

75. Marvick, in this volume.

76. Consult overviews of the subfield found in Leon D. Epstein, "The Scholarly Commitment to Parties," in *"Political Science: The State of the Discipline*, ed. Ada Finifter (Washington, D.C.: American Political Science Association, 1983), 127–54; and Epstein, "Political Parties," in Greenstein and Polsby, *Handbook of Political Science, Volume 4: Nongovernmental Politics*, 229–77.

77. See discussion in Crotty, *The Party Game*, ch. 9.

78. Eldersveld, *Political Parties in American Society*, 155–56.

79. Ibid., 156.

80. Ibid., 143.

81. See the chapter on the Chicago parties in this volume.

82. See the chapters on parties in Houston, Los Angeles, and Nashville in this volume.

83. See the chapter on the Detroit parties in this volume.

84. For one comparison of California's political patterns with those of a more traditional eastern state see Jeffrey M. Stonecash, "Party Systems, Electoral Be-

havior, and Political Communication: A Comparison of Connecticut and California" (Paper prepared for Annual Meeting of the Midwest Political Science Association, Chicago, April 1985).

85. The best discussion is V.O. Key, Jr., *Southern Politics in State and Nation* (New York: Knopf, 1949).

86. The evidence is summarized in Crotty, *American Parties in Decline*. Also see Wattenberg, *Decline of American Political Parties*.

87. The reference is to the body of research by Cotter et al. See: Cotter et al., *Party Organizations in American Politics*; Cotter and Bibby, "Institutional Development of Parties and the Thesis of Party Decline"; Cornelius P. Cotter, James L. Gibson, Robert J. Huckshorn, and John F. Bibby, "The Condition of the Party Organizations at the State Level: State-Local Party Integration" (Paper prepared for Annual Meeting of the Southern Political Science Association, Savannah, Nov. 1984); Gibson et al., "Assessing Party Organizational Strength"; Gibson et al., "Whither the Local Parties?"; Gibson et al., "Party Dynamics in the 1980s"; James L. Gibson and Gregg W. Smith, "Local Party Organizations and Electoral Outcomes: Linkages Between Parties and Elections" (Paper prepared for Annual Meeting of American Political Science Association, Washington, D.C., Sept. 1984); Bibby, "Party Renewal in the National Republican Party."

88. Eldersveld, *Political Parties in American Society*, 147. See also Eldersveld, "The Condition of Party Organization at the Local Level," 16.

CHAPTER 2

# The Emergence of Two-Party Competition
# in the Sunbelt: The Case of Houston

*Richard W. Murray and Kent L. Tedin*

Over the last twenty years many observers have noted, often with alarm, that the fortunes of American political parties are on the decline. Numerous studies have documented the falling percentages of self-identified partisans and the accompanying rise in split-ticket voting. Increasingly, political scientists and election commentators talk of the "new politics," wherein most of the important tasks traditionally performed by parties (recruiting candidates, raising funds, communicating with voters, etc.) have been assumed by a candidate's personal organization and/or special interest groups. Even those last survivors of party organizational strength, the urban machines, are described as being in retreat. In view of many, these developments indicate a "party system in crisis."[1]

Without disputing the specific evidence cited in support of the party decline thesis, we nevertheless believe that the recent literature overstates the weakness of American political parties. Most voters still think of themselves as Democrats or Republicans, and no other organization performs the range of functions undertaken by parties in the electoral process. Party voting can still be quite robust.

There has been change in the party system, but not necessarily atrophy. A close look at trends around the country since the 1950s reveals a pattern of party development more mixed than the one presented in the party decline literature. The viability of the party system has, in fact, increased in many parts of the United States. In northern New England and the Plains states, the Democratic party has emerged as a strong competitor to the long-dominant Republicans. Of more importance has been the rise of the Republican party in the modern South. From Arizona to Virginia, a massive regional political shift has been occurring since the 1950s, and it is a shift in which political parties have played a major role.

From the late 1800s through the 1940s, Democratic nominees were routinely elected in southern states, which meant, as V.O. Key, Jr., observed, that the region really had a "no party" politics, centering on personalities and factions.[2] In the 1980s this characterization is no longer accurate. White southerners have become the most Republican of voters in presidential elections, and almost all the GOP's recent electoral gains have come from the party's improved showing in border and southern states.[3] Importantly, beneath this visible pattern of Republican electoral success one finds a degree of party organization not seen in the South since the days of the Whigs and the Democrats in the 1840s.

In this essay we shall examine the party organization in Harris County (Houston), Texas.[4] It is a study in the resurgence of a party system. Throughout most of the twentieth century it has not been meaningful to talk of interparty competition in the region or metropolitan area. However, by the 1980s the competition between Republicans and Democrats in Houston and Harris County was more than sufficient to warrant an analysis of "two-party" politics. Given the scholarly and popular concern with "parties in decline," a study of "party renewal" should provide an instructive contrast.

We begin by reviewing the development of competitive party politics in the Houston metropolitan area. Then, drawing on data from a 1980 survey of Democratic and Republican precinct committee members and several surveys of Houston and Texas voters carried out by the Center for Public Policy at the University of Houston, we describe the general characteristics of local activists, their levels of organizational effort in the 1980 presidential election, and their motivations for party work.[5]

### The Partisan Context

Harris County, Texas, which includes most of the Houston urban area, has been one of the most dynamic urban centers in the country since World War II. In 1950 there were barely 800,000 people in the county, but by 1970 the population had more than doubled to 1,741,000. The 1980 census counted 2,409,000 residents, of which 20 percent are black, 15 percent Hispanic, and 62 percent white. The Houston Standard Metropolitan Statistical Area (SMSA) has about 2.9 million people as of 1980 and experienced the second largest population gain (46 percent) since 1970 of any SMSA

Table 2.1.  Voting Patterns in Harris County, 1948–1980.

| Year | Republican Percentage of Two-Party Presidential Vote | Republican Percentage of Two-Party Congressional Vote | GOP Performance in County Races | | |
| | | | Number Contested | Number Won | Mean GOP Percentage |
|---|---|---|---|---|---|
| 1948 | 42.4 | 14.5 | 5 | 0 | 12 |
| 1952 | 57.6 | — | 0 | — | — |
| 1956 | 61.1 | 38.6 | 0 | — | — |
| 1960 | 53.1 | 34.5 | 0 | — | — |
| 1964 | 40.4 | 35.1 | 0 | — | — |
| 1968 | 52.5 | 48.0 | 2 | 0 | 38.3 |
| 1972 | 62.9 | 49.0 | 4 | 0 | 37.1 |
| 1976 | 52.6 | 52.5 | 3 | 0 | 43.4 |
| 1980 | 60.3 | 60.7 | 21 | 10 | 48.7 |

Source: Official Records, Harris County Clerk.

in the country. This population growth reflects a booming local economy. No-one comes to the "Golden Buckle of the Sunbelt" (as the local Chamber of Commerce dubs Houston) for its cool summer breezes, scenic vistas, clean air, or winter sports. Houston has grown because, in an era of general urban stagnation, the local economy has generated about 70,000 new jobs a year since 1970. The reasons for this economic boom are several, but principal among them is the fact that the products which undergird the economy (petroleum and natural gas) have increased tenfold in value since 1973. The prosperity of the petroleum industry has brought not only growth to Houston, but also affluence. In 1970 the median family income in the Houston SMSA was $10,191, or 101 percent of the national median. In 1980 the median income was $23,959, or 120.3 percent of the national level.[6] These figures placed Houston tenth among the thirty-eight metropolitan areas with a population of one million or more, but when one controls for the lower cost of living (primarily due to low property taxes and no state income tax), Houston is clearly among the most affluent urban areas in the nation.

The growth of Houston and its increased affluence have been accompanied by substantial political changes as well. Like the rest of Texas and most of the South, Harris County was solidly Democratic well into the 1940s. In 1948 Republican presidential nominee Thomas Dewey won the affluent west-side suburban precincts of the county, but as Table 2.1 indicates, Democrat Harry Truman still carried the county by a healthy margin. The local Republican candidate for Congress received less than 15 percent of the vote. Presidential Republicanism took firm hold in 1952, when Dwight Eisenhower received nearly 58 percent of the vote in Harris County and carried the state—a victory he repeated in 1956. Since Eisenhower, only native son Lyndon Johnson, who taught school in Houston in the early 1930s, has carried the county for the Democrats. In congressional voting, the Republicans achieved parity in the late 1960s, forged ahead of the Democrats in the 1970s, and now hold three of the four local seats.

The Republicans have also made inroads in county politics. From the 1940s to the 1970s, the local Republican party was basically concerned with national politics and an occasional statewide contest for governor. Few candidates ran for local office on the GOP ticket outside of a handful of heavily Republican legislative districts, and those who did run usually got little support from the party. Even during the 1972 Republican landslide, when Richard Nixon took 63 percent of the county vote, the few GOP contestants for county office averaged only 37 percent of the vote. This figure increased slightly in 1976, but in 1980 the Republicans achieved parity with the Democrats in county elections as well. As can be seen in Table 2.1, Republicans contested twenty-one county-level offices, winning ten with an average vote of 49 percent.

The dramatic Republican gains in presidential, congressional, and finally local elections reflect several factors. The leftward movement of the national Democratic party on racial issues in the 1940s and on economic policy in the 1950s and 1960s alienated some white conservatives traditionally active in Democratic politics. The increased affluence of Houston, with its burgeoning middle-class suburbs, constituted fertile soil in which a genuinely conservative local Republican party could set its roots and grow. Finally, the in-migration of sizable numbers of professional and technical workers from the Northeast and Midwest yielded many new voters with traditional Republican ties.

Aside from national political trends and demographic shifts, local Republicans have enjoyed another advantage over the once dominant Democrats—they are much better organized as a political party. Whether one speaks of raising money, maintaining a headquarters staff, recruiting campaign workers, or providing candidates with technical and managerial support services, the Harris County Republican party has achieved a substantial lead over its Democratic competitors.[7]

One factor that has contributed to this gap is the different electoral orientations of the two parties. Texas Republicans have traditionally viewed themselves as an embattled minority struggling to bring a two-party system into the state. GOP leaders have worked hard to hold down intraparty strife while focusing party efforts on beating the Democrats in November. By contrast, Texas Democrats have little tradition of party unity or cohesion in state or local politics.[8] The Democratic party has been a loosely knit umbrella association where most attention and effort has centered on battles between personalities and factions. These differences were fought out in the May primaries, and relatively little attention was paid to the November general elections. Instead of joining forces to fight Republicans, both liberal and conservative Democrats have been quite willing to ally themselves with the GOP to gain an edge in their intraparty squabbles.[9]

As long as the Democrats controlled virtually all state and local offices, this nonpartisan approach to elections posed little risk. However, that condition no longer prevails. Republican Bill Clements captured the Texas governorship in 1978, becoming the first GOP governor in over one hundred years, largely because the divisions in the Democratic primary carried over into the general election.[10] At the local level, Republicans are not only making inroads in Houston, but are challenging Democratic control in Dallas, Bexar (San Antonio), and several other urban counties in the state. Democratic leaders are aware of the costs of placing personality and faction ahead of party unity, but efforts to recast the party in a more competitive mode have not gone well.[11]

We see in Texas, therefore, a situation where both parties are in transition. The Republicans are a rapidly expanding minority party that has achieved striking success in recent state and local elections. Organizationally, the state GOP appears to be a disciplined, unified party that is far more effective in partisan matters than are the Texas Democrats. The Democratic party retains a sizable advantage among the state's voters in terms of party identification, and at least 95 percent of all state and county officials were elected as Democrats. However, the Democrats have not been able completely to shake the legacy of one-party politics, even as they face a new set of political realities.

## Party Activists in Houston

The basic unit of electoral and party organization in Texas is the voting precinct. There are about 6,000 precincts in the state, and there were 520 in Harris County in 1980. Typically, a Houston precinct includes between one and two square miles and has 2,000 or so registered voters. State law provides for the election of a Democratic and a Republican committee member in the biennial party primaries. The person elected serves for the next two years on the party's county executive committee, holds the party election in her or his precinct, and serves as temporary chair at the party mass meeting held on the evening of primary day. Legal duties aside, the precinct leaders are the key organizational operatives for the Texas parties both during and between electoral campaigns.

In March and April 1981, personal interviews were conducted with 140 precinct leaders in Harris County. The committee members were randomly selected, and of those contacted 82 percent agreed to be interviewed. The sample consists of 75 Democrats and 65 Republicans and is representative in that it reflects the sexual, racial, and areal distribution of the county executive committee.

*Personal Characteristics*

The background characteristics of the sample are summarized in Table 2.2. In general, one finds a pattern consistent with other studies of party activists. Precinct leaders tended to be of high socioeconomic status, the

**Table 2.2. Personal Characteristics of Party Activists (In Percent)**

|  | *Republican* | *Democratic* | *Sample* |
|---|---|---|---|
| *Sex* |  |  |  |
| Male | 65 | 72 | 69 |
| Female | 35 | 28 | 31 |
| *Age* |  |  |  |
| Under 30 | 5 | 9 | 7 |
| 30–39 | 15 | 7 | 11 |
| 40–49 | 23 | 32 | 28 |
| 50–59 | 54 | 33 | 43 |
| 60+ | 3 | 19 | 11 |
| *Ethnicity* |  |  |  |
| White | 95 | 77 | 86 |
| Black | 3 | 19 | 11 |
| Hispanic | 2 | 4 | 3 |
| *Occupation* |  |  |  |
| Professional/technical | 59 | 29 | 37 |
| Teacher | 8 | 7 | 7 |
| Sales, clerical | 11 | 7 | 9 |
| Skilled blue-collar | 3 | 15 | 9 |

**Table 2.2.  Continued**

|  | Republican | Democratic | Sample |
|---|---|---|---|
| Service worker | 0 | 7 | 4 |
| Retired | 2 | 16 | 9 |
| Housewife | 19 | 15 | 16 |
| Student | 0 | 5 | 3 |
| *Marital Status* | | | |
| Married | 97 | 81 | 90 |
| *Educational Level* | | | |
| Less than high school | 0 | 6 | 3 |
| High school graduate | 15 | 21 | 19 |
| Trade or business school | 0 | 4 | 2 |
| 1 or 2 years college | 31 | 23 | 26 |
| 3 or 4 years college | 35 | 36 | 36 |
| Post graduate work | 19 | 11 | 14 |
| *Family Income* | | | |
| Less than $10,000 | 0 | 7 | 4 |
| $10,000–20,000 | 3 | 16 | 10 |
| $20,000–30,000 | 9 | 12 | 11 |
| $30,000–40,000 | 29 | 13 | 21 |
| $40,000–50,000 | 6 | 11 | 9 |
| Over $50,000 | 37 | 27 | 15 |
| Refused | 15 | 14 | 15 |
| *Years in Houston* | | | |
| Less than 5 | 0 | 3 | 1 |
| 5 –9 | 2 | 4 | 3 |
| 10–14 | 14 | 13 | 14 |
| 15–20 | 6 | 9 | 8 |
| 20–29 | 37 | 23 | 29 |
| 30 or more | 42 | 48 | 45 |
| *Religious Preference* | | | |
| Catholic | 9 | 30 | 20 |
| Episcopal/Presbyterian | 17 | 14 | 15 |
| Baptist | 42 | 12 | 26 |
| Methodist | 5 | 36 | 21 |
| Other Protestant | 12 | 1 | 7 |
| Jewish | 0 | 3 | 2 |
| None | 15 | 4 | 9 |

majority was male (although over 30 percent were women), and most were in their forties and fifties. Ninety percent were married, and most had lived in Houston at least twenty years.

As one might expect with people who volunteer much time and effort for little or no financial reward,[12] the parties in Houston attract men and women with the time and financial resources to afford politics, the information to understand it, and the skills to be useful. In terms of occupation, 37 percent of our sample were employed in professional or technical jobs, 16 percent were in other white-collar jobs, and 16 percent were housewives. Only 13 percent held blue-collar or service jobs. Three-fourths of the sample had attended college, with half having gone at least three years. Only 14 percent fell below the local 1980 median family income of $24,000. Eighty-six percent of the precinct leaders were white, compared to 62 percent of the county population. Catholics, Baptists, and Methodists were represented in the sample at about their proportions in the overall population, Episcopalians and Presbyterians were overrepresented, and fundamentalist Protestants were underrepresented.

Republican precinct leaders, compared with Democrats, are older, drawn more from professional and technical fields, have higher incomes, are more likely to be married and almost universally are white.

The Democrats are more typical of the general population. Blacks are represented in approximate proportion to their numbers in the population. There is also a noticeable minority of Democratic workers with low levels of formal education, income, and job status, as well as more retired persons. These differences reflect the electoral bases of the parties. In terms of votes, the Republican party gets almost all its support from whites, and the great majority of that from the middle- and upper-middle-class whites.[13] The mass base of the Democratic party is blue-collar whites, blacks, and Hispanics, with a small contingent of middle-class whites.

### Political Background

While precinct committee positions might be thought of as basic "entry level" posts in partisan politics, the holders of these positions in Houston have generally had extensive political experience. Table 2.3 reports their political backgrounds. Most precinct leaders have been active in party politics for many years. Seventy-six percent were active ten years or more and 39 percent had twenty years of party activity. The Democrats have been active longer than the Republicans, with 43 percent of the former claiming over twenty years of activity, compared to just 19 percent of the latter. This is hardly surprising, given that the Texas Republican party was little more

**Table 2.3. Political Background of Precinct Leaders (In Percent)**

|  | Republican | Democratic | Sample |
|---|---|---|---|
| *Years Active in Party* | | | |
| Less than 5 | 9 | 8 | 9 |
| 5–9 | 20 | 11 | 15 |
| 10–14 | 32 | 20 | 26 |
| 15–19 | 11 | 12 | 11 |
| 20–29 | 19 | 43 | 31 |
| 30 or more | 9 | 7 | 8 |
| *Party Positions Held* | | | |
| Local club official | 51 | 56 | 54 |
| District party post | 38 | 31 | 34 |
| Texas convention delegate | 81 | 73 | 77 |
| National convention delegate | 11 | 9 | 10 |
| *Non-Party Positions Held* | | | |
| Appointive, non–civil service | 13 | 11 | 12 |
| Civil service | 0 | 4 | 2 |
| Elective city office | 2 | 5 | 4 |
| School board | 2 | 5 | 4 |
| State legislature | 0 | 0 | 0 |
| Other local office | 14 | 12 | 13 |

than an organizational framework for dispensing a few federal patronage posts until the late 1950s. Over three-fourths of the activists have been delegates to state conventions, and more than half have experience as a local party club official.

The non-patronage base of Texas party organizations is reflected in the absence of precinct leaders that have held appointive, non–civil service government jobs. In the Houston area, party work does not lead to public sector employment. The great majority of party workers havé non-political occupations and volunteer their time to the parties, and most of the others are housewives or retirees. Thus there is little difference in the political backgrounds of the precinct leaders along party lines, except that the Democrats have been active longer than the Republicans.

*Campaign Activities in the 1980 Election*
We have noted that Republicans in Houston are generally conceded to have a more potent campaign organization than the Democrats. This view was

confirmed in our queries about the 1980 campaign effort made by each party. Table 2.4 presents an assessment of the precinct activities carried out by the precinct committee members. One obvious Republican advantage is that their efforts focused almost entirely on the November general election, while the Democrats were still expending considerable energies in the spring primary battles. For example, when asked their most important political activity during 1980, a plurality of the Democrats (31 percent) identified working in the primary, while only 3 percent of the Republicans mentioned primary activity. The legacy of one-party politics dies hard, even though the real political competition has clearly shifted to the general election contest.

Republican strength is also reflected in the fact that GOP workers were much more active than their Democratic counterparts. The latter reported slightly more work on voter registration and "get out the vote" efforts, but in all other areas of traditional party work the Republicans maintained a clear advantage. In particular, the Republicans reported considerably more effort in the areas of fundraising—obviously an important key for a minority party challenging a long-entrenched majority party.

The superior focus and resources of the local Republican organization are further highlighted by the general assessments of the quality of the campaign effort. When asked if their precinct organization had made a maximum effort in 1980, could have done a better job, or was pretty non-

**Table 2.4. Level of Precinct Campaign Activity in 1980 (In Percent)**

|  | Republicans | Democrats |
|---|---|---|
| *Most Important Activity* | | |
| Working for candidates | 24 | 10 |
| Telephone canvassing | 18 | 5 |
| Voter registration | 16 | 24 |
| Door-to-door canvassing | 11 | — |
| Combination of several | 8 | 5 |
| Recruiting volunteers | 5 | 2 |
| Working in primary | 3 | 31 |
| Informing voters | — | 5 |
| Not active | 5 | 15 |
| *Activities Engaged in During 1980 Campaign* | | |
| Voter registration | 77 | 80 |
| Door-to-door canvassing | 49 | 36 |

**Table 2.4. Continued**

|  | Republicans | Democrats |
|---|---|---|
| Telephone canvassing | 71 | 48 |
| Distributing literature | 77 | 59 |
| Recruiting volunteers | 69 | 49 |
| Fundraising | 65 | 37 |
| Putting up signs, posters | 82 | 60 |
| Getting out the vote | 43 | 47 |
| Other activities | 20 | 8 |
| *How Many People Worked for Local* | | |
| *Organization During 1980 Campaign* | | |
| Five or fewer | 10 | 24 |
| Six to ten | 18 | 42 |
| Ten to twenty | 36 | 23 |
| Twenty to thirty | 24 | 8 |
| Over thirty | 13 | 3 |
| Mean | 18 | 7 |
| *General Assessment of Local Organization* | | |
| *During 1980 Campaign* | | |
| Made a maximum effort | 43 | 14 |
| Could have done better | 46 | 58 |
| Pretty much nonexistent | 11 | 29 |
| *Characterization of Local Organization's* | | |
| *Role in 1980 Campaign* | | |
| The most important group working for the party's candidates | 29 | 8 |
| One of several important groups working for the party's candidates | 51 | 32 |
| Not an important factor in local campaigning | 21 | 47 |
| Inactive in 1980 campaign | 0 | 13 |
| *Evaluation of Current Precinct Organi-* | | |
| *zation Compared to 5 to 10 Years Ago* | | |
| Now significantly stronger | 40 | 9 |
| Now somewhat stronger | 29 | 19 |
| Little change | 25 | 23 |
| Now somewhat weaker | 0 | 20 |
| Now significantly weaker | 6 | 17 |
| Not sure, cannot compare | 0 | 12 |

existent, 43 percent of the Republicans said their group had made the maximum effort, while only 14 percent of the Democrats would make this claim. Twenty-nine percent of the Democrats said their organizational effort was pretty much nonexistent. This assessment reflects the fact that the Republican workers had more help in their precincts than did the Democrats, with the GOP reporting a mean of 18 workers per precinct compared to only 11 for the Democrats. It is not surprising, therefore, that 80 percent of the Republicans see their organization as either the most important or one of the most important groups in the 1980 campaign. Just 40 percent of the Democrats make this claim. The Republicans also see their organizational effort as improving, while the Democrats see theirs as either stable or on the decline.

*Motivation and Commitment to Party*

Precinct leaders in Houston fit Frank Sorauf's observation that "the desire to use the party as a means to achieve policy goals appears to be the major incentive attracting individuals to party work these days."[14] When asked why they worked in party politics, the local activists overwhelmingly chose nonpersonal, public reasons for their political involvement. Almost no one indicated that he or she was active because of an expectation of tangible reward.

The reasons stated for being politically active are presented in Table 2.5. Influencing the government was most frequently mentioned (62 percent), followed by a sense of community obligation (54 percent), and politics as part of one's lifestyle (49 percent); 44 percent said their strong sense of party attachment was important. Among the reasons least mentioned were a feeling of recognition provided by party work (14 percent), desire to be close to influential people (13 percent), and using political activity to build a political career or make business contacts (2 percent).

Republican and Democratic precinct leaders, however, were not necessarily active for the same reasons. The Republicans were somewhat more inclined to cite the opportunity to influence public policy, while Democrats said that party work fulfilled a sense of community obligation and that political work was a way of life for them. The Democrats were also much more "socially" oriented, citing the fun and excitement of campaigns, social contacts, and personal friendships with candidates to a greater extent than did the Republicans. Basically, the Democrats were about equally motivated by the desire to influence public policy and by a traditional commitment to partisan activity, while a strong secondary support came from social rewards. For Republicans, the desire to influence public policy was

**Table 2.5.  Reasons For Party Work**

| | Percentage Saying Very Important | | |
| --- | --- | --- | --- |
| | Republicans | Democrats | Sample |
| My personal friendship for a candidate | 25 | 36 | 30 |
| Active political work is part of my way of life | 45 | 54 | 49 |
| I am strongly attached to my political party | 43 | 45 | 44 |
| I enjoy the friendships and social contacts I have with other party workers | 12 | 44 | 29 |
| I like the fun and excitement of campaigns | 22 | 43 | 33 |
| I am trying to build a personal career in politics | 0 | 1 | 1 |
| I see campaign work as a way of influencing the policies of government | 68 | 58 | 62 |
| I like the feeling of being close to influential people | 9 | 16 | 13 |
| Party work helps me make business contacts | 0 | 4 | 2 |
| Party work helps me fulflll my sense of community obligation | 49 | 57 | 54 |
| Party work gives me a feeling of recognition in my community | 5 | 22 | 14 |

clearly the most important incentive, with somewhat less commitment to party or political work per se and very little importance attached to social payoffs.

We were also interested in how the precinct leaders normatively evaluated party operations. It is clear that most activists view their parties as vehicles for self-expression rather than as disciplined electoral organizations. As Table 2.6 shows, winning is clearly not the only important thing. By a margin of 60 to 33 percent, local activists rejected the view that "controversial positions should be avoided in party platforms in order to insure party unity." Sixty-nine percent agreed that local party activities should be conducted free from state party direction, and 74 percent felt no obligation

**Table 2.6. How Parties Should Conduct Their Affairs**

| | Percent Agree | | Percent Disagree | | Percent |
|---|---|---|---|---|---|
| | Strongly | Somewhat | Strongly | Somewhat | Not Sure |
| Controversial positions should be avoided in a party to insure party unity. | | | | | |
| Republican | 0 | 25 (25)* | 41 | 29 (70)* | 8 |
| Democrat | 18 | 23 (41) | 43 | 8 (51) | 8 |
| All | 9 | 24 (33) | 42 | 18 (60) | 8 |
| Local party activities should be conducted free of state party direction. | | | | | |
| Republican | 11 | 55 (66) | 23 | 0 (23) | 11 |
| Democrat | 25 | 47 (72) | 21 | 4 (25) | 4 |
| All | 18 | 51 (69) | 22 | 2 (24) | 7 |
| Good precinct chairs should support party nominees even if they disagree with their views. | | | | | |
| Republican | 9 | 5 (14) | 48 | 39 (87) | 0 |
| Democrat | 17 | 15 (32) | 51 | 11 (62) | 3 |
| All | 14 | 12 (26) | 49 | 24 (73) | 1 |
| Except under unusual circumstances a precinct committeeman should remain officially and unofficially neutral even if they have a personal preference. | | | | | |
| Republican | 8 | 8 (16) | 49 | 35 (74) | 0 |
| Democrat | 16 | 34 (50) | 25 | 19 (44) | 6 |
| All | 12 | 22 (34) | 36 | 27 (63) | 3 |
| Party organization and unity are more important than free and open discussion of issues which may divide the party. | | | | | |
| Republican | 0 | 6 ( 6) | 45 | 49 (94) | 0 |
| Democrat | 11 | 19 (30) | 53 | 9 ( 9) | 9 |
| All | 6 | 13 (19) | 49 | 27 (75) | 5 |

**Table 2.6.  Continued**

| | Percent Agree | | Percent Disagree | | Percent Not Sure |
|---|---|---|---|---|---|
| | Strongly | Somewhat | Strongly | Somewhat | |
| Candidates should not compromise their basic values even if such compromise is necessary to win. | | | | | |
| Republican | 43 | 35 (78) | 8 | 9 (17) | 5 |
| Democrat | 35 | 48 (83) | 11 | 1 (12) | 5 |
| All | 39 | 42 (81) | 9 | 5 (14) | 5 |

*The number is the combined "strong" and "some" agree/disagree.

to support party nominees with whom they disagreed. Most did not feel they should remain neutral in primary contests, and overwhelmingly (76 percent) they rejected the view that "party organization and unity are more important than free and open discussion of issues that may divide the party." Eighty percent believed that candidates should not compromise their basic values to win elections. One clearly sees among Houston activists a strong devotion to the politics of principle above party. Most precinct leaders are party loyalists, but not to the point that they are willing to sacrifice those policy goals which are the important reason for their party work in the first place.

Table 2.6 also demonstrates that the commitment to principle is particularly strong among Republican precinct leaders, while there is more of a commitment to the party itself among the Democrats. Given the great time and effort the Republicans give to their party, one might expect that they would have a stronger sense of party loyalty than the Democrats. However, it was the Democrats who were more inclined (41 to 25 percent) to agree that party platforms should avoid controversial positions. Thirty-six percent of the Democrats would support the nominees of their party regardless of issue disagreements; just 14 percent of the Republicans would do so. Fifty percent of the Democrats would stay neutral in primary fights, compared to 16 percent of the Republicans. Just six percent of the Republicans thought party organization and unity were more important than free discussion of issues, but 30 percent of the Democrats agreed with that view. Thus the Republicans seem a much better fit than the Democrats with that group of party activists referred to in the academic literature as "purists." That is, they are more concerned with advancing their issues and concerns

**Figure 2.1.  Ideological Distribution of Precinct Leaders, by Party (In Percent)**

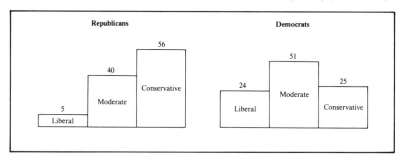

within the party than they are with maintaining an effective organizational structure for winning elections. Many political analysts see these sorts of incentives as having negative consequences for the party system.[15] We shall return to this point later in the chapter.

*Ideology and Issue Positions*

Precinct leaders were asked to rate themselves on a seven-point scale, from very liberal (1), through moderate or middle of the road (4), to conservative (7). This data is presented in Figure 2.1 (collapsing together categories 1 and 2 for liberals; 3, 4, and 5 for moderates; and 6 and 7 for conservatives). The contrast is striking. The Democrats roughly approximated the national ideological distribution—about 25 percent said they were liberal, another 25 percent were conservative, and half were moderates. The Republican distribution was strongly skewed to the right, with only 5 percent placing themselves at the liberal end of the scale, 40 percent in the moderate range, and 56 percent in the conservative categories.

These ideological differences take on more meaning when one looks at the responses to questions dealing with specific issues. Presented in Table 2.7 are views on eleven policy issues. What emerges is a pattern of substantial issue consensus among Republican activists that is not present among Democrats. This difference is particularly notable with regard to economic issues, where over 80 percent of the Republicans took the conservative position on repealing the windfall profits tax, Medicare, and cuts in the social service budget.

The Democrats were far more divided. Thirty-nine percent would repeal the windfall profits tax, but 53 percent were opposed. Forty-three percent were in favor of government health insurance, but 56 percent opposed the idea; the party workers divided about evenly on the social services item.

**Table 2.7. Precinct Workers' Positions on Issues, by Party (In Percent)**

| Issue | Party | Strong Favor | Some Favor | | Some Oppose | Strong Oppose | | Unsure |
|---|---|---|---|---|---|---|---|---|
| A constitutional amendment making abortion illegal | Rep. | 25 | 31 | (56)* | 15 | 22 | (37)* | 8 |
| | Dem. | 16 | 17 | (33) | 23 | 41 | (64) | 3 |
| Repealing windfall profits tax on gas and oil | Rep. | 61 | 28 | (89) | 6 | 0 | ( 6) | 5 |
| | Dem. | 23 | 16 | (39) | 20 | 33 | (53) | 8 |
| Increasing military spending | Rep. | 65 | 31 | (96) | 5 | 0 | ( 6) | 0 |
| | Dem. | 13 | 28 | (41) | 32 | 19 | (51) | 3 |
| Repealing 55 MPH speed limit | Rep. | 14 | 6 | (20) | 42 | 26 | (68) | 12 |
| | Dem. | 13 | 28 | (41) | 19 | 32 | (51) | 8 |
| Ratifying the Equal Rights Amendment | Rep. | 17 | 2 | (19) | 11 | 57 | (68) | 14 |
| | Dem. | 32 | 27 | (59) | 9 | 21 | (30) | 11 |

| Position on Scale Contrasting Public Policy** Alternatives | Party | Percent Taking | | |
|---|---|---|---|---|
| | | One | Two | Three |
| Continue reliance on a volunteer army (1) or Reinstate draft (3) | Rep. | 14 | 23 | 60 |
| | Dem. | 33 | 9 | 58 |
| Continue building nuclear power plants (1) or Rely on conservation (3) | Rep. | 57 | 17 | 25 |
| | Dem. | 56 | 4 | 40 |
| U.S. should increase its military presence around the world (1) or Support nonintervention (3) | Rep. | 38 | 16 | 45 |
| | Dem. | 57 | 8 | 24 |
| Gov't medical insurance plan (1) or Private medical insurance (3) | Rep. | 2 | 17 | 81 |
| | Dem. | 43 | 1 | 56 |
| Protect legal rights of accused (1) or Concentrate on stopping crime even if it reduces respect for the rights of the accused (3) | Rep. | 15 | 13 | 72 |
| | Dem. | 34 | 11 | 56 |
| Spend less and reduce social services (1) or Continue to provide such services (3) | Rep. | 83 | 3 | 16 |
| | Dem. | 43 | 11 | 43 |

\* Total of strong and some favor/disfavor.

\*\* Alternative two is *neutral* or no position on issue.

One can see that the disarray that plagued congressional Democrats in the 1980s (and particularly characterized the large Texas delegation) is reflected in basic divisions among party workers back home.

On military defense issues, the Republican leaders again reflected a strong conservative consensus. They were united behind increasing military spending; they would rely more on a strong military presence abroad as opposed to a noninterventionist and pro human rights policy; and they would reinstate the draft. Democrats also leaned toward increased military spending and the draft, but by much smaller margins; and they were slightly more favorable to the noninterventionist/human rights position than to an expanded military presence.

On social issues, the conservative consensus among Republicans was less pronounced. The GOP workers favored cracking down on suspected criminals, even at the risk of reducing the rights of the accused. They tended to support a constitutional amendment prohibiting abortions and opposed ratification of the Equal Rights Amendment (ERA). Democrats expressed a different view on these matters, with a majority opposed to an abortion amendment and favoring the ERA. Like the Republicans, however, they favored a get-tough posture on crime.

The clear message of the data was that the Republican activists were basically united in their support for a strongly conservative political program. There were few, if any, Republican dissidents among the party activists. The Democrats, however, were very catholic in their political preferences. There was no Democratic orthodoxy.

### An Interpretation of Party Change in Houston

The Republican party nationally has staged a remarkable resurgence in recent years. In addition to winning the presidency and control of the Senate in 1980, current poll data show the minority party has narrowed the Democratic lead in party identification as well.[16] Much of this improvement comes from the Republican party's dramatic gains in the South. An April 1981 CBS/*New York Times* poll, for example, showed that among whites in the region, 46 percent identified themselves as Republicans or independents leaning to Republicans, compared with 44 percent who were Democrats or leaned Democratic.[17] Even with blacks included, a higher percentage of southerners (41 percent) favored or leaned to the Republicans than was the case in traditional GOP strongholds like the Northeast (40 percent) and the Midwest (38 percent).

National political analysts also point out that the Republican party now enjoys a number of advantages over the Democrats: far superior financial resources, a better candidate recruitment operation, and the psychological advantage of being a party on the upswing.[18] Our data suggest that in Sunbelt cities like Houston, the Republican party also has a big edge in the trenches. The GOP can rely on a larger, more active, and better-disciplined corps of party workers than can the Democrats.

Table 2.8. Issue Positions of Party Precinct Workers and Party Voters

| Policy Position | Party | Percent of Workers | | Percent of Voters | |
|---|---|---|---|---|---|
| | | Favor | Oppose | Favor | Oppose |
| A constitutional amend- ment making abortions illegal | Rep. | 56 | 37 | 39 | 51 |
| | Dem. | 33 | 64 | 38 | 47 |
| Repealing windfall pro- fits tax and oil and gas | Rep. | 89 | 6 | 55 | 25 |
| | Dem. | 39 | 53 | 43 | 35 |
| Increasing military spending | Rep. | 96 | 5 | 88 | 9 |
| | Dem. | 61 | 36 | 81 | 11 |
| Repealing 55 MPH speed limit | Rep. | 20 | 68 | 29 | 63 |
| | Dem. | 41 | 51 | 38 | 55 |
| Ratifying the Equal Rights Amendment | Rep. | 19 | 68 | 41 | 40 |
| | Dem. | 59 | 30 | 67 | 19 |

In trying to explain the recent Republican success, we can reject one hypothesis—that Republican activists are more committed to party per se than are the Democrats. The Houston data show the reverse to be true. We would argue that the Republican advantage reflects the fact that, in an era when the motivations of party workers are largely purposive and ideological as opposed to social or material, the GOP has been able to rely on a cadre of activists who share a common faith. The Democrats, in contrast, are a much more diverse organizational party, whose workers do not share quite the missionary zeal that characterizes many of the Republican workers.

This, of course, leads to the next question: What accounts for the high degree of issue consensus among Republican precinct workers, compared to Democrats? Two possible explanations can be advanced. The first is that local Republican activists simply reflect the high degree of issue agreement that exists among GOP voters in the area. The second possibility is that the Republican activists are an atypical subset of partisans that have, through selective processes, come to dominate the party organization.

Survey data collected in 1980 by the Center for Public Policy at the University of Houston can help us choose between these two hypotheses. This poll of the public was conducted just before the 1980 presidential election and contained many of the same items that were used in the activists' survey. Table 2.8 compares the workers of each party and the party identifiers in the mass public.

In general, the Republican electorate was much less united behind conservative issue positions than were the party activists. Leaving aside the 55 m.p.h. speed limit, which seems devoid of ideological content, the GOP voters were less conservative than the activists on every item, although the differences on military spending were not large. On the social issues, Republican voters were equally divided on ratifying the ERA, and a majority opposed passing an anti-abortion amendment. Over 50 percent of the workers, on the other hand, took the conservative position on both these issues. Similarly, while party voters favored repeal of the windfall profits tax, they did so by a margin of only two to one (55 to 25 percent), compared to fifteen to one (89 to 6 percent) among the precinct workers. On the Democratic side, the same issue disagreements that characterized the activists also characterized the mass base. The single exception was military spending, where a majority of workers favored increases, but by a smaller margin than the Democratic voters.

Nonsurvey electoral evidence can also be marshalled in support of the argument that Republican activists are much more conservative than the electorate. In 1980 the Republican state and local party organization unquestionably favored Ronald Reagan for the presidential nomination. The state party adopted a primary plan favorable to Reagan, and 61 of 62 state executive committee members indicated a preference for the former California governor. Locally, at least two-thirds and possibly three-fourths of the precinct leaders favored Reagan. Nevertheless, in the May primary, when Reagan faced only the faltering candidacy of George Bush, he could win barely 52 percent of the vote statewide and took less than 35 percent in the Houston area.

The survey and electoral evidence strongly supports the position that, when compared to Republican voters, Republican party workers are atypically conservative. It is our contention that the dynamics involved in the creation (or recreation) of a competitive political party accounts for this asymmetry. More specifically, one can point to the critical role of the party primaries.

The Texas Democratic primary has lost its electoral monopoly, yet it remains something of a "general" election. That is, competition in these primaries is still fierce, and voters of every political persuasion continue to participate. In nonpresidential years the Texas Democratic primary attracts between 1.5 and 2 million voters, or about a third of those registered. In contrast, the Republican primary draws about 150,000 voters, or about 3 percent of the qualified voters. The large Democratic primary electorate reflects the general issue disagreements of the populace, but the very small Republican primary is largely composed of very committed conservatives who resemble the party workers. This similarity is not an accident. The primary electorate not only decides who will carry the party colors in the November general elections, but also defines the party's organizational makeup. The tiny Republican primary electorate determines the precinct committee members and county chairs, and only primary voters can attend the political meetings that select delegates to county, district, and state conventions.

The reason primary participation is so low in the modern Republican party in states like Texas is that the party has been concerned almost exclusively with national political issues. By not concerning itself with local issues nor burdening itself with local responsibilities, the nascent GOP became a party dedicated to the conservative faith. In Texas the touchstones of this faith have been right-wing economic policies and a hawkish position on defense issues. Most voters, regardless of their political ideology, remained interested in state and local affairs and chose to continue voting in the Democratic primary where relevant decisions in these arenas were made. This left the Republican party almost solely to the ideological conservatives.

The ineffectiveness of the Republican party in local politics was demonstrated in the 1981 election for mayor of Houston. The incumbent mayor, Jim McConn, was in deep political trouble and probably could not have been reelected (in fact, he got only 13 percent of the vote). Early in the campaign, the executive committee and the county chairman of the Harris County Republican party endorsed former city council member Louis Macey for mayor. Despite this endorsement, a poll conducted by the Center for Public Policy two weeks before the election showed only 10 percent of the Republican party identifiers in the city favored Macey. And the post-election poll showed that only 20 percent of the city's Republicans voted for Macey, placing him third in the race, following Harris County Sheriff Jack Heard and the ultimate winner, Kathy Whitmire. The national concerns that motivate local Republicans cannot be translated to local elections — at least as long as there are no economic or defense issues involved.

The clear conclusion from this data is that the Republican party as an organization has great difficulty marshalling its forces when the national issues about which they feel so strongly are not at stake. It is also apparent that in many ways the Republican party in Houston is simply a convenient vehicle for a small group of ideological purists to use in attempting to advance its political views. The Republican workers show a greater loyalty to their commonly shared ideology than to the Republican party. It is somewhat ironic that even though the Democrats are much more prone to issue disagreement and factional infighting, they are more loyal to their party than the highly homogeneous, nonfactionalized Republicans.


## Conclusion

Electoral circumstances in Texas have changed recently, but both parties are experiencing a "time lag" in adjusting to the new realities. The Democrats are having great difficulty in shifting their focus to the general election, while the Republican party organization remains dominated by an atypical minority. It is important to note that in Houston, as in most areas, party activists have been active in their parties for a number of years. The typical Republican precinct leader became active in the 1960s, when the local party was a lonely band of missionaries bringing the gospel according to Barry Goldwater to the land of Lyndon Johnson and Ralph Yarborough. The Republican party electorate is vastly different in the 1980s, but the GOP organization retains the ideological flavor of an earlier day.

One can speculate that the ideological consensus observed among local activists will be difficult to maintain. With Ronald Reagan in office and conservative majorities in both houses of Congress, the inevitable complexities and disappointments that come with holding power will be likely to tarnish some of the luster of conservative appeals. Successes at the state and local level are already beginning to attract a more diverse and pragmatic element to the party, a process that will challenge the homogeneity of the party electorate and party organization. Factional and personality clashes within the party are already beginning to occur, in much the same way such clashes have evolved in Florida.[19] It may well be that a resurgent party goes through a series of stages, beginning with a small band of true believers leading an organization with almost no members. As the party becomes successful in electing candidates, the true believers still control the party machinery, remain motivated by instrumental goals, and are atypical of the party's mass base. But as the party continues to be viable electorally, a more heterogeneous group of people is attracted to the party organization —a group concerned about winning elections at all levels and with a greater commitment to the party as an organization. In Houston for the present, this last stage has yet to be reached, and the organizational Republican party very much fits Edmund Burke's definition of a political party as "a body of men united, for promoting by their joint endeavors the national interest, upon some particular principle in which they are all agreed."[20]

# Notes

1. The recent "party decline" literature includes Ruth K. Scott and Ronald J. Hrebenar, *Parties in Crisis: Party Politics in America* (New York: Wiley, 1979); Kirkpatrick, *Dismantling the Parties*; Gerald Pomper, "The Decline of Party in American Elections," *Political Science Quarterly* 92 (1977), 21–42; and Walter Dean Burnham, "Revitalization and Decay: Looking Toward the Third Century of American Electoral Politics," *Journal of Politics* 38 (1976), 146–72; and Crotty, *American Parties in Decline*, 2nd ed.

2. Key, *Southern Politics*, 15–18.

3. The extent to which national GOP electoral success rests upon gains in the South is suggested by the following data. After the 1960 election, the Republican party held 36 U.S. Senate seats, compared to 64 held by the Democrats, and the minority party had 174 House seats, while the Democrats had 263. After the 1980 election, the Republicans held 53 Senate seats and had reduced the Democratic House margin to 243 to 192. After the 1960 election, the Republicans held none of the 22 Senate seats from the old confederate states, while today they hold 10. Thus, about 60% of the Republican gain has come from the southern states, and the remainder from the Mountain West. In the House, where the Mountain West has very few seats, the Republican gain has been entirely dependent upon better success in the South. In fact, the GOP actually did less well in the non-South in 1980 than it did in 1960 (winning 153 of 327 seats, or 46%, compared to 167 of 331 seats, or 50.5%). However, in the 11 southern states, the Republicans improved from winning 7 of 106 in 1960 (6.6%), to capturing 39 of 108 in 1980 (36.1%).

4. The study focuses on Harris County rather than the city of Houston because in Texas political parties are organized along county rather than municipality lines.

5. Later in the chapter we will refer to three surveys. The first of these is a statewide survey conducted in mid-October 1980. The sample was drawn from the list of registered voters and was stratified to be representative of the state electorate. The sample size was 800. Two other surveys were conducted before and after the 1981 election for mayor of Houston. The samples were again drawn from the list of registered voters and stratified to be representative. The pre-election survey had 400 respondents and the postelection survey 360. Telephone interviews were used in all three surveys.

6. The 1970 data is from the 1970 *Census of Population and Housing, Census Tracts; Houston Texas PHO(1)-89* (Washington: Bureau of the Census, 1972), 100. The 1980 data is from the *Houston Post*, 26 Apr. 1982, A5.

7. The apparent Republican organizational success led local Democratic activists in 1981 to invite Russ Mather, the Harris County Republican chairman, to discuss factors accounting for his party's success. Mather mulled it over, then declined the opportunity.

8. For a review of the background of partisan politics in Texas, see James R. Soukup, Clifton McCleskey, and Harry Holloway, *Party and Factional Division in*

*Texas* (Austin: Univ. of Texas Press, 1964). For a more recent overview, see James Anderson, Richard Murray, and Edward Farely, *Texas Politics: An Introduction* (New York: Harper and Row, 1980), 61–81.

9. Perhaps the most famous instance of this occurred in 1961, when conservative Democrat William Blakley opposed Republican John Tower for the U.S. Senate seat vacated by Lyndon Johnson. A number of liberal Democratic leaders, including Ronnie Dugger, editor of the *Texas Observer*, urged their fellow partisans to vote Republican or "go fishing" on election day. Voting was extremely light in the special runoff election (886,000 cast ballots, compared to 2,312,000 in the previous general election), and Tower defeated Blakley by 10,443 votes.

10. The 1978 Democratic primary for governor matched incumbent Dolph Briscoe against Attorney General John Hill in a typical party battle. Hill edged Briscoe in the primary but lost to Republican Bill Clements in the general election, by less than 1%. Hill's loss may be attributed partly to overconfidence (no Democrat had lost in Texas in more than a hundred years), but Briscoe's refusal to campaign for Hill undoubtedly hurt, since about half of Briscoe's supporters in the primary voted for Clements in the general election. See Kent L. Tedin and Richard W. Murray, "Dynamics of Voter Choice in a State Election," *Journal of Politics* 43 (1981), 435–55.

11. The 1981 Texas legislature's redistricting efforts clearly revealed the Democrats' inability to pull together in the face of a rising Republican challenge. Despite huge margins in the state senate (23 of 31 seats) and house (112 of 150), enough Democrats voted with Republicans on crucial ballots to give the minority party a substantial influence over plans approved by the legislature. See, for example, Ruperto Garcia, "Congressional Redistricting," *Texas Observer*, 14 Aug. 1981, 5–7.

12. Precinct committee members receive no direct compensation, but some small material rewards come with the positions. They conduct the parties' primary election and receive a per diem payment, and they can usually employ several clerks for the election. The committee member of the dominant local party typically is appointed to conduct the general election as well and again can employ several clerks for this task.

13. The very different electoral bases of the parties in Houston are suggested by the following analysis done by Richard Murray of presidential voting in 32 homogeneous precincts in 1980. The Republican share of the two-party vote in 1980 was 92% in affluent areas, 83% in upper-middle-class white areas, 70% in middle-class white areas, 56% in lower-middle-class white areas, 46% in working-class precincts, 20% in predominantly Hispanic precincts, and 4% in black precincts. Put another way, about 95% of the total Republican vote came from whites in Harris County, with about 3% from Hispanics and 2% from blacks. On the Democratic side, whites (about 70% of the voting adults) contributed about 52% of the Democratic vote for president, compared to 38% from blacks and 10% from Mexican Americans.

14. Frank J. Sorauf, *Party Politics in America* (Boston: Little Brown, 1980), 90.

15. Kirkpatrick, *Dismantling the Parties*; Nelson W. Polsby and Aaron Wildav-

sky, *Presidential Elections: Strategies of American Electoral Politics* (New York: Scribners, 1980).

16. See Karlyn H. Keene, ed., "Opinion Roundup," *Public Opinion*, April/May 1981, Vol. 4, No. 2, 29–31.

17. See Adam Clymer and Kathleen Frankovic, "The Realities of Realignment," *Public Opinion*, June-July 1981, Vol. 4, No. 3, 44–45.

18. Thomas Mann and Norman Ornstein, "The 1982 Election: What Will it Mean?" *Public Opinion*, June-July 1981, Vol. 4, No. 3, 50.

19. For a description of the factionalism that emerged in the Florida Republican Party in the 1970s, see Manning J. Dauer, "Florida: The Affluent State," in *The Changing Politics of the South*, ed. William Havard (Baton Rouge: Louisiana State Univ. Press, 1972), 144–46.

20. Edmund Burke, "Thoughts on the Cause of the Present Discontents," quoted in Sorauf, *Party Politics in America* (1980), 7.

CHAPTER 3

# Campaign Activities and Local Party Organization in Nashville

*Anne H. Hopkins*

The Nashville metropolitan complex is a bustling southern urban area which includes the Tennessee state capitol and the home of the Grand Old Opry. In 1962, the City of Nashville and Davidson County consolidated city and county government functions. Although Tennessee and Davidson County only marginally participate in the phenomenal Sunbelt population growth, both have experienced considerable population expansion in recent years. In Davidson County, the last three decades have produced a 32.6 percent increase, although the growth rate declined to only 6.3 percent between 1970 and 1980. In 1980, the county's population stood at 478,000. Politically Davidson County has been predominantly Democratic since the time of the Civil War. Suburban growth in the 1960s and 1970s, especially in the southwestern part of the county, led to the development of some Republican electoral strength, but the county remains heavily Democratic.

This essay addresses the strength and activities of party organization and its competitor organizations at the grassroots level in Davidson County. Democratic party local units are the focus of analysis since, as in many other southern states, the Republican party has not matured to the point of organizing geographically-based units below the county level.[1] In 1980 the smallest unit of organization for the Republican party in Davidson County was a seven-member executive committee with no within-county geographical representation. In contrast, the Democratic party was organized geographically on the basis of 35 county council districts. Each of these districts has two representatives (a committeeman and a committeewoman) who collectively compose the Davidson County Democratic Executive Committee. These Democratic officials were queried about party and other political organizations within their districts, in terms of their activities during the 1980 election.


**The Context**

A brief overview of electoral trends in Davidson County will provide a context within which to examine party and other organizational activities during the 1980 election. There are two types of offices with which to examine these trends. The first set of trends is examined in Figure 3.1 and includes the elections for three major, highly visible offices—president, governor, and U.S. senator—from 1936 to 1978. The second type of office is presented in Table 3.1 and includes elections to the less visible offices of Tennessee Public Service Commission, U.S. Congress, and upper and lower houses of the state legislature (General Assembly) from 1970 to 1978.

Viewed simultaneously, Figure 3.1 and Table 3.1 reveal the bifurcation of Davidson County electoral behavior, characteristic in much of southern politics, between more and less visible offices. Presidential, senatorial, and gubernatorial voting, although somewhat erratic, shows declining support for Democratic candidates for president since the 1950s and for senator and governor since the 1960s. It was not until 1968, however, that a Democrat received less than 50 percent of the vote for president in Davidson County, and in this case the plurality voted for Wallace. In 1972 two Republicans, Richard Nixon and Howard Baker, carried Davidson County, the first time Republicans had triumphed there in recent history. Davidson County Democrats recouped in 1974 and 1976, carrying the county for both gubernatorial and senatorial candidates. In 1978 Republicans were again successful, carrying the county for both the gubernatorial and senatorial candidates. Viewed in terms of these visible offices, Davidson County Democratic activists in 1980 seem likely to have recognized Republican candidates as potential victors in their county. This likelihood needs to be qualified, however, since in the 1980 election, of these three offices, only the presidency was at stake, and the incumbent Carter had carried the county in 1976 with over 60 percent of the vote.

If one examines electoral trends in Davidson County with regard to less visible offices, quite a different picture emerges. Table 3.1 examines the voting for four different offices—Public Service Commission, U.S. Congress, state house, and state senate—between 1970 and 1978. The data are reported in a different form than those in Figure 3.1 because the Democratic Party is so consistently dominant as to make the comparison of elec-

**Figure 3.1. Democratic Percentage of the Total Vote, Davidson County, Tennessee, 1936-1978**

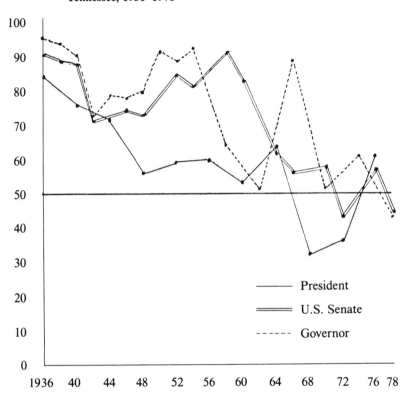

**Table 3.1. Democratic Victories, Davidson County, 1970–1978**

| | Public Service Commission | Congress | General Assembly | | Totals |
|---|---|---|---|---|---|
| | | | House | Senate | |
| **1970** | | | | | |
| No. of positions | 1 | 1 | 8 | 2 | 12 |
| No. of Dem. victories | 1 | 1 | 8 | 2 | 12 |
| No. uncontested | 0 | 0 | 7 | 0 | 7 |
| **1972** | | | | | |
| No. of positions | 1 | 1 | 10* | 2 | 14 |
| No. of Dem. victories | 1 | 1 | 9 | 2 | 13 |
| No. uncontested | 0 | 0 | 3 | 2 | 5 |
| **1974** | | | | | |
| No. of positions | 1 | 1 | 11* | 3** | 16 |
| No. of Dem. victories | 1 | 1 | 10 | 3 | 15 |
| No. uncontested | 0 | 1 | 7 | 1 | 9 |
| **1976** | | | | | |
| No. of positions | 1 | 1 | 11 | 2 | 15 |
| No. of Dem. victories | 1 | 1 | 10 | 2 | 14 |
| No. uncontested | 0 | 0 | 9 | 2 | 11 |
| **1978** | | | | | |
| No. of positions | 1 | 1 | 11 | 2 | 15 |
| No. of Dem. victories | 1 | 1 | 10 | 2 | 14 |
| No. uncontested | 0 | 0 | 5 | 2 | 7 |

\* The number of seats changed due to reappointment.
\*\*Three senate seats were filled because of mid-term vacancies.

toral trends inappropriate. Instead, Table 3.1 presents the number of positions to be filled, the number of positions won by Democrats, and the number of positions which were *not* contested by the Republican Party. The main finding stressed in Table 3.1 is that Democrats won virtually every contest throughout the entire period. The only exception is a single state legislative seat captured by the Republicans in 1972 and maintained since that time. In the contests in which the Republicans did field candidates, none of the contending candidates came within a reasonable distance of the Democratic victors. Striking is the large number of contests (ranging from five out of fourteen, to eleven out of fifteen) in which Republicans did not even provide token opposition to Democratic candidates. Thus the picture of recent local partisan strength in Davidson County in Table 3.1 is of a highly dominant Democratic party virtually unchallenged by the Republicans.

Thus the full partisan context of the 1980 election was divided, depending on which level of office is considered. For a highly visible office race such as the presidential contest between Carter and Reagan, the Republicans had some chance of carrying the county or at least providing a strong showing. But while in the less visible races for Public Service Commission, Congress or the state legislature, Democrats were likely totally to dominate the electoral outcomes.

Since the strength of the two parties varies within Davidson County and because our level of analysis of party organization is the council district, it is also appropriate to elaborate upon the geographical basis of this partisan context. Figure 3.2 presents a map of Davidson County and its 35 Metropolitan Council Districts. The shading on the map indicates the relative strength of the Democratic Party as an average of five statewide contests between 1974 and 1978. The five elections which were averaged were those for 1974 governor, 1974 U.S. senator, 1976 president, 1978 U.S. senator, and 1978 governor. We selected elections held immediately prior to the election under study because they seemed likely to form the basis for political activists' perception of potential threats and opportunities in the 1980 election. To permit a later examination of party variance in relation to campaign activities, only visible offices were utilized. These five elections showed almost a 20 percent variance in Democratic fortunes. In 1974, the Democratic candidate for governor carried Davidson County with over 62 percent of the vote; similarly, the 1976 votes for president and U.S. senator produced 62 and 58 percent Democratic majorities. In contrast, 1978 was a much more Republican year with the Democratic gubernatorial and U.S. senate candidates receiving only 43 percent and 46 percent respectively. Seventeen of the 35 council districts averaged 55 percent or more Democratic for the five races, twelve were fairly competitive, and six were Republican. The areas of Republican strength lay in the more affluent western and southern suburban areas. These are also the areas of largest population growth, suggesting the potential for greater Republican strength in the future.

## Democratic Party Officials

In the week following the 1980 election, questionnaires were sent to the members of the Davidson County Democratic Executive Committee.[2] Of these, 37 percent responded; if the unit of analysis is considered to be the council district, the response was a more reasonable 57 percent. Council

**Figure 3.2.  Partisan Strenth in Davidson County, Tennessee, for
Selected Offices, by Council Districts, 1974–1978**

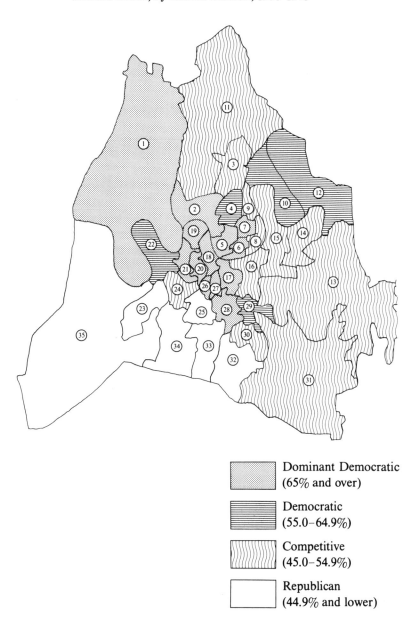

districts not responding were predominantly from the more rural, less-populated areas of the county, a fact that reduces the problem of bias because of the larger comparative city focus of the study.

Two general types of information were sought from the Democratic committeemen and committeewomen: (1) the nature of and reasons for the respondents' participation in electoral politics, and (2) the campaign activities engaged in by a variety of organizations within their districts during the 1980 election. This section focuses on the types of individuals who serve as local Democratic party officials, including related demographic factors, party experience and loyalty, and motivational patterns. Following this we explore the respondents' own campaign activities. The final section examines the range of campaign activities conducted by organizations within the council districts.

Table 3.2 presents a summary of the demographic characteristics of the council district committee members. The average Davidson County council district party official was a longterm resident; worked in a professional, technical, or managerial position; had an income between $20,000 and $29,999 per year; attended graduate or professional school; and was a white Protestant.

A large number of previous studies of local party activists have found upward status bias relative to the general population. This bias was evident in this study relative to occupation, income, and education. Professionals were substantially overrepresented among party activists, as were those with higher incomes, and those who had attended graduate or professional school. Although many cities are largely nonwhite and/or have large ethnic populations, Davidson County does not have a majority black population and is not an ethnic city. Interestingly, over 80 percent of the respondents answered a question about their ethnicity by identifying themselves as Americans. Our respondents were 28 percent black, a slightly larger proportion than in the county population. Consistent with the characteristics of the general population, the respondents were overwhelmingly Protestant, with large proportions either Baptists or members of the Church of Christ.

Additional background information on the council district party leaders is provided in Table 3.3, which characterizes the respondents' party experience and party loyalty. The bulk of the activists had worked for the Democratic Party for a number of years, with small proportions having held other party positions, sought public office, or held appointive office. It appears that those who hold positions as members of the Democratic County Executive Committee remain for a fairly long period but generally do not use the office as a springboard to other party or public office. There

**Table 3.2.  Characteristics of Democratic Committee Members
and General Population, Davidson County (1980)**

|  | Percentage of Party Respondents | Percentage of General Population |
|---|---|---|
| *Years in County* | | |
| Less than 10 | 8 | — |
| 10–19 | 20 | — |
| 20+ | 78 | — |
| *Years in Neighborhood* | | |
| Less than 10 | 24 | — |
| 10–19 | 24 | — |
| 20+ | 52 | — |
| *Occupation* | | |
| Professionals | 32 | 14 |
| Technical/managers | 36 | 47 |
| Operators/laborers | 14 | 39 |
| Homemaker | 14 | — |
| Student | 5 | — |
| *Family Income* | | |
| Under $10,000 | 15 | 20 |
| $10,000–19,999 | 15 | 31 |
| $20,000–29,999 | 60 | 24 |
| $30,000– | 10 | 25 |
| *Education* | | |
| H.S. or less | 8 | 66 |
| Some college | 32 | 15 |
| College graduate | 12 | 10 |
| Grad. or prof. school | 48 | 9 |
| *Religion* | | |
| Protestant | 68 | — |
| Catholic | 8 | — |
| Jewish | 12 | — |
| Other/none | 12 | — |
| *Sex* | | |
| Male | 44 | 47 |
| Female | 56 | 53 |
| *Race* | | |
| White | 72 | 77 |
| Black | 28 | 22 |
| *Union Membership* | | |
| Member | 20 | — |
| Nonmember | 80 | — |

Table 3.3.  **Party Experience and Party Loyalty of Democratic Leaders, Davidson County (In Percent)**

| | |
|---|---:|
| *Party Experience* | |
| *Years Previous Party Experience* | |
| 0–4 | 24 |
| 5–9 | 8 |
| 10–14 | 28 |
| 15+ | 40 |
| *Party Positions Held* | |
| County party committee/official | 68 |
| Congressional district committee/official | 16 |
| State central committee/official | 0 |
| County convention delegate | 20 |
| State convention delegate | 16 |
| National convention delegate | 28 |
| *Public Office Sought* | |
| County level | 12 |
| Other local official | 4 |
| State legislature | 4 |
| Congress | 4 |
| *Appointive Office* | |
| Hold now | 16 |
| Held at one time | 9 |
| Never held | 75 |
| *Party Loyalty* | |
| *Strength of Democratic Partisanship* | |
| Very strong | 76 |
| Moderate | 16 |
| Weak | 8 |
| *Loyalty as a Reason for Involvement* | |
| Very important | 63 |
| Somewhat important | 25 |
| Not important | 12 |
| *Would Consider Splitting the Ticket in Voting* | |
| Yes | 56 |
| No | 36 |
| Don't Know | 8 |

are of course some exceptions, the most common being those who serve as a party convention delegate or hold appointive office. It is also important to note that almost one-quarter of the activists were relatively new to the job, suggesting that this is not a static or unchanging party grouping.

Several indicators of party loyalty are also included in Table 3.3. As

**Table 3.4.** **Motivational Patterns of Democratic Activists,**
**Davidson County (In Percent)**

|  | Very Important | Somewhat Important | Not Important |
|---|---|---|---|
| *Philosophical / Ideological* |  |  |  |
| Influence policies of government | 67 | 29 | 4 |
| Community obligation | 64 | 32 | 4 |
| Party attachment | 63 | 25 | 13 |
| Part of my way of life | 54 | 29 | 17 |
| *Personal* |  |  |  |
| Friendships and social contacts | 58 | 17 | 25 |
| Fun and excitement | 39 | 48 | 13 |
| Personal career in politics | 29 | 38 | 33 |
| Personal recognition | 26 | 57 | 17 |
| Close to influential people | 24 | 40 | 36 |
| Business contacts | 17 | 42 | 42 |
| *Friendship for a Candidate* | 28 | 36 | 36 |

Note: Respondents answered the question, "In examining why *you* have been active in organized politics in recent years, how important are these reasons?"

would be expected, Democratic council district leaders were fairly strong partisans, and over 60 percent of them saw loyalty as a very important reason for their involvement. Party attachment, however, was not inviolate —almost 40 percent did not see loyalty as a very important reason for their involvement, and well over half of the activists would consider splitting their tickets. This finding is consistent with the general patterns of split-ticket voting described in Figure 3.1 and Table 3.1 and reflects the differential partisan support patterns of the general electorate when different kinds of offices are being contested.

Differential loyalties raise the issue of why political activists become involved in politics. Numerous studies of political participation have sought self-defined motivations for that participation. Davidson County Democratic party officials were asked to assess the importance to them of eleven motivations for their party participation (see Table 3.4). Four of the motivations—influence policies, community obligation, party attachment, and "part of my way of life,"—seem to reflect philosophical or ideological reasons for political involvement, and fairly substantial proportions of the activists claimed these were very important to them.

The second block of motivations presented in Table 3.4 is more personal in nature and includes such factors as friendship and social contacts, fun and excitement, desire for a personal career in politics, personal recognition, to be close to influential people, and to enhance business contacts. With the exception of the desire for friendship and social contacts, the other five personal motivations were very important to a substantially smaller proportion of party activists. A third kind of motivation was suggested by those who responded that they were active in politics out of personal friendship with a candidate. Very important to 28 percent of the activists, friendship with a candidate as a motivator seems likely to produce somewhat different campaign behavior on the part of the party activist.

Given the differential loyalties indicated in Table 3.3, it seems useful to examine the relationship between the importance attached to various motivations and both strength of partisanship and willingness to split a party ticket. On the whole there were not very large differences in the motivations of strong partisans and ticket splitters. Strong partisans, however, were somewhat more likely to identify motivations that are philosophical or ideological (influencing governmental policies, community obligation, or lifestyle) as being more important to them. This finding contradicts the popular belief that party activists are drawn to politics primarily for personal gain and recognition. Potential ticket splitters were less likely to identify philosophical or ideological motivations (particularly party attachment and lifestyle) and more apt to select being close to influential people as an important motivator.

Overall, the characteristics of Davidson County Democratic activists roughly paralleled the nature of the county population, but with an upward status bias in terms of education, income, and occupation. Typically these activists had worked for the party for a number of years, and only a small minority held or had held other political positions. Council district leaders were generally very strong partisans, but a number would upon occasion consider splitting their tickets. Philosophical and ideological motivations for participation tended to dominate, rather than more personal incentives.

## Campaign Activity of Democratic Committee Members

Although it is important to examine the background characteristics and motivations of our respondents, the primary focus of this essay is to expand our understanding of the activities of parties and other organizations in campaign and related activities. Campaign activity is examined in two major ways in this study—by reviewing the activities engaged in by the

**Table 3.5. Campaign Activity by Democratic Leaders, Davidson County (In Percent)**

| *Hours Worked Per Week* | | | | |
|---|---|---|---|---|
| 10 or less | | | | 32 |
| 11–30 | | | | 36 |
| 31+ | | | | 32 |
| *Personally Engaged In:* | | | | |
| Voter registration | | | | 88 |
| Literature distribution | | | | 84 |
| Fundraising | | | | 72 |
| Face-to-face canvassing | | | | 68 |
| Getting out vote | | | | 56 |
| Telephone canvassing | | | | 32 |
| *Focus of Activity* | | | | |
| Candidate | | | | 17 |
| Party ticket | | | | 75 |
| Both | | | | 8 |

| *Interactions with Other Party Leaders* | *One or Two a Week* | *One or Two a Month* | *One or Two a Year* | *Hardly Ever* |
|---|---|---|---|---|
| Council district leaders | 26 | 68 | 5 | 0 |
| County level | 6 | 78 | 17 | 0 |
| State level | 0 | 14 | 64 | 21 |

respondents in their capacity as council district party leaders, and, in the next section, by shifting the analysis to the full range of campaign activities within each council district.

Previous studies have reported a wide range of campaign activities by party workers, engaged in with varying degrees of effort. Table 3.5 reports the time spent, kinds of activities pursued, and the focus of campaign work by the Democratic council district leaders in the 1980 election. Nashville local party leaders span the full range of effort and activities. In terms of time commitment, party workers ranged from little effort to virtually full-time activity. Traditional activities such as voter registration and literature distribution head the list of frequent campaign activities. It is interesting to note that a large percentage of respondents were involved in fundraising, an activity usually associated with a fairly narrow participation base.[3] The more traditional party organization activities, get-out-the-vote efforts and telephone canvassing, are the least frequently pursued. The council district party leaders were also asked for whom they specifically worked in the 1980 election. An overwhelming majority responded "for the party ticket" or both "for the party ticket" and "for one candidate." Of those who said they worked for one candidate, over half worked in the presidential campaign of Democratic candidate Jimmy Carter.

Council district leaders were also asked about the frequency of their interactions with other party leaders. The most involved activists, and potentially the most influential with the local party organization, seem likely to be those that interact most frequently with other party leaders. Table 3.5 presents the frequency with which council district leaders interact with other district leaders, countywide leaders, and statewide leaders. As might be expected, interactions are less frequent as one moves farther from the district level, although almost 80 percent of the district leaders interacted with county leaders once or twice a month and only about 15 percent met with state leaders that often.

The variation in the frequency with which campaign activities were performed by the district leaders raises a question about the nature of these variations. Since there was a wide spread in terms of the time spent by the workers, it was expected that time would be related to some campaign activities and not to others. Party leaders who spend more time at their jobs were more apt to raise funds and do face-to-face canvassing. It was also expected that some campaign activities would have a traditional sex stereotype or bias attached to them; for example, fundraisers might tend to be men. In practice, male council district leaders were slightly less likely to distribute literature or to work in voter registration than women, but there were no other sex differences. Finally, the high proportion of district leaders who espoused a desire to influence public policy suggests that such people might selectively pursue certain campaign activities to that end. The only large difference between those who did and did not see influencing policy as a reason for participating in party politics existed in fundraising. Those who sought to influence policy were less likely to engage in that activity.

To facilitate an examination of the correlates of differences in campaign activity, an index of campaign activity was created. Index scores are based on a summation of the number of different kinds of activities (voter registration, fundraising, getting out the vote on election day, and face-to-face or telephone canvassing) participated in by each respondent. Those employed in technical and managerial occupations were the least active, those with lower incomes were more active, education was unrelated to activity scope, blacks and men were somewhat more active than whites or women, and liberals were less active than moderates or conservatives. Party leaders who

saw influencing policies or a sense of community obligation as very important motivations were much less likely to be active, whereas those who
identified friendship and social contacts, building a personal career, personal recognition, and business contacts as very important were apt to be
more active. Thus, extended activism seemed more characteristic of those
who were primarily motivated by personal goals and who belonged to up-
wardly mobile groups.

## Campaign Activities Within Council Districts

Candidates' reliance on their own campaign organizations, multiple offices
being contested simultaneously, and the growth of political action committees (PACs), make surveying all electorally involved organizations prohibi-
tive. Thus, the council district committeemen and committeewomen were
asked to act as informants or experts in answering a range of questions
about campaign activities conducted within their council districts. There
are, of course, both advantages and limitations to using such respondents
as informants. On the one hand, it seems reasonable to expect that an
individual with both a personal commitment and a formal position is likely
to be fairly well informed, not only about their own immediate activities
but about those of others operating on the same turf. On the other hand,
however, it is clear that both the quality of information a given informant
has and individual perceptual skills may vary substantially among the respondents. It seems plausible that such informants are likely to be more
knowledgeable about some aspects of campaign activities than others. For
instance, the quality of information held by Democratic activists about
their own party is likely to be higher than that about the Republicans. Even
given these limitations, though, the use of informants seems essential if we
are to determine what is happening on the local level. And the smaller the
unit one is asked to address (for example, the council district as opposed
to the county), the more likely it seems that better quality information will
be obtained.

Respondents were asked (see Appendix) how much campaign activity
took place in their council district in relation to voter registration, fundraising, getting out the vote, face-to-face canvassing, and telephone canvassing; and by whom the activity was conducted—party organization,
candidate organization, or PAC. Distinctions were also made by level of
party organization, particular candidate race, and type of PAC involved. It
should be noted that a good number of the respondents left blank a con-

siderable portion of the matrix provided for answers. Although it is possible that complexity reduced the responses, it seems likely that blank spaces indicate lack of knowledge. This lack of information may exist because the respondent really did not know what was going on in the district or, more likely, that nothing was being done in the district by a particular group or with regard to a particular activity. Thus in the analysis which follows, if a respondent filled out at least part of the matrix, missing information was assumed to be part of the total response rather than excluded.

Table 3.6 summarizes the information provided by the Democratic council committee members acting as informants about what campaign activities were conducted by which groups at what level of intensity in their district. The percentages in each cell in Table 3.6 indicate the proportion of all respondents who indicated that *much*, as opposed to *not much* (or blank), of each of the five campaign activities was being done in their districts by the various organizations (party organizations, candidate organizations, and PACs).

With regard to party organization (the top three lines of Table 3.6), the countywide Democratic organization, and to a lesser extent the Republican organization, was more active in more districts in carrying out campaign activities than were the council or subcouncil district organizations. Democratic organizations, no matter at which level of party organization, were substantially more active in more districts than their Republican counterparts. Although this reported lower Republican activity may be to a certain extent a function of having only Democratic informants, it is also consistent with the continuing minority status of the Republican party in Davidson County. Consistent with this minority status and with recent attempts to improve their electoral success, Republican organizations were proportionately more likely to engage in fundraising activities than were Democratic organizations. Interestingly, the kind of activity engaged in by these party organizational units differed from that of the individual district leaders (see Table 3.5), who emphasized getting out the vote on election day more than fundraising.

Coterminous with the campaign activities of party organizations are candidate-based and PAC organizations. The intensity and scope of the activity of organizations centered on presidential candidates were by far the strongest among these latter two types, roughly comparable to the activity levels of the countywide party organization. Candidate-based organizations for Congress were also fairly active—more active than one might have expected in a presidential election year, but perhaps understandable in an urban congressional district similar to the county party unit. Substantially

**Table 3.6. Campaign Activities in Council Districts, Davidson County (In Percent)**

| Carried out by | Democratic | | | | | Republican | | | | |
|---|---|---|---|---|---|---|---|---|---|---|
| | Voter Regis-tration | Fund Raising | Face-to-Face Canvas-sing | Getting Out Vote | Tele-phone Canvas-sing | Voter Regis-tration | Fund Raising | Face-to-Face Canvas-sing | Getting Out Vote | Tele-phone Canvas-sing |
| Subcouncil District | 36 | 12 | 12 | 20 | 16 | 16 | 12 | 8 | 8 | 12 |
| Council District | 48 | 28 | 24 | 36 | 32 | 12 | 12 | 4 | 12 | 8 |
| Countywide | 64 | 40 | 36 | 52 | 48 | 12 | 24 | 8 | 16 | 16 |
| Carter/Reagan for President | 60 | 44 | 36 | 56 | 48 | 16 | 20 | 4 | 20 | 16 |
| Democrat/Republican for Congress | 44 | 40 | 32 | 48 | 40 | 8 | 16 | 4 | 4 | 8 |
| Democrat/Republican for State Legislature | 16 | 12 | 24 | 20 | 12 | 16 | 8 | 12 | 16 | 4 |
| Labor PACs | 12 | 16 | 8 | 12 | 20 | — | — | — | — | — |
| Business PACs | 4 | 12 | 4 | 4 | 4 | — | — | — | — | — |
| Professional PACs | 4 | 8 | 4 | 16 | 8 | — | — | — | — | — |

**Table 3.7. Campaign Intensity, by Type of Organization (In Percent)**

|  | Campaign Intensity | | |
|---|---|---|---|
|  | Low | Medium | High |
| Democratic Party Organization | 36 | 28 | 36 |
| Democratic Candidate Organization | 28 | 36 | 36 |
| PACs | 74 | 24 | 0 |

less campaign activity was attributed to PACs and candidate organizations for state legislators. As with the Democratic party organizations, Democratic candidate organizations were substantially more active than their Republican counterpart organizations.

In order to assess the relative strength of campaign activities conducted by the organizations within the council districts, a campaign activity intensity score was developed.[4] Campaign intensity scores were calculated simply by summing across different types of campaign activities conducted by the three levels of party organization, by the three types of candidate organizations, and by the three kinds of PACs.[5] Given the sparse responses relative to Republicans[6] and because of a desire to focus on the traits of the dominant organization, only Democratic party and candidate organizations were considered in developing campaign intensity scores.

Table 3.7 presents a simple comparison of campaign intensity scores for Democratic party organizations, Democratic candidate organizations, and PACs. Campaign intensity scores are grouped into high, medium, and low categories. A low campaign activity intensity indicates that virtually none of the campaign activities (voter registration, fundraising, face-to-face canvassing, getting out the vote, and telephone canvassing) were perceived to be conducted within the districts[7] by a given type of political organization (party, candidate, PAC). A low campaign intensity score indicates that only one or none of the fifteen possible campaign activities was assessed as "much." A medium campaign intensity score indicates slightly more activity, with three to seven of the possible activity-organization combinations appraised as "much." Finally, a high campaign activity intensity score is based on eight or more of the fifteen possibilities' having been viewed as conducted.[8]

Table 3.7 suggests that, overall, Davidson County experienced a moderate amount of Democratic campaign-related activity in the 1980 election. Moderate proportions (36 percent for party and candidate organizations) of the respondents perceived a fairly high intensity of campaign activities in their council districts. A fair number of additional districts were seen to have experienced medium levels of Democratic party and candidate organization activity. Table 3.7 indicates that Democratic candidate-based organizations were only slightly more active in campaigning than their party organization counterparts. This is somewhat surprising, given that Tennessee's campaign style is generally recognized to be based on individual personalities.[9] Finally, Table 3.7 strongly suggests that PACs hold a very weak position in the overall campaign picture in Davidson County.

Earlier in this essay (see Figure 3.1), the geographical basis of the the partisan situation in Davidson County was reviewed briefly. Since campaign activities are ostensibly conducted to maximize electoral success, it seems plausible that there would be a relationship between district competitiveness and campaign effort. The nature of such a relationship may differ, however, given variations in the electoral context. As we have discussed above, in Davidson County the electoral context varies with the level or visibility of the office, as well as across districts. Because of the dominance of the Democrats in Davidson County, one might expect a certain degree of complacency on the part of both Democratic candidates and the Democratic party organization in the general election. However, in areas in which electoral party competitiveness is the norm, or where Republicans have experienced recent growth, one might expect substantially more activity by all kinds of political organizations.

Given these variations in context, the relationship between competitiveness and Democratic campaign activity can be anticipated. In areas of Davidson County which have been dominated by the Democratic party, campaign activity will likely be lower, out of both habit and lack of a perceived threat. In competitive areas, one anticipates increased activity by both Democratic party organizations and Democratic candidate organizations, as they see a challenge to their ability to either elect candidates or maintain their share of the vote. This anticipation seems plausible, since all of the competitive council districts have only become competitive relatively recently (in the last fifteen years). By contrast, activity levels in solidly Republican areas are more difficult to anticipate, since two possibilities arise. First, Democratic organizations may simply write off such areas as hopeless causes and ignore them in their electoral efforts. Or second, the Democrats may recognize more clearly in such areas a threat to their electoral dominance on the county or state level and heighten campaign activities. We cannot document here the process which may lead to one or the other of these reactions to electoral threat. We can, however, examine locationally the match between actual electoral performance and campaign ac-

**Table 3.8.  Democratic Party Organization Campaign Intensity,
by District Competitiveness (In Percent)**

| Campaign intensity | District Competitiveness | | |
| | Republican | Competitive | Democratic |
|---|---|---|---|
| Low | 11 | 44 | 57 |
| Medium | 33 | 22 | 29 |
| High | 56 | 33 | 14 |

**Table 3.9.  Democratic Candidate Organization Campaign Intensity,
by District Competitiveness (In Percent)**

| Campaign Intensity | District Competitiveness | | |
| | Republican | Competitive | Democratic |
|---|---|---|---|
| Low | 0 | 44 | 43 |
| Medium | 56 | 22 | 29 |
| High | 44 | 33 | 29 |

tivity levels, making inferences about the process which might lead to such relationships.

Past electoral party performance seems to be the best indicator of the electoral context of campaign activities. Using the data in Figure 3.1, the percentage Democratic for each of the five races (U.S. senator, president, governor, 1974–78) was averaged for each council district and matched with the informant's responses about campaign activities.[10] Utilizing data from these elections should approximate the recent electoral experiences of both the party activists who are serving as informants and the organizational activities they are depicting.

Tables 3.8 and 3.9 examine the relationship between competitiveness and campaign intensity scores for Democratic party organization and Democratic candidate organization. Party organizational campaign activity among Democrats in 1980 (see Table 3.8) fits the expectations outlined above, with the highest proportion of low levels of campaign activity occurring in Democratic districts. Conversely, the highest proportion of high campaign activity intensity scores occurs in Republican districts, supporting the idea that Democratic activists may feel most threatened, and hence be most apt to put forth effort, in areas of recent weakness.

Democratic candidate organizational campaign activities (Table 3.9) show much the same pattern, although the contrasts are less clear-cut. Among Democratic candidate organizations, the most common pattern within Republican districts is a medium level of campaign intensity. Similar to the practice of party organizations, Democratic candidate organizations tend to put least effort into dominantly Democratic districts.

Another way of viewing the electoral context is to look at changes in the relative electoral strength of the two political parties over time. If electoral fortunes within given districts have declined, then the level of campaign activity may be altered to meet the new electoral context. To examine this possibility, an indicator of electoral change was developed by calculating the difference between the average Democratic vote for the most recent electoral contests (the 1978 contests for governor and U.S. senator) and those in the two preceding elections (1976 president, 1976 U.S. senator, and 1974 governor). In the average Democratic vote countywide, the two 1978 elections reflected a decline of 16 percent from the 1974 and 1976 contests; losses by council districts ranged from 5 percent to 27 percent. The relationship between electoral change and party competition is best summarized by the Democrats' average district losses: in Republican districts, 13 percent; in competitive districts, 19 percent; in Democratic districts, 22 percent; and in dominant Democratic districts, 13 percent. Democrats are clearly most vulnerable in districts that are competitive or that are Democratic but not dominantly so. If party and candidate organizations note these altering electoral fortunes and adopt new campaign strategies to fit the new circumstances, then we anticipate a relationship between the degree of electoral change and campaign intensity scores. In particular one would expect greater campaign activity to occur in those districts subject to the greatest shifts in electoral outcome and less activity in more stable districts. Alas, this expectation is not confirmed (see Table 3.10). Indeed, to the extent that there is any relationship between electoral change and campaign intensity, it is a weak inverse relationship, with those districts which experienced the greatest change showing the lowest campaign intensities. Of course, it may be that by 1980 Democrats had already written off such districts, or it may be that the data simply is insufficiently sensitive to indicate such perceptions of electoral change.

Use of these respondents as informants about their council districts is not without limitations; but a number of interesting findings are evident. In general, the council district committeemen and committeewomen provided a fairly full view of the campaign activities conducted within their districts by each type of political organization. The analysis of competitiveness indicates that contextual variations explain a portion of the variance

Table 3.10.  **Relation Between Electoral Shifts and Campaign Intensity, Davidson County (In Percent)**

| Campaign Intensity | Partisan Change | | |
|---|---|---|---|
| | Less Chg. | Avg. Chg. | More Chg. |
| *Democratic Party Organization* | | | |
| Low | 36 | 25 | 50 |
| Medium | 27 | 25 | 33 |
| High | 36 | 50 | 17 |
| *Democratic Candidate Organization* | | | |
| Low | 27 | 38 | 50 |
| Medium | 46 | 25 | 33 |
| High | 27 | 38 | 17 |
| *PACs* | | | |
| Low | 73 | 75 | 0 |
| Medium | 27 | 13 | 17 |
| High | 0 | 13 | 0 |

in campaign activity intensity. The analysis of electoral change was less fruitful, but the possibility that recent electoral shifts may affect activist perceptions of threat and thus alter their campaign activity warrants further investigation.

## Conclusion

This chapter briefly has described the kinds of individuals who act as local council district party leaders in Davidson County and the campaign activities engaged in by them, their party organizations, candidate-based organizations, and PACs. In general, the characteristics of these leaders appear consistent with those identified in other studies of local party activists. The investigation of reasons leaders have for being active in party politics revealed an emphasis on philosophical and ideological motivations.

As for personal investments of time and energy in the 1980 campaign, the district leaders ranged from little time and effort to virtually fulltime, broad-scale campaigning. Voter registration and literature distribution were the commonest activities. Leaders tended to work for the whole party ticket rather than for individual candidates. Considerable variation existed in the degree of interaction with other party leaders.

The most interesting findings were obtained when the district leaders acted as informants about the extent of campaign activities conducted in their council districts by party organizations, candidate organizations, and PACs; and when the relationship of these activities to district competitiveness was analyzed. This data permit a preliminary assessment of party and candidate organizational and campaign strength. The strongest efforts seem to have been made by countywide party organizations and presidential campaign organizations. Not surprisingly, the Democratic party and candidate organizations clearly overshadowed their Republican counterparts. It is somewhat surprising that the Reagan organization did not surpass the county Republican organization. The second level of campaign activity seemed to be carried out by council district organizations and the candidate-based organizations of congressional candidates. PACs were active in some areas, but clearly were weak relative to other more traditional organizations. The frequency of types of activity varied, too. The Democrats tended to be strongest in fundraising and weakest in face-to-face canvassing. Republicans evinced the most activity in fundraising (more, proportionately, than the Democrats) and in voter registration. PAC activities varied by the orientation (labor-business-professional) of the groups involved.

The campaign activity intensity scores reflect the rough equality of efforts in the campaign by Democratic party and candidate organizations. The examination of the relationship between campaign activity intensity and competitiveness roughly fit the expectation that Democratic organizations (whether party or candidate-based) are least likely to be active in strong Democratic areas and most likely to be active in Republican areas. It is possible that the perception of relative threat posed by Republican opposition in recent elections may promote greater Democratic activity. The Republican electoral areas are also the areas of greatest population growth, a fact which suggests that more trouble may be ahead for the Democratic party.

What does this limited exploration of party campaign activity suggest about the state of political parties on a more general level? Many locales are like Davidson County in having a long tradition of electoral dominance by one political party. One usually associates such dominance with inactive or nonexistent party organizations. The variance in activity levels across Davidson County, depending on the districts' relative degree of recent competitiveness, indicates that activity is reduced in areas of electoral dominance. But the countywide picture of campaign activity suggests a more complex reality. Democratic party organizations exist in every council district, and they seem to co-exist at roughly comparable activity levels with candidate-based organizations. In other words, although one might expect candidate organizations to replace the party organization where the latter is inactive, this seems not to happen. Democratic dominance seems to reduce activity levels for both types of organizations. Of course, it is possible that Democratic candidate and party organizations work against each other in competitive and Republican districts, but there is no evidence from party leaders of that kind of problem. Potential Republican party growth seems to be the common enemy to both organizations. Although historical data is lacking and our test of the impact of electoral change did not produce the expected results, it still seems likely that the Republican party's fortunes —both real and feared—have a major impact on the activities of the Democratic party. If this is correct, then it may be erroneous to view the Democratic party as dominant in Davidson County.

### Notes

1. The Republicans have fared well electorally in Tennessee in recent years. Organizational efforts outside of traditionally Republican East Tennessee have predominantly stressed candidate recruitment and statewide campaigns rather than grassroots party organizational development. See Anne H. Hopkins and William Lyons, "Toward a Classification of State Electoral Change: A Note on Tennessee, 1837–1976," *Journal of Politics* 42 (1980), 209–26, for a historical overview of electoral party development and change in Tennessee.

2. The questionnaire was mailed in three waves, including a postcard reminder, and was sent immediately following the election.

3. There are only two studies of campaign financing in Tennessee. See William Buchanan and Agnes Bird, *Money As a Campaign Resource: Tennessee Democratic Primaries, 1948–1964* (Princeton: Citizens' Research Foundation, 1966), and Anne H. Hopkins and Ruth S. Jones, "State Campaign Fund Raising: Targets and Response," *Journal of Politics* 47 May 1985, 427–49.

4. The idea of developing such an index was suggested by Dwaine Marvick's analysis of Los Angeles in this volume, although the method of calculation differs.

5. For example, the fifteen instances (five campaign activities by three levels of organization) of possible Democratic party organization indicators are summed (1–much activity; 0–not much activity or blank), yielding party organization campaign activity scores ranging from 0 to 15.

6. As mentioned above, it is also possible that Democratic party activists simply know less about Republican party organizational and candidate-based activity than they do about Democratic party activity. It is not possible to determine this from the available data.

7. In interpreting the analysis which follows, it is important to note that the

unit remains the individual party official, not the council district. There are four instances of two respondents from the same district; the remaining respondents are from different council districts.

8. Although this may appear to be a rather generous categorization of high campaign activity intensity, it should be remembered that five different kinds of campaign activity are incorporated in the scoring. Not all of these activities had to be conducted for a relatively strong effort to have existed. In fact, if all five activities were pursued, it might seem that insufficient targeting of energy and resources had occurred.

9. See Lee Seifert Greene, David H. Grubbs, and Victor C. Hobday, *Government in Tennessee*, 3d. ed. (Knoxville: Univ. of Tennessee Press, 1975).

10. The actual distribution of districts included in the analysis differs from the total council district data in that the respondents do not perfectly mirror the total district competitive distribution.

# CHAPTER 4

# The Party Activist in Detroit and Los Angeles: A Longitudinal View, 1956–1980

*Samuel J. Eldersveld*

The state of American party organization today, viewed in longitudinal perspective, has elicited the concern of scholars and politicians. The assumption in certain quarters is that there has been a change for the worse—"a decline," "decomposition," "deterioration," or "dismantling." While others see less of a "deinstitutionalization" than a "reorientation" (in new functional directions, or in the "sharing" of functions of party organizational leadership with campaign specialists and special interest groups), the observation widely made is that for ten years or more, party structures have been weakening. There are those, of course, who see countertrends. Thus, it is alleged that the National Committees have become more assertive and powerful—the Republican one because of the party's 1970s organizational rebuilding, and the Democratic one through its control over the delegate selection process. Research by scholars of state party organization has also demonstrated an apparent increase, and not a decline, in the funding and staffing of most of these state committees since the 1960s.[1] Nevertheless, the lament about what is happening to our parties has continued for some time, in the absence of solid empirical evidence—particularly empirical evidence about the condition of party organization and campaign efforts at the local level.

It is obvious to anyone actively involved in our parties that they are in the throes of significant modification, embracing changes in formal structure, elite recruitment, activist involvement, campaign effort, and relationship with the public. The reform movement in both parties since the late sixties has led to improvement in the representative character of party conventions, to changes in the composition of central committees and in the roles of party organs (such as the Democratic Caucus) in the Congress, and to the utilization of new technological approaches to campaigning. Yet from press reports about such reforms, one gets very limited insight into what has been happening at the infrastructural level of our parties. What *has* been the nature of party organizational change at the base of party organizations—in the precinct, ward, assembly district, club, town committee, or other similar base unit of the party? Our knowledge of what has been occurring at this vital level is limited, usually dating from studies which precede the reform period. The aim of the analysis presented here, relying on interviews with local party organization leaders at time points from the 1950s to 1980, is to fill that gap for two cities, Detroit and Los Angeles.

Linked to our interest in documenting the state of the party organization over time is a concern over the extent of local party adaptiveness to changes in the environment. Insofar as changes in party organization occur, they can, of course, be the product of a variety of forces, internal as well as exogenous to the party. Since we assume that our parties are relatively "open" structures, decentralized and power maximizing, we would expect parties to change by responding to population change, to perceptions of changes in the nature and strategy of their opposition, and to awareness of new approaches, techniques, and challenges for mobilizing public support. Indeed, we are inclined to assume that in democratic societies parties will be, must be, socially and politically adaptive if they are to survive. The style and pace of party responsiveness, as well as its genuineness, will of course vary from one community to another. And it is this aspect of comparative longitudinal analysis which must be kept in mind. Here we shall present some data relevant to this question of organizational adaptiveness.

The data are for the Republican and Democratic party base-unit personnel in Detroit and Los Angeles over a twenty-five year timespan. In analyzing these data, our objectives are:

1. To describe the social background and demography of these activists, noting changes in patterns of social recruitment.
2. To attempt in a preliminary analysis to link such changes to the changes in the population in these cities and in the neighborhoods in which these leaders are working.
3. To assess the nature of the activists' involvement with the party organization over time, as well as their experience in party work.
4. To describe and evaluate the extent of motivational change, that is, the reasons activists had for (a) becoming active and (b) remaining active.
5. To report in some detail the uniformities and variations in campaign activity over time, and the extent of the campaign effort by different interest subgroups within the parties.
6. Finally, to assess, based on these data, the extent of party "decline."

The data sets we utilize are unique. In Detroit we interviewed a sample of precinct leaders for the city in 1956 and 1980. In these and in intervening years we have, in addition, data for a set of thirty-eight key precincts in identical neighborhoods for elections in 1956, 1964, 1972, and 1980. Thus two types of analyses are possible for Detroit: (1) for the entire city sample of Republican and Democratic precinct leaders in 1956 and 1980; and (2) for a selected set of thirty-eight precincts at eight-year intervals. The original research in Detroit in 1956 included interviews with precinct leaders (total N = 281), an adult cross-section, and district-level leaders in the six congressional districts.[2] In 1964 we returned to the original eighty-seven precincts to interview again at the precinct level only (a new set of leaders, since only four had held their positions from 1956 on). In 1972, we interviewed once more in as many of these precincts as we could, within the limits posed by precinct boundary changes and the inaccessibility of precinct leaders.[3] In 1980 we included these key precincts in the total Detroit sample selected at that time.

Due to limited resources, we could not personally interview most of the respondents in Detroit in 1980, as we had in 1956; therefore we used a mail questionnaire for many of them. This strategy affected the response rate considerably. Whereas in 1956 we completed 85 percent of our interviews, in 1980 the response rate was 35 percent for mail questionnaires and 60 percent for personal interviews.

Our 1980 Detroit precincts fairly well matched the voting behavior of the city:

|  | City | Average for Sample of 202 Precincts |
|---|---|---|
| Percent of Democratic Vote for Carter for President | 78.50 | 78.58 |
| Turnout—Percent of Registered Voters Voting | 65.82 | 57.32 |

The vote for U.S. president was mirrored well in our sample precincts. We did "undersample" high-turnout precincts somewhat, though not seriously.

In 1980, under the direction of Dwaine Marvick, a study was conducted in Los Angeles, including interviews with a sample of 474 club presidents and county committee members (elected from the assembly districts). Over 80 percent of these interviews were personal ones with a representative sample of the universe of party activists at these levels in the Los Angeles area. The interviews can be compared with samples from earlier studies Marvick has done in the Los Angeles area since 1956.[4]

**Table 4.1.  Social Backgrounds of Detroit Precinct Leaders, 1956 and 1980
(Percentage Based on City of Detroit Data Only) (In Percent)**

|  | Democrats | | Republicans | | Totals | |
|---|---|---|---|---|---|---|
|  | *1956* | *1980* | *1956* | *1980* | *1956* | *1980* |
| *Sex* | | | | | | |
| Male | 85 | 58 | 80 | 62 | 81 | 59 |
| *Age* | | | | | | |
| Up to 40 | 36 | 32 | 28 | 35 | 32 | 32 |
| *Race* | | | | | | |
| Black | 26 | 59 | 20 | 35 | 23 | 52 |
| *Education* | | | | | | |
| No college | 65 | 20 | 47 | 14 | 55 | 17 |
| *Occupation* | | | | | | |
| White-collar | 44 | 50 | 75 | 68 | 60 | 56 |
| *Religion* | | | | | | |
| Catholic | 46 | 32 | 23 | 39 | 34 | 34 |
| *Labor* | | | | | | |
| Union members | 60 | 70 | 25 | 32 | 42 | 60 |
| Union activists | 47 | 66 | 8 | 24 | 26 | 54 |

## Basic Trends in Social Profiles
## of the Party Cadres: Continuous Diversification

Social demography data indicate that in Detroit the precinct leadership is
as diversified as before, if not more so (see Table 4.1). Lower status groups
have as good an opportunity now as in the 1950s to get precinct positions—
52 percent of these leaders are black, 44 percent are not white-collar, 60 percent are from the unions. The Democratic party is more "open" in certain
respects than the Republican, but the latter also has a diversified leadership,
in terms of social backgrounds—32 percent union members, 35 percent
black, and, surprisingly, 39 percent Catholic (more than among Democrats!). Women are represented better nowadays in both parties, and the
younger age groups are holding their own, doing particularly well among
Republicans. Most striking are the penetration of the precinct cadres by the
unions, the increased educational level in both parties, the great rise of
blacks in the Democratic party, and the movement of Catholics to the
Republicans. Despite these trends, the heterogeneity of these cadres is very
noticeable, and hence the possibility of social group tensions within the
parties must be recognized.

Table 4.2.  Social Backgrounds of Los Angeles Activists, 1963–1980 (In Percent)

| | Republicans | | | | | | | Democrats | | | | | | |
|---|---|---|---|---|---|---|---|---|---|---|---|---|---|---|
| | 1963 | 1968 | 1972 | 1976 | 1978 | 1980 | | 1963 | 1968 | 1972 | 1976 | 1978 | 1980 |
| *Sex* | | | | | | | | | | | | | |
| Male | 78 | 79 | 67 | 76 | 61 | 63 | | 82 | 75 | 77 | 70 | 68 | 63 |
| *Age* | | | | | | | | | | | | | |
| Up to 40 | 42 | 37 | 31 | 25 | 26 | 27 | | 40 | 36 | 41 | 33 | 40 | 36 |
| *Education* | | | | | | | | | | | | | |
| No college or only some college | — | 35 | 43 | 43 | 31 | 30 | | — | 43 | 35 | 31 | 31 | 29 |
| *Occupation* | | | | | | | | | | | | | |
| Professional | 39 | — | 38 | 37 | 42 | 34 | | 47 | — | 48 | 46 | 55 | 38 |
| Executive, business, and other white collar | 36 | — | 41 | 32 | 47 | 47 | | 28 | — | 32 | 23 | 24 | 40 |
| *Religion* | | | | | | | | | | | | | |
| Catholic | 14 | 12 | 15 | 19 | 19 | 19 | | 27 | 25 | 19 | 20 | 22 | 16 |
| Jewish | 2 | 4 | 3 | 2 | 3 | 7 | | 23 | 21 | 23 | 22 | 27 | 19 |
| Protestant | 75 | 73 | 77 | 67 | 69 | 65 | | 39 | 37 | 37 | 27 | 28 | 40 |

**Table 4.3.  Social Profiles of Party Activists, Detroit and Los Angeles, 1980 (In Percent)**

|  | Republicans 1980 | | Democrats 1980 | |
|---|---|---|---|---|
|  | *Detroit* | *Los Angeles* | *Detroit* | *Los Angeles* |
| Black | 35 | 2 | 59 | 10 |
| Jewish | 5 | 7 | 4 | 19 |
| Union members | 32 | 15 | 60 | 47 |
| Protestant | 41 | 65 | 44 | 40 |
| Blue-collar workers | 16 | 19 | 26 | 22 |
| Graduate or professional education | 37 | 48 | 36 | 47 |

The social characteristics of the Los Angeles club presidents and county central committee members reveal certain similarities to those in Detroit, but also some sharp differences (see Table 4.2). As in Detroit, women have taken a larger proportion of these positions; Catholics have shown an increase in the Republican party and a decrease in the Democratic party; and the educational level of these activists has risen. The differences between the two cities are in the high proportion of black activists in Detroit and Jewish ones in Los Angeles, the differential involvement of labor union members, and the higher socioeconomic status of the Los Angeles leaders.

While change has occurred in both cities, in 1980 the party cadres had distinctive social profiles. The penetration by blacks and union members in Detroit stands out, while the dominance of well-educated white Protestants and Jews in Los Angeles is striking. The contrasts in 1980 are clear, as Table 4.3 indicates.

## The Adaptiveness of Local Party Leadership to Population Changes

The linear increase in black leadership in Detroit can be seen from data on "key precincts" in Tables 4.4 and 4.5. Although these precincts were not representative of the entire city, they indicate the crucial shifts over each eight-year span of time. We note a gradual decline in male dominance of precinct positions; a gradual increase in the proportion of young activists;

**Table 4.4.  Aggregate Changes in the Social Profiles of a Segment of Detroit's Precinct Leaders, 1956–1980 (Percent Based on Leader Interviews in 38 Key Precincts)**

|  | 1956 | 1964 | 1972 | 1980 |
|---|---|---|---|---|
| *Race* | | | | |
| Black | 32 | 40 | 45 | 54 |
| *Sex* | | | | |
| Male | 79 | 63 | 63 | 58 |
| *Age* | | | | |
| Below 40 | 26 | 39 | 35 | 42 |
| 55+ | 26 | 26 | 34 | 33 |
| *Education* | | | | |
| Primary plus some high school | 26 | 21 | 21 | 31 |
| Some college | 58 | 58 | 50 | 38.5 |
| (Completed college) | (40) | (26) | (29) | (31) |
| *Religion* | | | | |
| Protestant | 68 | 57 | 63 | 61.5 |
| *Occupation* | | | | |
| Blue-Collar | 28 | 38 | 43 | — |
| Professional-Managerial | 61 | 57 | 32 | — |
| *National Origin* | | | | |
| Central, Eastern, Southern Europe | 35 | 23 | 20 | 16 |
| North and Northwest Europe | 34 | 34 | 28 | 30 |
| *Residence* | | | | |
| Native Detroiters plus those 20 or more years in Detroit | 64 | 87 | 77 | 96 |
| *Union Member* | | | | |
| Labor union affiliation | 26 | 21 | 53 | 55 |

and a jump in labor union membership (primarily but not exclusively confined to the Democrats), from 26 percent in 1956 to over 50 percent in 1972 and still rising in 1980. Further, the social status of precinct leaders may have improved somewhat, but there remained a fairly large minority (up to 30 percent) with no college education and with blue-collar jobs.

A central query in all of this, of course, is whether these changes are associated with population changes in Detroit. During this period the population of the city of Detroit was undergoing major change, as census data reveal:

|                              | 1950  | 1960  | 1970  | 1980  |
|------------------------------|-------|-------|-------|-------|
| Population (in Thousands)    | 1,850 | 1,670 | 1,511 | 1,203 |
| Percent Change               | —     | −9.7  | −9.5  | −20.0 |
| Percent of Population Black  | 16.2  | 28.9  | 43.7  | 63.1  |

Proportionately, Detroit had a much larger black population than Los Angeles, which also grew during this era. In Los Angeles blacks constituted 13.5 percent in 1960, 17.9 percent in 1970, and 17 percent in 1980. In addition, of course, Los Angeles had a larger number of Mexicans and other nonwhites. The proportion of Detroit's 1970 population which was "native" (not foreign-born nor of foreign or mixed parentage) was 77 percent, while in Los Angeles it was 66 percent. And of course the city of Detroit's population has been steadily decreasing. This has not been true of the city of Los Angeles, where preliminary 1980 figures indicated a 5.5 percent increase (to a total of 2,966,763).

The extent of organizational adaptation by the Detroit parties in response to population shifts can be examined more precisely by reference to neighborhoods than to gross changes for the entire city. Census tract data for individual precincts were not available. But we did ask our precinct leaders to inform us about the social complexion of their precincts and about whether their precincts were changing (in terms of race, class, reli-

**Table 4.5. Percentage Aggregate Changes in Characteristics of Detroit Precinct Leaders, by Party, 1956–1980 (38 Precincts) (In Percent)**

|                          | Republican | | | | Democrats | | | |
|--------------------------|------|------|------|------|------|------|------|------|
|                          | 1956 | 1964 | 1972 | 1980 | 1956 | 1964 | 1972 | 1980 |
| *Race*                   |      |      |      |      |      |      |      |      |
| Black                    | 22   | 22   | 22   | 25   | 40   | 55   | 65   | 67   |
| *Sex*                    |      |      |      |      |      |      |      |      |
| Male                     | 89   | 72   | 61   | 63   | 70   | 55   | 65   | 56   |
| *Age*                    |      |      |      |      |      |      |      |      |
| Below 40                 | 17   | 40   | 34   | 43   | 35   | 40   | 35   | 41   |
| 55 plus                  | 22   | 45   | 28   | 29   | 30   | 10   | 40   | 29   |
| *Education*              |      |      |      |      |      |      |      |      |
| Primary and some high school | 17 | 22 | 17 | 25 | 35 | 20 | 25 | 33 |
| Attended or completed college | 67 | 55 | 50 | 75 | 50 | 60 | 50 | 67 |

**Table 4.6.  Racial Changes in Detroit Precinct Leadership, As Linked to Perceived Changes in the Population (In Percent)**

|  | 1956–1964 | 1964–1972 | Total Period 1956–1972 |
|---|---|---|---|
| *Precincts with a Reported Increase in Black Population* | | | |
| Percentage of Leaders Who Were Black: | | | |
| In first year | 17 | 25 | 23 |
| In second year | 67 | 38 | 46 |
| Net Change to Black Leadership | +50 | +13 | +23 |
| *Precincts Where No Change in Black Population Was Reported* | | | |
| Percentage of Leaders Who Were Black: | | | |
| In first year | 33 | 56 | 41 |
| In second year | 33 | 56 | 41 |
| Net Change to Black Leadership | 0 | 0 | 0 |

gion, etc.). On the basis of these informant reports, it was possible for us to classify our precincts according to whether the precinct was changing or not and whether it was increasing, decreasing, or remaining stable in the proportion of these subgroups in its population. We could then link these reports of trends in the social composition of the individual precinct to precinct leadership change.

The data in Table 4.6 reveal that, in those precincts where our informants claimed that the black population was increasing, there was a significant shift to black leadership. This was particularly true in the Democratic party, as the following summary shows.

Percentage Net Change to Black Leadership

|  | Democrats | Republicans |
|---|---|---|
| In Precincts Becoming More Black in Population | +60 | −8 |
| In Precincts Not Becoming More Black in Population | −4 | +5 |

Table 4.7.  Organizational Involvement and Party Experience
in Detroit (In Percent)

| | Demo-crats | | Repub-licans | | All Precinct Leaders | |
|---|---|---|---|---|---|---|
| | 1956 | 1980 | 1956 | 1980 | 1956 | 1980 |
| *Experience* | | | | | | |
| Years in party work: | | | | | | |
| 0–4 | 44 | 21 | 47 | 42 | 46 | 30 |
| 5–8 | 11 | 17 | 18 | 6 | 15 | 15 |
| Total Recently Active | 55 | 38 | 65 | 48 | 61 | 45 |
| *Interaction Frequency* | | | | | | |
| With other leaders, % seeing leaders once or twice/month or more frequently (1980), compared to "often" (in 1956): | | | | | | |
| – Precinct leaders | 41 | 62 | 42 | 39 | 42 | 54 |
| – District level leaders | 57 | 63 | 29 | 32 | 40 | 53 |
| – County level leaders | 31 | 31 | 6 | 19 | 18 | 27 |
| – State level leaders | 23 | 28 | 6 | 11 | 14 | 23 |
| *Attachment to Party Was "Very Important" Reason for Becoming Active* | 57 | 42 | 50 | 30 | 53 | 38 |
| *Would Consider Splitting the Ticket in Voting* | 46 | 69 | 70 | 80 | 58 | 73 |
| *Aspire to Higher Position in the Party Organization* (if had the opportunity) | 51 | 74 | 62 | 81 | 57 | 75 |
| *Morale in Organizational Role* | | | | | | |
| Wants more say | 45 | 66 | 56 | 59 | 51 | 63 |
| Precinct leaders have a say in running the district party's organization: | | | | | | |
| – A "great deal" | 35 | 16 | 15 | 16 | 25 | 16 |
| – A "fair amount" | 18 | 18 | 17 | 23 | 17 | 20 |
| Total—Have a say | 53 | 34 | 32 | 39 | 42 | 36 |

There is a strong suggestion here that the Democratic organization was, through self-conscious recruitment or "natural selection," adapting to population change, but such adaptation was far less evident for the Republicans in Detroit.

By 1980 Detroit blacks had already assumed leadership in a large number of precincts. Again the differences by party are significant. Of those precincts which our informants described as predominantly black, only 10 percent had white Democratic leadership but 33 percent had white Republican leadership. On the other hand, none of the white precincts had black Republican leaders while 9 percent had black Democratic leaders. To turn the analysis around, in 1980 we found:

|  | Republicans | Democrats | Totals |
|---|---|---|---|
| Percentage of White Leaders in Black Precincts | 22 | 12 | 16 |
| Percentage of Black Leaders in White Precincts | 0 | 2 | 2 |

While there was some overlap or lag in the emergence of black leaders in black precincts, by 1980 the linkage of race to precinct type was very high, suggesting that the parties had indeed "responded" to population change.

**Party Experience, Loyalty, and
Organizational Involvement**

Not all activists are strongly committed or deeply involved with the organization. Different measures are used here to determine the level of that involvement. Table 4.7 presents these data for Detroit. "Behavioral" measures, such as length of time in party work, suggest two observations. One is that a large proportion of Detroit activists are relative newcomers, but there was a decline in this proportion from 1956 to 1980. Still, in 1980, 30 percent had entered party work only in the last four years and 45 percent in the past eight years. This was to be expected, since for many activists party work is a marginal and tentative responsibility. In Los Angeles we found a fairly stable pattern in the 1960s and 1970s, one which revealed more continuity and expertise than in Detroit.[5] The contrast is as follows:

Percentage with More Than Eight Years in Party Work (1980)

|              | Republicans | Democrats |
|--------------|-------------|-----------|
| Los Angeles  | 72          | 74        |
| Detroit      | 52          | 62        |

This stability might have been expected in Los Angeles, since the sample of activists consisted of club presidents and county committee members, who stay in their party positions for long periods of time. The turnover among Detroit activist leaders was much greater.

The behavioral measure of frequency of contacts with other leaders suggests not a decline in such interaction in the past twenty-five years, but rather an increase. Apparently up to 50 percent of these leaders in Detroit saw other precinct and district leaders quite frequently. But the pattern found in 1956—that for the large majority these interactions are confined to the local stratum of politics—was borne out in 1980. This was true for both Detroit and Los Angeles samples. In Los Angeles, the county was the most proximate local stratum of the party, since for the most part these were county-centered committee activists. In Detroit, by contrast, the precinct and district levels were most relevant, since our activists were precinct delegates to district conventions. Keeping these parallels in mind, we find the following similar patterns of contact:

Monthly or Weekly Contacts of Local Activists (1980) (In Percent)

|              | At County (L.A.) or District (Detroit) Level | | At State Level | |
|--------------|-------------|-----------|-------------|-----------|
|              | Republicans | Democrats | Republicans | Democrats |
| Detroit      | 32          | 63        | 11          | 28        |
| Los Angeles  | 68          | 71        | 29          | 35        |

Local level contacts remained more frequent than contacts at the state level. And Democrats in the two cities were similar, while the Detroit and Los Angeles Republicans differed considerably.

When we look at more "attitudinal" measures of organized involvement, we find evidence of both strong commitment and limited liability. On the one hand, a very high percentage in both cities aspired to higher positions in the organization. When asked whether they would take a more responsible position if given the opportunity, over 70 percent said "yes." This is an amazing find, particularly for those who think local parties are atrophying.

Percentage of Activists Who Would Take Another Position (1980)

|  | Definitely Yes | Probably Yes | Total Yes |
|---|---|---|---|
| Democrats: |  |  |  |
| Los Angeles | 37 | 34 | 71 |
| Detroit | 39 | 33 | 72 |
| Republicans: |  |  |  |
| Los Angeles | 43 | 31 | 74 |
| Detroit | 35 | 45 | 80 |

Party work was still fascinating to these people. And the trend data reveal that this aspiration level has not declined. In Detroit, 57 percent said "yes" to this question in 1956, while 75 percent did in 1980. The 1976 Los Angeles data are almost identical to those for 1980.

It is particularly interesting to note that certain groups that one might not expect to be "at home" in a party ("deviant social groups," in party recruitment terms) in 1980, in both Detroit and Los Angeles, were exceedingly interested in continuing party activity:

Percentage Aspiring to a Higher Party Position

|  | Los Angeles | | Detroit | |
|---|---|---|---|---|
|  | Republicans | Democrats | Republicans | Democrats |
| Activist Subgroups |  |  |  |  |
| Catholics | 77 | 75 | 93 | 69 |
| Jews | 80 | 77 | — | — |
| Blacks | — | — | 89 | 73 |

Obviously there was considerable desire, irrespective of subgroup, for recognition in the party, and hence considerable latent internal pressure among the social groups of each party's coalition. All of this again suggests that at the local level in these two cities the dynamism of party operations has not disappeared.

While a large majority of these workers likes to stay in the party organization, their loyalty to the party may be suffering a minor erosion. In a battery of questions dealing with reasons for getting involved in party work, we included an item on the importance of "party loyalty" for such involvement. In both cities we found a decrease in the rating of this reason as "very important":

Percentage Citing "Party Loyalty" as Motivation

|  | 1956 | 1980 |
|---|---|---|
| Detroit | 53 | 38 |
| Los Angeles | 69 | 50 |

We also can look at trends in the strength of partisan commitment of the
activists from the 1960s to 1980 in Los Angeles (see Table 4.8). There was
a small decline in strong partisanship in 1980 among Democrats, but an
increase among Republicans. Both Los Angeles cadres were very loyal compared to the Detroit precinct leaders, a large proportion of whom rated
themselves as less partisan than the Los Angeles leaders. Again, this difference was probably linked to the higher position and longer party experience
of the Los Angeles activists.

Another measure used in the Detroit study was whether the respondent
would consider deserting the party and "splitting the ballot," voting for a
candidate of the opposition. The incidence of this was already high in 1956

**Table 4.8.  Strength of Partisanship of Activists Over Time
(Based on an 8-Point Scale) (In Percent)**

|  | Highest Two Categories | Middle Three Categories | Lowest Three Categories |
|---|---|---|---|
| *Los Angeles Dems.* |  |  |  |
| 1980 | 71 | 22 | 7 |
| 1976 | 77 | 21 | 2 |
| 1974 | 73 | 26 | 1 |
| 1972 | 76 | 21 | 3 |
| 1968 | 73 | 24 | 3 |
| *Los Angeles Reps.* |  |  |  |
| 1980 | 81 | 15 | 4 |
| 1976 | 70 | 28 | 2 |
| 1974 | 71 | 26 | 3 |
| 1972 | 71 | 26 | 4 |
| 1968 | 76 | 20 | 4 |
| Detroit Dems.—1980 | 53 | 41 | 6 |
| Detroit Reps.—1980 | 34 | 52 | 14 |

(particularly among Detroit Republican activists, 70 percent of whom said "yes"), and in 1980 it was 69 percent for Democrats and 80 percent for Republicans. Thus, in these senses, loyalty was less salient for the activists than before.[6] Yet they did want to stay on in party work. And they did want more "say" in the decision-making process in their district organizations in Detroit (Table 4.7). If anything, this demand was greater in 1980 than previously. A minority (about one-third) felt they had enough say, and 60 percent wanted more influence. This result attested to the existence of a cadre of activists who, while perhaps more independent than previously, were still committed to exercising a role in the party organization.

## Motivational Directions:
## Remarkable Uniformity Over Time

A varied set of queries can be posed in considering the incentives for being a party activist in 1980 as compared with the 1950s and 1960s. Did the same level of general idealism pervade explanations for becoming active as we found in earlier research? And did we find the same low salience of ideological purposiveness when activists were asked to discuss current satisfaction? Was politics still meaningful for many because of social friendships, campaign excitement, "inside dopesterism," and social recognition? These and other queries can be tested with our data. In both cities we have already noted a decline in the importance of party loyalty as a reason for becoming active. What other trends appear?

The uniformities in incentives for involvement over a twenty-five year period are nothing short of remarkable (see Table 4.9). When asked to tell us what reasons were "very important," the 1956 and 1980 activists gave us very similar answers over this timespan, and very similar answers in both communities. Thus, two reasons considered very important (ranking close to ratings 1 and 2) in both cities—"to influence the policies of government" and a "feeling of community obligation"—produced these similar responses:

|  | Detroit | | Los Angeles | |
|---|---|---|---|---|
|  | 1956 | 1980 | 1956 | 1980 |
| Percentage Citing Influence Politics | 58 | 65 | 74 | 71 |
| Percentage Citing Community Obligation | 65 | 58 | 59 | 50 |

**Table 4.9.  Relative Importance of Incentives for Becoming Active (All Party Activists) (Percentage of Sample Saying Motivation Was "Very Important")**

| Incentives | Detroit | | Los Angeles | |
|---|---|---|---|---|
| | *1956* | *1980* | *1956* | *1980* |
| Personal friendship for a candidate | 23 | 24 | 20 | 27 |
| Politics is my way of life | 43 | 50 | 43 | 56 |
| Party loyalty | 53 | 38 | 69 | 50 |
| Social friendships and contacts | 56 | 41 | 32 | 33 |
| The fun and excitement of politics | 34 | 42 | 33 | 36 |
| Building a personal career in politics | 11 | 19 | 11 | 19 |
| Desire to influence the policies of government | 58 | 65 | 74 | 71 |
| Desire to be close to influential people | 34 | 20 | 7 | 14 |
| Feeling of community obligation | 65 | 58 | 59 | 50 |
| Belief it will help with business contacts | 6 | 16 | 5 | 8 |
| Desire for recognition in the community | 20 | 27 | — | 16 |

And the reason which ranked lowest in both cities—"help in making business contacts"—also has similar proportions (below 20 percent in both cities). The rank orders are presented in Table 4.10, revealing a close coincidence.

The changes in these incentives overall are not very large or significant. If one grouped these reasons into the types of categories normally employed ("purposive," "solidary," and "material"), it would be hard to discern any major trend. Thus, in Detroit there was a slight increase in "purposive" responses (to "influence policies" and "politics is my way of life"). There was also some decline in emphasis on social contacts (a "solidary" incentive), but this was balanced by an increase in interest in campaign "fun" and a desire to be close to influentials. Similarly, in Los Angeles the "purposive" incentive patterns held up pretty well over this timespan. While there was slightly less feeling of community obligation, there was a stronger feeling that being in party work is "my way of life." Thus, on balance, in the

**Table 4.10. Motivations for Involvement in Party Work, Detroit and Los Angeles, 1956–1980 (Rank Order)**

| | Detroit | | | Los Angeles | |
|---|---|---|---|---|---|
| | 1956 | 1980 | | 1956 | 1980 |
| Community obligation | 1 | 2 | Policies | 1 | 1 |
| Desire to influence policies in government | 2 | 1 | Loyalty | 2 | 3 |
| Social contacts and friendship | 3 | 5 | Community obligation | 3 | 3 |
| Party loyalty | 4 | 6 | Politics my way of life | 4 | 2 |
| Politics my way of life | 5 | 3 | Fun and excitement | 5 | 5 |
| Fun and excitement | 6 | 4 | Social contacts | 6 | 6 |
| Desire to be close to influentials | 7 | 9 | Personal friendship for candidate | 7 | 7 |
| Personal friendship for candidate | 8 | 8 | Personal career | 8 | 8 |
| Desire for recognition | 9 | 7 | Close to influential people | 9 | 9 |
| Building a personal career in politics | 10 | 10 | Business contacts | 10 | 10 |
| Help in business contacts | 11 | 11 | | | |

basic character of motivation at the time of entrance into the party, very little change was apparent.[7]

This trend analysis can be pursued further with Detroit data, since at all time points we asked two questions:

1. Which one of these reasons *best* explains why you became active?
2. If you had to drop out of political activity tomorrow, what things would you miss most from such work?

Responses to these questions permit us to identify the most salient motives for activity. The first of these questions yielded the pattern of answers of Table 4.11. As was to be expected from our previous analysis, ideological-philosophical reasons were the "real" reasons reported for being active. The predominance of these increased in 1980, so that 77 percent of the Detroit activists cited such reasons as "the best reasons" for being active.

**Table 4.11.  Motivational Orientations of Detroit Party Activists (In Percent)**

|  | Demo-crats | | Repub-licans | | Totals | |
|---|---|---|---|---|---|---|
|  | 1956 | 1980 | 1956 | 1980 | 1956 | 1980 |
| Most Salient Reasons for Becoming Active (Percentage Considering It the Best Reason) | | | | | | |
| *Ideological/ Philosophical* | | | | | | |
| To influence policies | 19 | 40 | 25 | 29 | 21 | 36 |
| A sense of community obligation | 16 | 20 | 24 | 29 | 20 | 23 |
| "Politics is my way of life" | 16 | 16 | 7 | 6 | 11 | 13 |
| Party loyalty | 11 | 4 | 15 | 6 | 13 | 5 |
|  | 62 | 80 | 71 | 70 | 65 | 77 |
| *Personalized* | | | | | | |
| Social contacts, the fun and excitement of the campaign, being close to influentials, recognition in the community, and material rewards (as business gain and building a career in party politics) | 26 | 15 | 15 | 25 | 20 | 19 |
| *Friendship for a Candidate* | 12 | 5 | 14 | 4 | 12 | 5 |
| Reasons for Remaining Active ("What would you miss most if you had to drop out of activity tomorrow?") | | | | | | |
| *Ideological Concerns* | | | | | | |
| Working for issues; other general ideological concerns | 7 | 32 | 20 | 26 | 13 | 28 |
| *Personalized Concerns* | | | | | | |
| Social contacts and friendship | 63 | 39 | 47 | 44 | 55 | 41 |
| Fun and excitement, plus other personalized incentives | 13 | 18 | 9 | 22 | 10 | 20 |
| *Nothing Would be Missed* | 15 | 10 | 22 | 7 | 19 | 10 |
| Total | 98 | 99 | 98 | 99 | 97 | 99 |

If we contrast such findings with those in the lower half of Table 4.11, we again find striking evidence of the phenomenon of "motivational reorientation," which we identified in our earlier Detroit analysis.[8] When pressed for the most important *current* satisfaction derived from party work, respondents named "personalized" concerns predominantly in 1980 as in 1956. Although there was less emphasis in 1980 on social contacts and friendships, these were still by far the most important satisfactions (55 percent in 1956 and 44 percent in 1980). When combined with other personally instrumental satisfactions such as the fun of campaigning, recognition in the community, and being close to influentials, the total proportion who emphasized instrumental motivations was 61 percent in 1980, compared to 65 percent in 1956. The extent of "motivational reorientation" from time of entrance can be summarized as follows:

| | 1956 | | 1980 | |
| --- | --- | --- | --- | --- |
| Percentage Citing | Demo-crats | Repub-licans | Demo-crats | Repub-licans |
| Began with Personalized Motivational Orientations | 26 | 15 | 15 | 25 |
| Currently Hold Personalized Motivations | 76 | 56 | 57 | 66 |
| Balance in the Direction of More Personalized Motivations | +50 | +41 | +42 | +41 |

This same finding has been supported by research in other parts of the United States. As in the 1950s, party activity in 1980, irrespective of ideological reasons for initial involvement, remained for many a satisfying "solidary" experience. After activists have been in the party, they clearly "learn" to see party work as socially rewarding and personally gratifying in terms of mobility and recognition needs. In 1980 fewer said that "nothing would be missed" if they had to leave the party (10 percent in 1980 compared to 19 percent in 1956, a drop particularly noticeable for Detroit Republicans). For those who stay, the party is a rewarding "social group."

## Levels and Patterns of Local Party Activity: How Much Organizational Slack?

In earlier research we discovered that in communities like Detroit and Los Angeles in the 1950s the nature of task performance was, on the one hand,

**Table 4.12.  Comparative Activity Levels: Three Critical Tasks,
1956 and 1980 (In Percent)**

|  | Detroit | | | | Los Angeles | |
|  | Demo-crats | | Repub-licans | | Demo-crats | Repub-lican |
|  | 1956 | 1980 | 1956 | 1980 | 1980 | 1980 |
|---|---|---|---|---|---|---|
| *Proportion of Activists Who Personally Engaged In:* |  |  |  |  |  |  |
| Voter registration | 93 | 42 | 80 | 19 | 60 | 72 |
| House-to-house canvassing | 46 | 60 | 32 | 61 | 53 | 48 |
| Election-day roundup of votes | 68 | 69 | 80 | 62 | 68 | 77 |
| Performed: |  |  |  |  |  |  |
| All 3 tasks | 17 | 30 | 25 | 16 | 31 | 35 |
| 2 of 3 tasks | 38 | 35 | 22 | 34 | 30 | 36 |
| Total | 55 | 65 | 47 | 50 | 61 | 71 |

not intensive and, on the other hand, characterized by improvisation and autonomy. Party activists were pretty much left to organize their own operations, and therefore the level of performance was minimal. In Detroit we concluded that in 1956 no more than 55 percent of the Democratic precinct leaders and 47 percent of the Republicans performed the critical vote mobilization tasks of the party. One should not assume therefore that "in the past" local parties were extremely efficient. They may have been so in such machine oases as Chicago or Philadelphia or Jersey City, but normally the level of efficiency in task performance had always been low. And hence the potential for activating the local activists was great.

Similar types of data are available for 1980 and for earlier years. For Detroit we can compare the proportions of activists who engaged in the critical tasks of registering voters, house-to-house canvassing, and the election day "round up" of votes (see Table 4.12). There seems to have been a slight decline in task performance in 1980 in Detroit, primarily due to the fact that for some reason much less effort was put into voter registration in that year. The reported effort in house-to-house canvassing rose considerably, and one could argue that such personal contacts (supplemented by another 40 percent who claimed they engaged in telephone canvassing) represented more significant measures of the level of party effort. Although we do not have trend data on these specific tasks for Los Angeles, the 1980 data reveal a much higher registration effort there than in Detroit, and very similar proportions of activists engaged in canvassing and "get out the vote" activities. In the 1963 Los Angeles study, respondents were asked if they had (ever) engaged in certain types of campaign work. Almost two-thirds of the Republicans and Democrats reported that they had done doorstep canvassing, just short of 50 percent had engaged in fundraising, and from one-third to one-half reported other publicity, organizational or speech-making activities.

One other comparison over time is possible for Los Angeles, using re-sponses to the question, "How many hours a week did you spend on the campaign?" This question was used in Los Angeles from 1968 on, and the trends are interesting to note (see Table 4.13). There seems to have been no diminution in time spent on party affairs, although of course there were low periods (e.g., the 1976 election). The proportion of activists who were "slackers" (giving less than ten hours a week) remained at about 45 percent over the last twelve years, while the proportion of "entrepreneurs" (spending over twenty hours a week) remained constant at about 35 percent. Further, the comparison with Detroit was very close—the Democrats were a bit more labor intensive in Detroit than in Los Angeles, the Republicans a bit less.

Who are those activists who are most energetic and committed to cam-paign activity, and do they differ much in 1980 from those in 1956? Analysis of activity levels by demographic subgroups in Detroit reveals very few significant changes (see Table 4.14). The black activists in Detroit were always hard workers in the Democratic party, and again in 1980 60 percent of them were very active (compared to 26 percent of whites, who were more active in 1956). Union members were relatively active in both parties, but among Democrats in 1980 not more active than non-members. Those with college educations were more active among Democrats, but not among Republicans (perhaps because there were so few *without* a college educa-tion in the Republican cadre). Age differences were not great. If one makes a precise break by age, the 1980 data suggest that middle-aged (Democrats) and older activists (Republicans) did better than young activists:

|  | Percentage High in Activity | |
|  | Republicans | Democrats |
| --- | --- | --- |
| Age Group | | |
| Up to 30 | 27 | 43 |
| 30 to 44 | 36 | 43 |
| 45 to 54 | 33 | 67 |
| 55+ | 41 | 38 |

**Table 4.13. Time Spent on Campaign Activities (Percentage of Activists)**

| Hours Worked | Los Angeles | | | | | | | | | | Detroit | |
|---|---|---|---|---|---|---|---|---|---|---|---|---|
| | Republicans | | | | | Democrats | | | | | Republicans | Democrats |
| | 1968 | 1972 | 1976 | 1978 | 1980 | 1968 | 1972 | 1976 | 1978 | 1980 | 1980 | 1980 |
| Up to 10 | 46 | 40 | 76 | 48 | 46 | 44 | 41 | 62 | 49 | 43 | 53 | 41 |
| 10–20 | 24 | 21 | 17 | 16 | 20 | 21 | 22 | 20 | 16 | 22 | 18 | 19 |
| Over 20 | 30 | 39 | 7 | 36 | 34 | 35 | 37 | 18 | 35 | 35 | 29 | 40 |
| Average | 18 | 20 | 9 | 20 | 20 | 20 | 20 | 13 | 19 | 20 | N = 57 | N = 135 |

**Table 4.14.  Activity of Social Subgroups Within Detroit Party Cadres, 1956 and 1980 (In Percent)**

| | High Activity | | Medium Activity | | Low Activity | | Ns | |
|---|---|---|---|---|---|---|---|---|
| | 1956 | 1980 | 1956 | 1980 | 1956 | 1980 | 1956 | 1980 |
| *Democrats* | | | | | | | | |
| *Union Membership* | | | | | | | | |
| Members | 58 | 47 | 22 | 18 | 19 | 35 | 41 | 45 |
| Non-members | 40 | 47 | 19 | 35 | 41 | 18 | 27 | 55 |
| *Education* | | | | | | | | |
| Less than college | 55 | 28 | 18 | 31 | 27 | 41 | 44 | 29 |
| College or better | 44 | 50 | 26 | 25 | 30 | 25 | 23 | 110 |
| *Age* | | | | | | | | |
| Under 45 | 51 | 43 | 18 | 21 | 30 | 36 | 33 | 53 |
| 45+ | 52 | 47 | 23 | 27 | 26 | 25 | 35 | 80 |
| *Race* | | | | | | | | |
| Blacks | 72 | 60 | 6 | 25 | 22 | 15 | 18 | 81 |
| Whites | 44 | 26 | 26 | 28 | 30 | 46 | 50 | 54 |
| *Republicans* | | | | | | | | |
| *Union Membership* | | | | | | | | |
| Members | 33 | 45 | 17 | 26 | 50 | 29 | 18 | 31 |
| Non-members | 20 | 30* | 23 | 30* | 56 | 40* | 56 | 10 |
| *Education* | | | | | | | | |
| Less than college | 27 | (50)* | 21 | (0)* | 51 | (50)* | 33 | (6) |
| College or better | 22 | 34 | 22 | 32 | 56 | 34 | 41 | 56 |
| *Age* | | | | | | | | |
| Under 45 | 27 | 31 | 17 | 34 | 54 | 35 | 29 | 29 |
| 45+ | 22 | 38 | 24 | 24 | 54 | 38 | 45 | 29 |
| *Race* | | | | | | | | |
| Blacks | 27 | 33 | 20 | 19 | 53 | 48 | 15 | 21 |
| Whites | 24 | 42 | 22 | 31 | 54 | 27 | 59 | 36 |

*Small N, hence caution is necessary in using results.
Note: The activity index in both years was based on summing up scores for three types of activities: registration, canvassing, and election-day roundup of the vote. In 1956, giving advice to constituents and activities between election years were included.

**Table 4.15.  The Relevance of Social Group Status for Political Activity in Detroit (Using "Difference Measures")**

|  | Democrats | | Republicans | |
| --- | --- | --- | --- | --- |
| *Relevance of:* | *1956* | *1980* | *1956* | *1980* |
| Union membership | +40 | −17 | +19 | +26 |
| College education | −14 | +38 | −10 | 0 |
| Race | +36 | +65 | + 4 | −20 |
| Middle age and older | + 5 | +15 | + 5 | + 4 |

Note: A "difference measure" is derived by subtracting the proportion with low activity from that with high activity.

Clearly, the most striking and consistent tendency is the high level of activity in the Democratic party by black precinct leaders. In the Republican party, blacks were not as highly active in 1956 (27 percent) or 1980 (33 percent). Republicans were consistently lower than Democrats in level of activity in all subgroups, except possibly the union members. The major contrasts can be presented most clearly by the "difference measures" in Table 4.15. Whereas race made the great difference for Democrats, the relevance of union membership fell off for them in 1980 but assumed a significant role in explaining Republican activism in 1980.

If we isolate ideology as a factor associated with levels of activity in Detroit, we find divergent developments in the two party cadres (see Table 4.16). In 1956 the "liberal" Democrats were rather active but not the hardest working, but in 1980 they definitely were (see Table 4.17). What apparently happened was that the moderates and conservatives among Democrats reduced their level of activity in 1980, while the liberals functioned at the same level as previously. The "difference measures" for liberal activists were −24 in 1956 but +40 in 1980. Among Republicans, however, both liberals and conservatives continued to function at practically the same levels over time, with the conservatives, on balance, doing a bit better than the liberals in 1980 (see Table 4.17). The Republican moderates, interestingly, were least active in 1980. Apparently the support for Reagan, as well as the considerable support for both Anderson and Bush in the primary battles, carried over to the campaign effort by both liberal and conservative wings.

Other factors linked to a high level of activity are: aspiration level of the activist, loyalty to the party, incentives which emphasize personally instrumental (or "solidary") satisfactions, and a sense of involvement in organizational decision making. The complete set of data is found in Table 4.18. We can summarize the findings and demonstrate the relevance of these

**Table 4.16.  Association of Activity Level and Ideology for Detroit Leaders (In Percent)**

|  | High Activity Levels | | Medium Activity Levels | | Lowest Activity Level | | Ns | |
|---|---|---|---|---|---|---|---|---|
|  | 1956 | 1980 | 1956 | 1980 | 1956 | 1980 | 1956 | 1980 |
| *Republican Leaders* | | | | | | | | |
| Liberals | 38 | 41 | 15 | 24 | 46 | 35 | 13 | 20 |
| Moderates | 28 | 30 | 24 | 23 | 48 | 47 | 25 | 13 |
| Conservatives | 26 | 34 | 33 | 41 | 40 | 25 | 15 | 22 |
| *Democratic Leaders* | | | | | | | | |
| Liberals | 50 | 50 | 22 | 27 | 28 | 23 | 36 | 98 |
| Others | 64 | 31 | 18 | 25 | 18 | 44 | 22 | 30 |

**Table 4.17.  Summary of Change in Detroit Leaders' Activity Levels (In Percent)**

| | 1956 | | 1980 | |
|---|---|---|---|---|
| *Republicans Who Are:* | Liberals | Conservatives | Liberals | Conservatives |
| Very active | 38 | 26 | 41 | 34 |
| Not active | 46 | 40 | 35 | 25 |
| "Difference" | − 8 | −14 | + 6 | + 9 |
| Net Measure | + 6 | | + 3 | |
| | (Pro Liberals) | | (Pro Conservatives) | |

| | 1956 | | 1980 | |
|---|---|---|---|---|
| *Democrats Who Were:* | Liberals | Others | Liberals | Others |
| Very Active | 50 | 64 | 50 | 31 |
| Not Active | 28 | 18 | 23 | 44 |
| "Difference" | +22 | +46 | +27 | −13 |
| Net Measure | −24 | | +40 | |
| | (Anti-Liberals) | | (Pro Liberals) | |

Note: The "net difference measure" is arrived at by comparing the "difference" (between very active and not active) for each ideological group. Thus, if the difference is minus 8 for the Liberals but minus 14 for the Conservatives, the net difference is +6 for the Liberals.

**Table 4.18. Relationship of Activity to Other Perspectives of Detroit Leaders (In Percent)**

| Perspectives: | High Activity | | Some Activity | | No Activity | | Ns | |
|---|---|---|---|---|---|---|---|---|
| | 1956 | 1980 | 1956 | 1980 | 1956 | 1980 | 1956 | 1980 |
| *Aspiration* | | | | | | | | |
| Interested in a position in the organization | | | | | | | | |
| Republicans | 38 | 39 | 42 | 30 | 21 | 31 | 48 | 54 |
| Democrats | 59 | 44 | 33 | 32 | 8 | 24 | 36 | 103 |
| Not interested, "non-aspirers" | | | | | | | | |
| Republicans | 28 | 22 | 21 | 22 | 50 | 56 | 28 | 9 |
| Democrats | 47 | 54 | 37 | 9 | 17 | 37 | 30 | 35 |
| *Loyalty* | | | | | | | | |
| Do not approve of splitting the ballot | | | | | | | | |
| Republicans | 39 | 55 | 39 | 9 | 22 | 36 | 23 | 11 |
| Democrats | 52 | 61 | 35 | 22 | 14 | 17 | 37 | 41 |
| Disloyal, do approve | | | | | | | | |
| Republicans | 30 | 34 | 35 | 34 | 35 | 32 | 54 | 50 |
| Democrats | 47 | 39 | 38 | 27 | 16 | 34 | 32 | 97 |
| *Morale* | | | | | | | | |
| Want more say | | | | | | | | |
| Republicans | 30 | 34 | 33 | 32 | 37 | 34 | 43 | 38 |
| Democrats | 57 | 52 | 37 | 29 | 7 | 19 | 30 | 93 |
| Seem satisfied | | | | | | | | |
| Republicans | 44 | 45 | 41 | 27 | 16 | 27 | 32 | 22 |
| Democrats | 44 | 32 | 39 | 21 | 17 | 47 | 36 | 38 |
| *Motivations* | | | | | | | | |
| Social contacts (current) | | | | | | | | |
| Republicans | 44 | 47 | 28 | 26 | 28 | 17 | 32 | 34 |
| Democrats | 61 | 55 | 31 | 24 | 8 | 21 | 36 | 67 |
| Ideological reasons | | | | | | | | |
| Republicans | 50 | 29 | 33 | 57 | 17 | 14 | 18 | 14 |
| Democrats | 61 | 41 | 23 | 32 | 15 | 27 | 13 | 34 |

**Table 4.19.  Relevance of Particular Perspectives For Explaining Levels of Activity (Using "Difference Measures")**

| Relevance of: | Democrats | | Republicans | |
|---|---|---|---|---|
| | *1956* | *1980* | *1956* | *1980* |
| Party loyalty (split ticket voting) | + 7 | +39 | +22 | +17 |
| Aspiration to take position in party organization | +11 | + 3 | +39 | +42 |
| Social contact and personal reasons for being involved (over ideological and more general philosophical reasons) | + 7 | +20 | −17 | +15 |
| Feeling of involvement in party decision making | — | +18 | — | +67 |
| Desire to have more say in party decision making | +23 | +48 | −35 | −18 |

Note: See Table 4.15 for explanation of "difference measure."

factors by using our "difference measure" (see Table 4.19). Aspiration was clearly strong as a relevant factor in both 1956 and 1980, particularly for Republicans. Party loyalty was also consistently relevant, but more so for the Democrats in 1980. "Social contact" incentives have become increasingly more important than "purposive" and ideological satisfactions in inducing greater activity. And so far as organizational involvement is concerned, *having* a sense of being taken into consideration was relevant for both parties, but *desiring* more "say" produced opposite results—"dissatisfaction" was associated with more activity for Democrats, but with less for the Republicans!

The model that appears to emerge from this 1980 analysis can, then, be diagrammed as shown in Figure 1.

## The Alleged Decline in Party Organization

It is difficult to get completely satisfactory evidence to support or refute claims about the disintegration of local parties. Even though we have two unique data sets for Detroit and Los Angeles, with data about the party activists which go back into the fifties, there are always gaps in the data; questions which were not asked, or not asked in an identical way; samples drawn differently; interviews conducted differently; and other variations in the data sets over time which pose problems for longitudinal analysis.

**Figure 4.1. Factors Influencing Detroit Leader Activity Level**

| Type of Variable | Both Parties | Democrats Only | Republicans Only |
|---|---|---|---|
| | | Factor Relevant for: | |
| A. *Social Status* | | | |
|    Age | X | | |
|    Union Membership | X | | |
|    Education | | X | |
|    Race | | X | |
| B. *Attitudes* | | | |
|    Aspiration | X | | |
|    Party Loyalty | X | | |
|    Motivations | | | |
|      (Social Contact) | X | | |
|    Ideology – Conservative | | | X |
|          – Liberal | | X | |

Nevertheless, the data we do have are indeed useful, often explicitly comparable over time, and in other respects similar enough to permit inferences about change and continuity. One must remember also that the persons constituting the Los Angeles sample were primarily county committee personnel, having a special status because they were elected to these positions and kept them over time; while in Detroit the sample consisted of precinct leaders who were usually elected as delegates to a district convention and hence did not hold positions which were fixed and prestigious in the same sense as those in Los Angeles.

One of the major tests concerning the state of the local organization would certainly be the level and nature of the activity of local leaders. As indicated above, there is no evidence that a significant decline in activity has occurred. In Detroit in 1956 we found that 14 percent of the Democrats and 30 percent of the Republicans, by their own admission, did practically no work. In 1980, 31 percent of the Democrats and 39 percent of the Republicans reported little or no work. This suggests a "decline" in 1980. Yet when we compared the performance level on particular tasks which are most critical in vote mobilization, we found a 1980 level of activity by no means below the 1956 level. On house-to-house canvassing, for example, the proportions reported in Detroit in 1980 were 60 percent (D) and 61 percent (R), compared to 46 percent (D) and 32 percent (R) in 1956. Another significant piece of evidence forms part of the Los Angeles data—the number of hours per week worked on the campaign. The key finding was that the 1980 proportion reporting twenty hours or more was 35 percent (D) and 34 percent (R), compared to the 1968 proportion of 35 percent (D) and 30 percent (R). As we reported in our earlier research, local party organizations have always been "slack" systems. It appears they were no more so in 1980 than previously.

Another key test of "decline" certainly lies in the organizational involvement of local party activists. Here the data were somewhat mixed, but they generally confirmed the interpretation that no major "decline" was in evidence. Five types of data were looked at: extent of party experience, loyalty to the party, aspiration to continue in the organization, frequency of interaction with other party leaders, and desire to be consulted in organizational decisions. The loyalty data may have suggested a decline for Detroit on some of the measure, but this certainly was not the case for Los Angeles if one looks at strength of partisanship over time. As for length of time in party work, we found relatively experienced cadres in both cities—62 percent (D) and 52 percent (R) had had more than eight years experience in Detroit, while in Los Angeles the proportions were over 70 percent. As for the level of aspiration in these cadres, in both cities it was truly remarkable. Most of these activists apparently enjoyed party work, found it challenging and satisfying, and said they wanted to stay on—true for over 70 percent, more than in 1956. The interaction data revealed no decline, although as in previous years the preponderance of interaction occurs at the lowest organizational strata.

In the third key area, motivations, we have argued that there has been remarkable uniformity over time in both cities leaders' reasons for becoming involved. In Detroit (where analysis of trend in *current satisfactions* was possible), there was some evidence that ideological and philosophical concerns were more important than previously. But we found, as in 1956, the same basic phenomenon of motivational reorientation in the direction of more personally instrumental (or "solidary") motivations *after* entrance into party life. There was certainly more continuity than discontinuity in these data.

Finally, our longitudinal data strongly suggest that the two party cadres in Detroit and Los Angeles in 1980 retained the "rival" and combative characters that we discerned in our earlier analyses. This becomes clear if one looks at their social backgrounds. In Detroit the contrasts on race and union membership were particularly noticeable. In Los Angeles the contrast on religion (the proportion of both Jewish and Protestant) stood out, as did the difference in union membership. In other respects, there was considerable homogeneity—in the educational level, age, sex, and occupations of these activists. But the two parties did appeal in certain seminal ways to different social groups, and as such appeared to be differently "adaptive" to the populations which they seek to recruit and mobilize.

The "rivalness" of these cadres in ideology, or in their positions on the issues of the day, was truly striking. A subsequent analysis will present these findings in detail. There was a somewhat less "liberal" orientation in both parties in 1980. But the polarization on racial questions was very high —in Los Angeles, 8 percent of the Republicans were liberal on such issues, while 60 percent of the Democrats were. In Detroit the matching proportions were 27 percent and 62 percent. And on conservation issues and redistributive policies affecting the poor, the polarization was also extreme.

Thus, in a variety of senses, and using a variety of indices, the two parties are competing as before. While never highly efficient systems, they clearly have not declined in the enthusiasm with which people enter party work, in their desire to stay in party work, in their performance of critical campaign tasks. The parties are competing today, it appears, with about the same effectiveness as previously.

## Notes

1. Cotter et al., *Party Organizations in American Politics.*
2. See Eldersveld, *Political Parties: A Behavioral Analysis.*
3. The "mortality" of cases in a study seeking to match precincts presents real problems. The disappearance of comparable precincts, plus the difficulty in getting comparable respondents, complicates the research greatly. Thus our 87 precincts dropped to 52 which were usable in 1964, then to 38 in 1972 and 1980. We have sought here to limit our analysis for the key precincts to the same ones which have remained usable throughout.
4. See Dwaine Marvick in this volume.
5. In a 1963 study of Los Angeles County committee members, 80% of the Republicans and 75% of the Democrats had spent ten years or more in partisan politics.
6. In the 1963 Los Angeles study, when asked whether they had ever split their tickets, only 35% of the Republican activists and 49% of the Democrats said "never."
7. Our analysis in Detroit in the interim years confirms the constancy of these response patterns. In our 38 "key precincts," for example, we found that the incen-

tive "to influence the policies of government" was considered very important by 62% in 1956, 63% in 1964, and 61% in 1972.

8. See Eldersveld, *Political Parties: A Behavioral Analysis*, 286–92. See also Conway and Feigert, "Motivation, Incentive Systems, and the Political Party Organization," 1159–73.

CHAPTER 5

# Stability and Change in the Views
# of Los Angeles Party Activists, 1968–1980

*Dwaine Marvick*

Every other year since 1968, an hour-long interview survey has been made
of several hundred Republican and Democratic party activists in Los Angeles County.[1] A cumulative data base for more than 3,000 informants has
resulted, containing information on their personal backgrounds, various
measures of their campaign efforts, organizational participation, and political activities, and data on their subjective views about American politics—
their concerns, beliefs, appraisals, and preferences. Selected findings about
these variables are discussed in this essay.

First, because participation was voluntary, attention is given to respondents' assessments of why people like themselves become active and later
sometimes cease to be active in grassroots politics. Over time, two sets of
questions on these points clarify both the essential stability of their motivational rationales and the extent to which Republican and Democratic activists concur in their emphases.

Second, since informants work in the same party units and interact with
fellow activists, it has been useful to ask what topics of conversation they
frequently engage in. Persistent differences were found between the rival
camps of Republicans and Democrats, as well as secular trends that make
the conversational agenda in both parties increasingly similar. In recent
years, that is, there has been a greater likelihood for discussion to be on
substantive topics than on organizational problems.

Third, knowing that party activists in the Los Angeles area are ideologically oriented toward the issues of the day, we regularly asked them to
characterize their ideological stance—as liberal, moderate, or conservative.
Year after year, by roughly two to one, each party split into a dominant

ideological wing and a smaller moderate wing. Of those interviewed in more than one year, half in each party reaffirmed a commitment to the dominant ideological wing, while a fourth repeated allegiance to the moderate ranks. And for the one person in every four among both sets of activists who changed her or his ideological self-description in a later interview, virtually as many moved to the left as to the right (conventionally speaking), thus leaving the alignments proportioned as before.

Fourth, activists were also asked each year a battery of questions about what role the federal government should play in coping with current problems of foreign and domestic policy, both social and economic. Each ideologically self-defined type scored distinctively on the full range of policy issues, so that as much ideological distance could be said to separate the two wings within each party as has persistently been found between the rival sets of party moderates.

These data thus permit study of what it means to join an organized party as a volunteer, to remain active over the years, to interact with fellow activists, to discuss issues and organizational problems, and to think about public issues in an ideologically predictable way. New complications arise when the question is raised of how activists view the local voters, those on whom their partisan success hinges. In each locality live many followers of the two major parties, ordinary voters who are largely content to make only informal efforts, if that, to change one another's voting plans. By contrast, to be an activist, almost by definition, is to think not only of one's personal choices of leaders and policies, but also to consider and perhaps try to modify the voting plans of one's fellow citizens. Even if activists engage in party work largely for social or idiosyncratic reasons, they find themselves making estimates about the policy views and voting plans of target publics, discussing shifts in public opinion, considering the popularity or name recognition of candidates, reacting to the demands of community groups, and making plans to mobilize and enlarge the party's local following.

To explore these matters, a fifth battery of questions regularly has been posed since 1968, asking how well various manipulative campaign tactics (such as emotionalizing or personalizing their appeals) can be expected to work in that locality. Over the span of years, a clear convergence has taken place. Republican and Democratic activists have come to evaluate the effectiveness of manipulative tactics quite similarly in the post-Watergate years, rather than in the contrasting ways they did before.

A sixth battery of questions—assessing the gullibility of voters, the culpability of politicians, etc.—has also been part of each survey. On these questions about political belief, stable levels of agreement over time, together with substantial concurrence across party lines, have prevailed.

When negative expectations about voter competence, officeholder selfishness, and the manipulative tendencies of those in politics were combined to
form an index of skepticism about electoral democracy, half of the party
activists in each party regularly scored on the skeptical (or perhaps realistic) side.

Other batteries of survey questions regularly used since 1969 asked the
party activists to estimate what stand on seven different public issues they
think "most Democratic voters" and (separately) "most Republican voters"
in their locality take toward federal governmental efforts to handle each
problem. In modal terms, party activists in both parties persisted in thinking that both sets of voters want more federal efforts (a leftist stance) on
"cost of living" and "pollution" control. On the issue of "curbing urban
violence," both voter blocs were also seen as wanting more federal action (a
rightist view). On four other issues—nuclear disarmament, cuts in defense
spending, help for poor people, and desegregation of schools and housing—
Democratic and Republican voters were most often seen by activists in
both parties as aligned in favor of leftist and rightist policies respectively.

When these expectations were keyed to our informant's own policy
preferences on the same issues, most Democratic activists were found, year
after year, to hold what we will call a "partisan leftist" view, while most
Republican activists were found to hold a "partisan rightist" perspective
toward the electoral alignment on the same issue. Lines were drawn on
these four issues in clear and simple fashion: us versus them.

Of course, in each party some activists held more complex "issue alignment perspectives." Thus, on all seven issues, a significant fraction of
Democratic activists took the stance of "isolated leftists"—that is, they personally wanted leftist federal action but viewed both Democratic and Republican voters as favoring a rightist policy.

Later, attention will center on such complications. Briefly, too, we will
consider results obtained when knowledgeable activists were persuaded to
provide detailed estimates of the various kinds of campaign efforts mounted
in their localities by units of their own party and its rival. First, however,
the partisan organizational arrangements in Los Angeles County call for
some attention, and the findings briefly noted above will receive a more
detailed discussion.

## Party Organizations in Los Angeles County

Party organizations in Los Angeles are loosely knit structures. At the
neighborhood level, membership in voluntary clubs and committees waxes

and wanes from one election to the next. There are nuclear groups of party activists at legislative district levels in most parts of the county. But there is no record of strong control or direction exercised by the countywide or statewide structures of either party. In neither party is the Los Angeles county committee a powerful entity. Its powers are ambiguous; its meetings bog down with trivia; its funds are limited and its patronage resources more so. In each party, rival factions time after time frustrate even the appearance of solidarity in supporting a full slate of party nominees. On the other hand, each party's central committee meets quite regularly. Its members come to know each other; exchange rumors and gossip; talk about party bigwigs, potential candidates, polling results, fundraising efforts, and the reputations of various campaign managers, staff people, new club leaders, and the like.

By law, all parts of Los Angeles County are represented on each party's county committee. Each of the thirty assembly districts sends a delegation of seven, elected at primary time for two-year terms. In both parties, it is not uncommon for ten to fifteen people—many of them presidents or active members of local party clubs—to compete for the county committee posts. In a number of districts, rival slates recurrently are fielded by intraparty factions. Turnover is substantial; in 1978 and 1980, for example, approximately 40 percent of the incumbents who sought reelection were not successful.

For research purposes, these county committees provide an excellent sample frame, especially when augmented by the officers of all chartered voluntary party organizations throughout the county. In the seven surveys since 1968, the University of California at Los Angeles (UCLA) project has used the rosters of these Republican and Democratic county committees as legally prescribed composite assemblies that are convenient grids for sampling equivalent sets of rival party activists. Not only does this sample frame guarantee geographical diversity, but it also reflects (with equivalent weight built in for each party) the varied patterns of apathy, rivalry, and complacency to be found in different localities. In other words, politically "sure" territory, doubtful terrain, and "lost" areas are represented in each party's roster in due proportion.

## Motivations for Political Participation

*Why People Join Party Organizations*
For three successive years, our informants were asked how important six considerations were in explaining why "people like them" were politically

Table 5.1.  Why People Like You Have Been Active in Organized Politics
(Percentage Saying "Very Important")

|  | Republicans | | | Democratic | | |
|---|---|---|---|---|---|---|
|  | 1978 | 1976 | 1974 | 1978 | 1976 | 1974 |
| *Impersonal Political Aims* | | | | | | |
| Influence election results | 91 | 88 | 82 | 87 | 77 | 83 |
| Shape public policies | 71 | 71 | 69 | 72 | 69 | 75 |
| *Personal Political Aims* | | | | | | |
| Gain voice in party affairs | 64 | 52 | 62 | 56 | 55 | 60 |
| Build own political career | 17 | 14 | 16 | 22 | 28 | 26 |
| *Personal Social Aims* | | | | | | |
| Achieve community recognition | 25 | 10 | 12 | 23 | 30 | 32 |
| Make social contacts | 21 | 7 | 9 | 18 | 19 | 16 |
| Cases | (87) | (165) | (139) | (110) | (181) | (125) |

active. More than three-fourths in each party stressed the "impersonal political aims" of influencing election results and shaping public policies; only
relatively small and varying fractions were willing to acknowledge personal
social aims such as "making social contacts" or "achieving community
recognition" or the personal desire to "build one's own political career." On
the other hand, fully half in each party acknowledged that activists commonly wanted to "gain a voice in party affairs."

Evidently, based on their own experience, respondents only infrequently
thought of fellow activists as more preoccupied with social or political ambitions or gratifications than with larger public purposes. The picture that
emerges is one of party activists who tend to harness their personal desire
for a voice in party decisions to political objectives that serve community-
wide needs. If anything, Republicans and Democrats are growing more
alike.

*Why People Cease to be Active in Organized Politics*
The other side of the coin—motivational considerations that help to explain why people sometimes quit politics—was also examined. Two kinds
of political considerations—"disillusioned about elections," which implies a
certain skepticism about how well political democracy is working, and "becoming tired of campaign work," which poses only a simple hedonistic
test—were regularly stressed by about two-thirds in each party. So was the
bland and enigmatic excuse of "no time to spare." Other considerations

**Table 5.2. Why People Like You Have Stopped Being Active in Politics (Percentage Saying "Very Important")**

|  | Republicans | | | Democrats | | |
|---|---|---|---|---|---|---|
|  | *1978* | *1976* | *1974* | *1978* | *1976* | *1974* |
| *Political Considerations* | | | | | | |
| Disillusioned about elections | 74 | 68 | 60 | 65 | 64 | 70 |
| Tired of campaign work | 71 | 64 | 62 | 65 | 65 | 69 |
| *Social Considerations* | | | | | | |
| No time to spare | 70 | 59 | 66 | 65 | 61 | 65 |
| Other groups take up time | 53 | 51 | 63 | 54 | 50 | 53 |
| Prefer private way of life | 46 | 45 | 34 | 45 | 46 | 48 |
| Don't seem to fit in anymore | 33 | 33 | 26 | 31 | 46 | 39 |
| Cases | (86) | (159) | (132) | (106) | (164) | (119) |

more social than political were rated "very important" by roughly half of our informants. People said they quit because "other groups take up my time," which presumably means they continue to be involved in other formal organizations, or because they simply "prefer a private way of life," a response that suggests nonparticipation in group life and withdrawal. Finally, an explanation with somewhat poignant overtones—namely, "I just don't seem to fit in anymore"—suggests that the party milieu of activists itself has been undergoing significant change. About one-third of our rival party activists voiced such a thought.

In seeking to explain why people drop out, respondents understandably stress substantive political matters rather than social or personal gratifications. But not as markedly as one might have expected. Two conclusions seem warranted. First, the priorities are stable; party activists give predictably different weight to these motivational rationales. Moreover, year after year, the essential similarity of Republican and Democratic priorities is noteworthy.

## What Party Activists Discuss

A picture emerges of energetic and politicized campaign workers. Active because of some combination of public purposes, convivial needs, and personal aims, they work long hours in voluntary cooperation with fellow activists doing rather monotonous tasks—stuffing envelopes, answering phone calls, ringing doorbells, staffing party headquarters. Numerous chances arise for party workers to discuss both the substance of politics and the organizational work of the party.

In every survey since 1969, our informants were asked how frequently they discussed seven different topics with fellow activists. As Figure 5.1 shows, in both parties substantive topics (political leaders, public policies, or campaign strategies) have come to be discussed in recent years nearly twice as often as organizational matters (such as how to organize drives, where to raise funds, how to rate fellow workers). Criticism of a key figure in the rival party is clearly the most frequent theme, but in both parties by 1978 a majority of activists reported frequent criticism of a leader in one's own party. On both counts, this represented no difference among Democrats compared with earlier years. But both kinds of critical talk markedly increased among Republicans in the late 1970s.

The same points hold concerning the frequency with which party activists had arguments over some public policy, or voiced doubts about the efficacy or morality of some campaign strategy. Just under half in each party reported "often" having such conversations. Here again, these topics have substantially increased in frequency among Republicans, while among Democrats they have continued to be high.

## Ideological Thinking about Policy Issues

Among party activists the notion of ideology is often explicit. Sometimes, too, it can be inferred from the way they talk about candidates and issues. Using the UCLA party activist data, three rather different "styles" in ideological thinking were disclosed when activists were called upon to say what they meant by the terms "liberal," "moderate," and "conservative." Factor analysis of their responses yielded one group who stressed that such terms characterized how people "understood people," whether in dogmatic or tolerant fashion. Another group felt the terms clarified how different people "handled problems"—whether in doctrinaire or pragmatic ways. A third group used such terms to describe the "combative struggle" associated with public policy issues—between haves and have-nots, dominants and dependents.[2]

In each survey, activists also were asked to make self-characterizations of their ideology. Analysis revealed that Republicans called themselves "conservatives" rather than "moderates" by two-to-one margins, and rarely

**Figure 5.1.  Topics Frequently Discussed Among Activists**

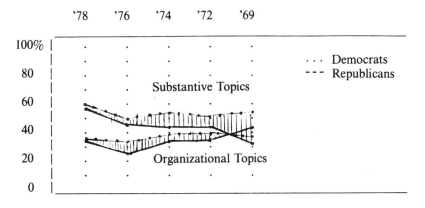

**Figure 5.2.  How Good Are Various Manipulative Tactics in Your Area?**
**(Percentage Rating Tactic "Good")**

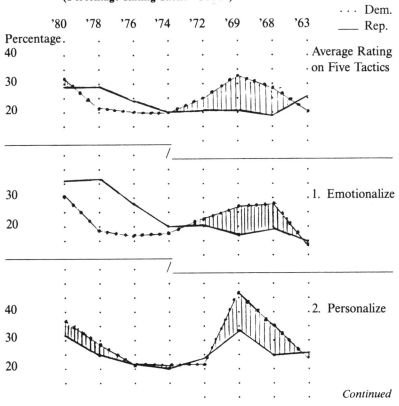

*Continued*

**Figure 5.2.** (*Continued*)

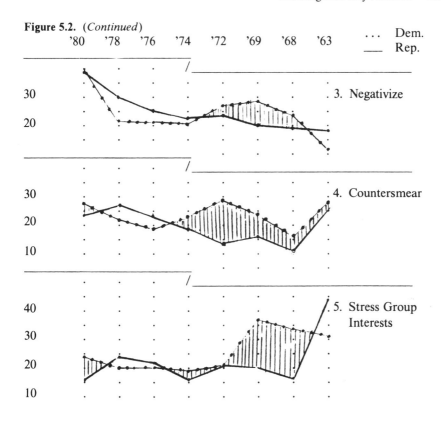

3. Negativize

4. Countersmear

5. Stress Group Interests

**Figure 5.3.  Indicators of Skepticism about Electoral Democracy
(Percentage Agreement with Belief Statement)**

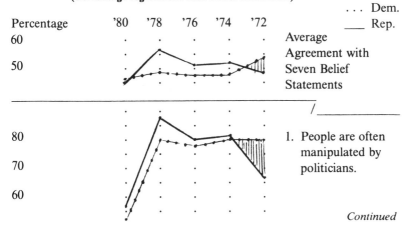

Average Agreement with Seven Belief Statements

1. People are often manipulated by politicians.

*Continued*

**Figure 5.3.** (*Continued*)

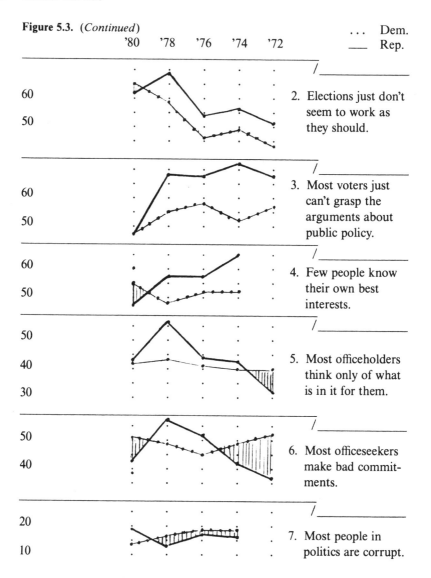

... Dem.
___ Rep.

'80    '78    '76    '74    '72

60
50

2. Elections just don't seem to work as they should.

60
50

3. Most voters just can't grasp the arguments about public policy.

60
50

4. Few people know their own best interests.

50
40
30

5. Most officeholders think only of what is in it for them.

50
40

6. Most officeseekers make bad commitments.

20
10

7. Most people in politics are corrupt.

**Table 5.3.  Topics Frequently Discussed with Fellow Activists**
**(In Percent)**

|  | Republicans | | | | | Democrats | | | | |
|---|---|---|---|---|---|---|---|---|---|---|
|  | 1978 | 1976 | 1974 | 1972 | 1969 | 1978 | 1976 | 1974 | 1972 | 1969 |
| *Substantive Topics* | | | | | | | | | | |
| Criticize rival party leader | 85 | 79 | 73 | 72 | 55 | 82 | 70 | 78 | 82 | 81 |
| Criticize own party leader | 54 | 39 | 45 | 32 | 20 | 58 | 47 | 49 | 44 | 49 |
| Argue about public policy | 47 | 39 | 28 | 29 | 33 | 55 | 43 | 49 | 44 | 50 |
| Question a campaign strategy | 42 | 26 | 30 | 17 | 20 | 60 | 50 | 53 | 51 | 54 |
| Average | 57 | 46 | 44 | 44 | 32 | 60 | 50 | 53 | 51 | 54 |
| *Organizational Topics* | | | | | | | | | | |
| How to run group activities | 48 | 42 | 49 | 51 | 60 | 45 | 44 | 56 | 49 | 46 |
| Where to raise party funds | 34 | 26 | 36 | 38 | 50 | 30 | 35 | 30 | 42 | 42 |
| How a fellow worker is rated | 18 | 11 | 13 | 12 | 19 | 26 | 23 | 30 | 26 | 23 |
| Average | 33 | 26 | 33 | 34 | 43 | 34 | 34 | 39 | 39 | 37 |
| (Cases) | 84 | 161 | 138 | 178 | 207 | 111 | 173 | 127 | 175 | 216 |

used the term "liberal"; Democrats, on the other hand, chose "liberal" over "moderate" by a similar ratio and avoided the term "conservative." Each party had two rather stable ideological wings.

Of course, over the eighteen years covered by these surveys, some activists changed their self-descriptions, while others steadfastly used the same terms to describe their way of thinking. Since more than 700 informants were interviewed in at least two different survey years, it is possible to compare self-ratings given by such persons in the earliest and most recent surveys in which they responded. As Table 5.4 shows, 48 percent of the Republicans called themselves conservative on both occasions, while 59 percent of the Democrats styled themselves liberal both times. As for the moderate wings, 25 percent were stable moderates in the Republican camp, while among Democrats, 22 percent were. In each party, this left only one in every four or five whose self-rating changed from the earliest interview to

**Table 5.4.  Stability and Change in Ideological Self-Ratings (In Percent)**

| *Republicans* | | | *Democrats* | | |
|---|---|---|---|---|---|
| | *Most Recent Self-Ratings* | | | *Most Recent Self-Ratings* | |
| *Earliest Self-Ratings* | *Conservative* | *Moderate* | *Earliest Self-Ratings* | *Liberal* | *Moderate* |
| Conservative | 48 | 14 | Liberal | 59 | 9 |
| Moderate | 13 | 25 | Moderate | 10 | 22 |
| N=390 | (Four cells add to 100%) | | N=385 | (Four cells add to 100%) | |

the most recent. Of equal importance to the net stability, in both parties the number of those who shifted to the right politically almost exactly matched the proportion who moved leftward.

In all years, Los Angeles activists were asked what role the federal government should take in coping with various policy issues. Certain aspects of stability and change in policy preferences are keyed to how those same activists saw the voting blocs in their areas as changing or not. These will be examined later. Here it is worth noting that each ideological type— both the dominant wing and its moderate counterpart in each party—had a distinctive pattern of issue preferences across foreign, domestic, military, economic, and social questions. Year after year each wing of each party registered its own pattern of emphases. As Table 5.5 shows, the ideologically dominant wing of the Republican party averaged 17 percent who wanted "more federal action" on six policy fronts in the 1968–80 period, while Republican moderates scored an average of 33 percent. Among Democratic moderates, the corresponding figure was 61 percent while fully 88 percent of the ideologically dominant liberal wing called for more federal effort. The ideological distance within each party is demonstrably as great as the distance between Republican and Democratic moderates. Although the full breakdown for each year is not shown here, and although in each party some issues caused more dissension than others and some became more troublesome over time while others grew less so,[3] the point to be emphasized is the essential stability in the predictive power of each ideological type.

## Special Concerns of the Political Activist

What is distinctive about being a political activist? Volunteering to work in a party, remaining active between elections, discussing with fellow activists

**Table 5.5.  Policy Preferences for More Federal Government Action
On Six Policy Questions (Composite of Seven Surveys,
1968–1980) (In Percent)**

| | Republicans | | Democrats | |
| --- | --- | --- | --- | --- |
| Policy Question | Conser-vatives | Moder-ates | Moder-ates | Liberals |
| Control the cost of living | 32 | 50 | 68 | 90 |
| Stop air and water pollution | 27 | 45 | 70 | 93 |
| Work for nuclear disarmament | 22 | 40 | 68 | 88 |
| Cut defense spending | 6 | 23 | 60 | 85 |
| Expand opportunities for poor | 8 | 20 | 61 | 91 |
| Desegregate housing and schools | 4 | 12 | 39 | 78 |
| Average on six issues | 17 | 33 | 61 | 88 |
| Cases | (948) | (390) | (412) | (900) |

both the organization's goals and the problems of implementation that must
be solved, even thinking in a patterned and predictable way about the
larger implications of one's participation—each of these aspects of organizational participation has its counterpart in other contexts than politics.
To study involvement in union affairs, church life, community betterment
efforts, environmental protection movements, or professional or trade association activities, one might well pursue similar lines of inquiry. What are
the more distinctive features of partisan organizational activity, for which
the counterpart in nonpolitical processes are harder to see? If we think in
terms of the functional requirements of electoral democracy, and especially
of how a model of serious electoral competition, on the order of those
developed by Schumpeter (1939), Dahl (1956), or even Downs (1957), must
function in order to vest hiring and firing power in the electorate on at least
some occasions, there appear to be at least two distinctive sensitivities that
party activists ought to reveal quite often: worrying about what the voters
think and want, since voters can wield decisive power in the electoral context; and worrying about what the major rival party is planning and doing,
since its efforts and attractiveness can make the crucial electoral difference.[4]

*How Party Activists Assess the Local Electorate*
In various ways, the efforts of grassroots personnel can and do shape the
campaigns waged by the two rival parties to capture key public offices.
First, local activists may not have the zeal to carry party messages into

lukewarm or even hostile quarters. Second, if they are ideologically rigid, or use arguments that seem unrealistic, they can seriously antagonize even potential supporters. Third, in face-to-face situations, they personalize the campaign themes and emphases that are broadcast to mass media audiences. When grassroots personnel contact their neighbors in campaign drives or talk politics with their daily associates, inevitably they convey more than just the basic campaign "image" created by their side. They also convey, by words and gestures, an ideological and ethical commentary. Moreover, in such face-to-face situations, their credibility depends on their social credentials—their age and sex, the hallmarks of their education, income, and occupation, the lifestyle they represent—as well as on their political persuasiveness.

Regularly since 1963, the UCLA party activist surveys have included a battery of questions asking informants to assess how well various controversial campaign tactics are likely to work, if directed at the local Republican and Democratic voters in their home legislative districts. Several points emerge when these data are examined over time.

To examine the trend line, Table 5.6 uses an index of partisan agreement about the efficacy of manipulative tactics. Metric weights are given to the ordinal categories—good, fair, or poor—used to evaluate each tactic. Figure 5.2 charts the percentage who rated each tactic as "good."

First, there has been a secular trend in both parties toward greater acknowledgment that manipulative tactics work. Second, in the Democratic party prior to 1974, appreciation of how effective such tactics could be seems to have been higher than in Republican ranks. Third, by 1980, the levels of "favorable" assessment in both parties were quite similar, where "favorable" of course refers to a utilitarian standard and not necessarily to an ethical acceptance. Indeed, this set of questions typically prompted many party activists to distinguish between what is a "fair" method and what "works." There are, however, multiple signs that activists nowadays acknowledge (even if grudgingly) that emotionalizing, personalizing, negativizing, stressing group interests, and countersmearing tactics work in their localities.

The appraisals made by party activists of how effective different campaign tactics seem to be, were not the only assessments of the gullibility of voters, the selfishness of officeholders, the culpability of officeseekers, or the manipulative tendencies in American politics that our informants were asked to make. Regularly since 1972, a battery of propositions about the political scene has been posed and informants asked to agree or disagree with each item. Figure 5.3 reports the percentage agreement on each proposition over the five surveys involved. It discloses what many will consider

**Table 5.6. Acknowledgment of the Efficacy of Manipulative Tactics (Index of Partisan Agreement)**

| | 1980 | 1978 | 1976 | 1974 | 1972 | 1969 | 1968 | 1963 | Average |
|---|---|---|---|---|---|---|---|---|---|
| *Personalize* | | | | | | | | | |
| Stress a candidate's personality rather than his stand on issues. | | | | | | | | | |
| Republican | .47 | .42 | .39 | .36 | .38 | .43 | .36 | .36 | .40 |
| Democratic | .51 | .46 | .42 | .41 | .41 | .55 | .47 | .35 | .43 |
| *Emotionalize* | | | | | | | | | |
| Stir up strong hates and fears rather than be restrained. | | | | | | | | | |
| Republican | .50 | .50 | .45 | .38 | .35 | .23 | .34 | .18 | .33 |
| Democratic | .42 | .34 | .38 | .36 | .36 | .33 | .41 | .18 | .36 |
| *Negativize* | | | | | | | | | |
| Stress rival's bad record rather than own performance and plans. | | | | | | | | | |
| Republican | .52 | .46 | .42 | .36 | .38 | .30 | .31 | .28 | .37 |
| Democratic | .55 | .38 | .40 | .40 | .44 | .37 | .37 | .23 | .40 |
| *Group Link* | | | | | | | | | |
| Stress effects on groups rather than communitywide consequences. | | | | | | | | | |
| Republican | .27 | .42 | .37 | .33 | .37 | .27 | .27 | .56 | .36 |
| Democratic | .35 | .39 | .41 | .43 | .39 | .44 | .48 | .40 | .40 |
| *Countersmear* | | | | | | | | | |
| Meet smear attacks with counter-charges rather than ignore them. | | | | | | | | | |
| Republican | .41 | .41 | .37 | .33 | .29 | .23 | .19 | .37 | .32 |
| Democratic | .44 | .34 | .35 | .40 | .43 | .32 | .26 | .37 | .33 |
| *Index of Partisan Agreement* | | | | | | | | | |
| about the efficacy of manipulative tactics. | | | | | | | | | |
| Republican | .43 | .44 | .40 | .35 | .35 | .29 | .29 | .35 | .36 |
| Democratic | .45 | .38 | .39 | .40 | .41 | .40 | .40 | .31 | .39 |

Note: The index of partisan agreement is a weighted average of the assessment made on five questions: 1 if Good, 2 if Fair, 3 if Poor.

a disturbingly high level of skepticism—persistently about half of the activists in each party registered such a view—when it came to agreeing with such propositions as these:

—Elections just don't produce enough good leaders any more.
—To get nominated, most officeseekers make bad commitments.
—Most officeholders are thinking only of what's in it for them.

Other propositions set limits. Only about one in six activists are willing to endorse the view that "at least half of those active in American political life are corrupt." But even that proposition is persistently agreed to each year by a sizable minority of cynically-minded activists in both parties. At the other extreme, until 1980 sharply changed the pattern in both parties, well over three-fourths of our activist informants year after year did agree with the proposition that "people are often manipulated by politicians."

Consider the composite index of political skepticism. When responses on all seven questions were averaged to create such an index, it was found to hover persistently near the 50 percent agreement level. It is also apparent both from the index and from all component items save one that Republican activists were consistently more skeptical about the caliber of political leaders, the adequacy of the electoral process, and the competence of ordinary voters than their Democratic rivals.

Again, it should be noted that in 1980 the levels of agreement with each of these propositions were quite similar for Republicans and Democrats. It can be argued that such convergence perhaps reflects thoughtfulness and realism rather than stereotyping tendencies. In the absence of more evidence, any such argument is bound to be inconclusive.

What is clear from these data is that both party rosters in Los Angeles County include many who—despite the rather jaundiced view they hold of voters and politicians alike—are nevertheless willing to continue their efforts as activists at the organizational level of partisanship.

*How Local Voters Are Seen to Stand on Policy Issues*
The next two sets of data to be examined involve looking at how activists assessed the policy stands of Republican and Democratic voters in their home districts. On some issues, both voter blocs were seen by most activists as holding what is conventionally considered to be a leftist view about the desired federal governmental role. Thus, between 1969 and 1980, such was the typical view (45 percent for Republicans, 49 percent for Democrats) of what most voters wanted done to "control the cost of living." Again, most voters of both parties were seen as wanting federal action "to stop air and

**Table 5.7.  How Local Republican and Democratic Voters Were Perceived In Leftist-Rightist Terms on Seven Issues, 1969-1980 (In Percent)**

| | *Federal Governmental Policy Called For By* | | | | |
|---|---|---|---|---|---|
| Most Democratic Voters: | *Leftist* | *Leftist* | *Rightist* | *Rightist* | |
| Most Republican Voters: | *Leftist* | *Rightist* | *Leftist* | *Rightist* | |
| *As Seen By Rep. Activists* | | | | | |
| Control the cost of living | 45 | 35 | 13 | 7 | : 100 |
| Stop air and water pollution | 44 | 36 | 7 | 13 | : 100 |
| Get tough with urban violence | 6 | 32 | 9 | 53 | : 100 |
| Work for nuclear disarmament | 21 | 52 | 11 | 16 | : 100 |
| Expand help for the poor | 19 | 60 | 11 | 10 | : 100 |
| Make cuts in defense spending | 12 | 55 | 12 | 21 | : 100 |
| Desegregate housing and schools | 11 | 51 | 9 | 29 | : 100 |
| *As Seen By Dem. Activists* | | | | | |
| Control the cost of living | 49 | 41 | 4 | 6 | : 100 |
| Stop air and water pollution | 41 | 41 | 4 | 14 | : 100 |
| Get tough with urban violence | 4 | 19 | 8 | 69 | : 100 |
| Work for nuclear disarmament | 17 | 60 | 5 | 18 | : 100 |
| Expand help for the poor | 6 | 69 | 5 | 20 | : 100 |
| Make cuts in defense spending | 7 | 63 | 9 | 21 | : 100 |
| Desegregate housing and schools | 5 | 49 | 7 | 39 | : 100 |

water pollution." Such was the modal appraisal by activists, both Republicans (44 percent) and Democrats (41 percent). On both of these issues, trend analysis reveals, the perceived leftist consensus of voters seen in 1969 and 1972 was replaced by the mid-1970s, for many activists in both parties, by what they came to see as a left-right partisan alignment pitting Democrats against Republicans in the local electorate.

On another issue, the modal perception among both sets of party activists has persisted that local voters of both parties want more federal action to implement a rightist policy. In this case the call has been "to curb urban violence" by tougher methods, a policy formulation that would conventionally be classed as a rightist call for law and order. Accordingly, responses on this question were reverse scored for our purposes. In the early years, many liberal Democratic activists, who themselves disagreed with this policy and argued that violence was only symptomatic of bad living conditions, nevertheless acknowledged that their own party's voters as well as local Republican voters were in favor of rightist action. They felt themselves to be "isolated leftists" on this issue. After 1974, however, about half of these isolated leftists appear to have changed their personal policy preference to bring it into line with what they continue to see as a rightist consensus among their home district voters.

On the other four issues, the modal perceptions by most activists were that local Democratic voters are mostly leftist, while local Republican voters favor a rightist stand. This perception of a partisan left-right voter alignment was the mode on issues as different as (1) working for nuclear disarmament, (2) expanding help for the poor, (3) making cuts in defense spending, and (4) desegregating housing and schools. Since most Democratic activists personally took leftist stands on these issues and most Republicans favored rightist policies, each side could feel that the issues were suitably joined and that a partisan struggle was taking place at both activist and voter levels.

Still, in each party, a significant fraction saw the local voters of both parties to be rightist on these four questions. When keyed to their own policy preferences, such perceptions made many liberal Democrats feel themselves to be "isolated leftists." No such tension bothered the conservative Republican activists, who were able to see themselves as "mainstream rightists" on these issues.

### Issue Alignment Perspectives

When they size up the local electorate, some party activists, in short, must feel rather isolated and out of step. What most of the voters seem to want, they personally oppose. Other activists probably feel buoyed up as they watch a popular consensus emerge which calls for a public policy they support. To feel either isolated or part of the mainstream—these are the options when the public largely is seen as agreeing on what governmental action is wanted.

Alternatively, party activists may see the local electorate split along partisan lines, with their side largely taking one stand on the issue in question, but opposed by the followers of the rival party, most of whom take the opposite view. Finally, too, there are those who can be called "conflicted" advocates of a policy, because they find it is opposed by most local voters supporting their own party but liked and championed by the rival party's local supporters in the electorate.

Table 5.8. Issue Alignment Perspectives of Rival Party Activists in Los Angeles County, 1969–1980

| Issue Position Seen Taken By | Main-stream Left | Iso-lated Right | Parti-san Left | Con-flicted Right | Parti-san Right | Con-flicted Left | Main-stream Right | Iso-lated Left | |
|---|---|---|---|---|---|---|---|---|---|
| Own Party's Voters | L | L | L | L | R | R | R | R | |
| Rival Party's Voters | L | L | R | R | L | L | R | R | |
| Self | L | R | L | R | R | L | R | L | |
| *Republican Activists** | | | | | | | | | |
| Control cost of living | 33 | 12 | 10 | 3 | 30 | 5 | 5 | 2 | :100 |
| Stop air/water pollut. | 35 | 9 | 6 | 1 | 27 | 9 | 10 | 3 | :100 |
| Curb urban violence | 4 | 2 | 6 | 3 | 26 | 6 | 44 | 9 | :100 |
| Seek nuclear disarm. | 15 | 6 | 9 | 2 | 41 | 11 | 12 | 4 | :100 |
| Expand help for poor | 13 | 6 | 11 | 1 | 47 | 13 | 8 | 2 | :100 |
| Cut defense spending | 6 | 6 | 9 | 3 | 46 | 9 | 17 | 4 | :100 |
| Desegregate housing/ schools | 5 | 6 | 7 | 2 | 45 | 6 | 23 | 6 | :100 |
| *Democratic Activists** | | | | | | | | | |
| Control cost of living | 44 | 5 | 36 | 5 | 3 | 1 | 2 | 4 | :100 |
| Stop air/water pollut. | 38 | 3 | 40 | 1 | 2 | 2 | 2 | 12 | :100 |
| Curb urban violence | 2 | 2 | 15 | 4 | 5 | 3 | 43 | 26 | :100 |
| Seek nuclear disarm. | 14 | 3 | 55 | 5 | 3 | 2 | 4 | 14 | :100 |
| Expand help for poor | 6 | 0 | 65 | 4 | 4 | 1 | 2 | 18 | :100 |
| Cut defense spending | 5 | 2 | 57 | 6 | 6 | 3 | 4 | 17 | :100 |
| Desegregate housing/ schools | 3 | 2 | 44 | 5 | 5 | 2 | 7 | 32 | :100 |

*In percent.

These are what will be called "issue alignment perspectives," further characterized as leftist or rightist, and measured empirically by the response patterns to the relevant question batteries posed in each survey since 1969. Operationally defined, such issue alignment perspectives are the personal policy preferences of party activists, calling for more federal governmental action or less, when constrained by the expectations of those same activists about the current issue preferences of most Republican and most Democratic voters in their home district.

What do such perspectives tell us? On the one hand, they embody a personal preference; on the other, they entail a voting-bloc appraisal. Over time, either may change; on different issues in the same year, the same activist may hold quite different perspectives. Operationally, these perspectives are defined purely in issue-specific terms, without reference to which party one belongs to or how one characterizes one's ideological stance.

When specific issues are examined, the complex patterns of personal preference, coupled to expectations of support and opposition from relevant voting blocs which a given party activist might simultaneously be considering, can be appreciated, as in Table 5.7. And the transformation over time of one perspective into a quite different one can be traced, using Figure 5.4.

*Urban Violence*
In both parties by 1980, a substantial fraction held a mainstream leftist view. Among Republican activists, this way of looking at the controversy had been the mode as early as 1969. But among Democrats it came to be the mode only after 1974, as many Democrats, faced by what they acknowledged as a persistent and widely shared "rightist consensus" among the voters on this issue, apparently changed their "isolated leftist" posture and espoused a "mainstream rightist" perspective (Figure 5.4).

*Cost of Living*
In both parties, here, substantial fractions of activists have regularly seen both Republican and Democratic voting blocs positioned on the left; supported by such perceived public consensus, with which they agreed, the "mainstream leftists" predominated until the mid-seventies. Thereafter, in both parties a partisan left-right conception of where the voters stood became the mode. But since 1978 a mainstream leftist perspective has again predominated in both parties.

Assuming the same activists were involved, Democrats only had to change their minds about where Republican voters stood, and their "mainstream leftist" perspectives would become "partisan leftist" ones. On the other hand, Republican activists not only had to perceive the Republican voters as shifting from left to right—and, a few years later, back again—but also had to change their personal policy preferences correspondingly. Perhaps the impact of inflation, unemployment, and sluggish economic recovery during the late 1970s did cause numerous Republicans to think pragmatically about the appropriateness of federal efforts on this issue. In any case, surprisingly few Republican activists took the view that control of the cost of living was no business of the federal government. Nor did such respondents think that Republican voters held such a rightist position.

*Pollution Control*
On this policy front, as Figure 5.4 shows, prior to 1974, a mainstream leftist stance was often taken by activists in both parties. But thereafter a clear and stable left-right partisan alignment of views displaced it (although 1980 levels are slightly up). Again, most of the reassessment of personal views, and also of what the party faithful wanted, had to take place on the Republican side.

*Four Other Issues*
On the remaining four issues—nuclear disarmament, defense cuts, help for the poor, and desegregation—partisan cleavage was the modal pattern, with most Republicans taking partisan rightist views of the controversies, while most Democratic activists held partisan leftist perspectives on these issues. These are, so to speak, the bread-and-butter issues on which the rival parties confront each other.

Yet in each party, a significant number of activists felt that both Democratic and Republican voters preferred a rightist policy on these issues. For Republicans thus able to convince themselves that a "mainstream rightist" perspective correctly diagnosed the situation, it was no longer necessary to think in terms of mobilizing enough Republican voters to outnumber the opposition. Insofar as these issues looked like mainstream rightist cases, they could reasonably hope to mobilize erstwhile Democratic voters who were right-thinking on these questions. For the Democrats who saw both voting blocs as favoring rightist policies on these issues, the typical posture was that of an "isolated leftist," deserted by his own party's following in the electorate as well as opposed by the voters of the rival party. Yet, as Figure 5.4 shows, over the full time period, these Democrats were apparently willing to hold to their personal policy views, even though they acknowledged that both sets of voters opposed them.

Figure 5.4.  Issue Alignment Perspectives of Rival Party Activists, by Issue and Year

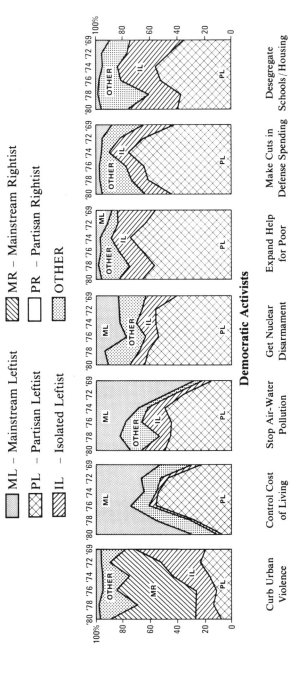

ML – Mainstream Leftist
PL – Partisan Leftist
IL – Isolated Leftist

MR – Mainstream Rightist
PR – Partisan Rightist
OTHER

**Democratic Activists**

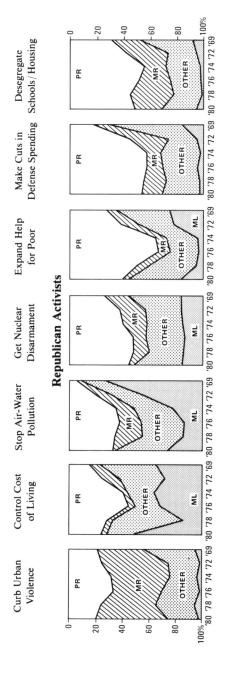

These fragmentary probes should serve to illustrate how a typology of issue alignment perspectives can enable us to monitor empirically the psychological adjustments which party activists periodically must make, between what they personally want the federal government to do and what they see the voters of their home districts as wanting—that is, between their ideological agenda and their political realism about what is feasible.

### Grassroots Partisan Efforts in 1980

In the 1980 UCLA party activist survey, an experimental data-gathering instrument was used to learn from the activists themselves—treated as "well-placed informants"—how much campaign activity was undertaken during the fall campaign weeks by each of the separately-run campaign apparatuses, party organizational echelons, and political action committees (PACs) that mounted any coordinated effort in each locality of the Los Angeles metropolitan area. Five kinds of campaign activity were distinguished—voter registration, fundraising, getting out the vote, face-to-face canvassing, and telephone canvassing.

Respondents were asked to say how much (if any) of each campaign activity was carried out by each candidate campaign unit (four were distinguished, for president, for U.S. senator, for Congress, and for the state assembly) and by four echelons of each party's regular organization, ranging from local clubs to the statewide organization. Also, equivalent information was sought about three kinds of PACs.

In the jumble of overlapping legislative constituencies and autonomous local governments found in Los Angeles County, there are typically rival candidates and hostile cliques seeking to capture the same office in each party. Officeseekers regularly organize their own campaign units and run their campaigns, often with the help of campaign management firms, but without much reliance on the party organization itself—local, districtwide, or higher.

In each of the thirty assembly districts in the county in 1980, we interviewed an average of seven Democrats and seven Republicans who were currently active in party work of some kind. Among other questions, they were asked to fill out (with prompting from the interviewer) the campaign efforts inventory reproduced in Figure 5.5. The form was admittedly elaborate, and sometimes it proved to be a daunting instrument. Informants were urged to leave items blank if the information was unknown to them.

**Figure 5.5.  Campaign Activity Form Used in 1980 Los Angeles Survey**

ESTIMATED LEVELS OF VARIOUS CAMPAIGN ACTIVITIES IN YOUR
STATE ASSEMBLY DISTRICT DURING THE FALL CAMPAIGN WEEKS

| Campaign Activities Carried Out by: | Voter Registration | | Fundraising | | Getting Out the Vote | | Face-to-face Canvassing | | Telephone Canvassing | |
|---|---|---|---|---|---|---|---|---|---|---|
| | Much | Not Much | Much | Not Much | Much | Not Much | Much | Not Much | Much | Not Much |
| **CANDIDATE CAMPAIGN UNITS** | | | | | | | | | | |
| Carter unit | — | — | — | — | — | — | — | — | — | — |
| Reagan unit | — | — | — | — | — | — | — | — | — | — |
| Anderson unit | — | — | — | — | — | — | — | — | — | — |
| D. Senate unit | — | — | — | — | — | — | — | — | — | — |
| R. Senate unit | — | — | — | — | — | — | — | — | — | — |
| D. Congress. unit | — | — | — | — | — | — | — | — | — | — |
| R. Congress. unit | — | — | — | — | — | — | — | — | — | — |
| D. Assembly unit | — | — | — | — | — | — | — | — | — | — |
| R. Assembly unit | — | — | — | — | — | — | — | — | — | — |
| **REGULAR PARTY ORGANIZATIONAL UNITS** | | | | | | | | | | |
| D. Local orgn. | — | — | — | — | — | — | — | — | — | — |
| D. District orgn. | — | — | — | — | — | — | — | — | — | — |
| D. County orgn. | — | — | — | — | — | — | — | — | — | — |
| D. State orgn. | — | — | — | — | — | — | — | — | — | — |
| R. Local orgn. | — | — | — | — | — | — | — | — | — | — |
| R. District orgn. | — | — | — | — | — | — | — | — | — | — |
| R. County orgn. | — | — | — | — | — | — | — | — | — | — |
| R. State orgn. | — | — | — | — | — | — | — | — | — | — |
| **POLITICAL ACTION COMMITTEES** | | | | | | | | | | |
| Labor PAC | — | — | — | — | — | — | — | — | — | — |
| Bus. PAC | — | — | — | — | — | — | — | — | — | — |
| Prof. PAC | — | — | — | — | — | — | — | — | — | — |

**Table 5.9.  Percentages in Each Party Claiming Some Knowledgeability
About Campaign Activities Undertaken by Various Groups**

| Campaign Unit | Kind of Campaign Activity Mounted by Specific Unit | | | | | | | | | |
| | Voter Registration | | Fundraising | | Getting Out the Vote | | Face-to-face Canvassing | | Telephone Canvassing | |
| | Rep. | Dem. | Rep. | Dem. | Rep. | Dem. | Rep. | Dem. | Rep. | Dem. |
|---|---|---|---|---|---|---|---|---|---|---|
| Carter | 46 | 73 | 42 | 69 | 43 | 69 | 40 | 67 | 40 | 66 |
| Reagan | 78 | 43 | 76 | 43 | 80 | 41 | 72 | 37 | 65 | 37 |
| Anderson | 42 | 40 | 39 | 41 | 39 | 39 | 37 | 39 | 36 | 36 |
| D. Senate | 42 | 62 | 40 | 63 | 38 | 62 | 38 | 60 | 36 | 58 |
| R. Senate | 68 | 34 | 66 | 35 | 67 | 35 | 66 | 33 | 68 | 33 |
| D. Congress | 47 | 67 | 45 | 66 | 44 | 66 | 42 | 66 | 40 | 65 |
| R. Congress | 73 | 42 | 72 | 43 | 73 | 41 | 70 | 40 | 71 | 40 |
| D. Assembly | 48 | 69 | 46 | 70 | 44 | 68 | 44 | 68 | 41 | 67 |
| R. Assembly | 73 | 41 | 72 | 43 | 72 | 41 | 70 | 41 | 71 | 39 |
| D. Local | 37 | 72 | 31 | 70 | 34 | 70 | 35 | 69 | 33 | 70 |
| D. District | 35 | 66 | 29 | 63 | 32 | 62 | 30 | 60 | 29 | 59 |
| D. County | 33 | 66 | 28 | 62 | 29 | 61 | 28 | 58 | 26 | 58 |
| D. State | 31 | 61 | 27 | 59 | 27 | 58 | 27 | 57 | 27 | 56 |
| R. Local | 71 | 27 | 64 | 25 | 69 | 25 | 65 | 24 | 51 | 25 |
| R. District | 66 | 24 | 61 | 24 | 64 | 23 | 61 | 22 | 61 | 23 |
| R. County | 71 | 27 | 67 | 25 | 68 | 25 | 63 | 25 | 66 | 25 |
| R. State | 64 | 25 | 61 | 25 | 62 | 23 | 58 | 23 | 59 | 23 |
| Labor PAC | 33 | 50 | 30 | 48 | 29 | 49 | 41 | 44 | 27 | 45 |
| Bus. PAC | 34 | 32 | 35 | 32 | 32 | 29 | 32 | 28 | 30 | 28 |
| Prof. PAC | 31 | 30 | 31 | 31 | 29 | 28 | 27 | 27 | 27 | 27 |

When they did respond on a particular point, a forced choice was all they
were given—"much" or "not much."

All told, 110 separately-run campaign efforts were pinpointed on the
inventory form. As we had expected, most individuals skipped whole sec-
tions. Yet, as Table 5.9 shows, our activist-informants proved to be selectively knowledgeable. Only 12 percent of the Republicans and 19 percent of

the Democrats were unwilling to provide estimates for any of the campaign efforts mounted by units of their own party or their party's nominees. Yet very few in either party systematically rated all of their own side's units on all counts.

When it was a question of rating the rival side's effort, 48 percent of the Republicans and 53 percent of the Democrats had nothing to contribute. Even those who did venture a few "guesstimates" seldom were knowledgeable about more than half of the rival party's efforts.

On average, 67 percent of our Republican informants gave appraisals about each unitary campaign effort on their side, while 64 percent of our Democrats typically rated each effort component undertaken by Democrats. Only about a third in each party was likely to rate any given element of the rival side's effort. As Table 5.10 shows, two-thirds in each party were prepared to rate their own side on any given count, while only one-third felt competent to rate the efforts of the rival camp. In short, a sizable number of these party activists were not very mindful of the organized competition, however hard they might work to win votes. At the same time, so far as their own side goes, each party's workers show a differentiated willingness to claim knowledge of a wide range of specific campaign activities.

How much of each kind of campaign effort were the various organized party units and candidate units seen as mounting? What were their "campaign intensity scores"? In the weighting scheme adopted for this analysis, the base for computing the intensity of each kind of campaign effort included only those who positively registered either a "much" or "not much" judgment on that count. Scored in a binary way, the resulting indicators can range from a low of 0 (should every judge in the panel say that "not much" effort had been expended) to a high of 1 (should all agree that "much" had been done). Table 5.10 provides the net assessments for each party's panel of self-described well-placed informants on each count.

Several features of Table 5.10 are noteworthy. First, almost without exception, Democratic informants attributed higher campaign intensities to the efforts of their party than did Republicans when evaluating Democratic efforts. In almost every case, too, Republican prowess was more highly rated by Republican informants than by Democrats; the only exceptions are starred, and concern the fundraising efforts of Republican local and countywide units, which Democrats rated more generously than did Republicans.

Second, on every count our informants rated the Republican effort more highly than the Democratic performance. Indeed, whereas our Republican informants uniformly were less generous than Democrats when rating

**Table 5.10.**  **Proportions of Knowledgeable Informants in Each Party Estimating High Levels of Campaign Effort on Each Count by Specific Units (Scaled from 0 to 1)**

| Campaign Unit | *Kind of Campaign Activity Mounted by Specific Unit* | | | | | | | | | |
|---|---|---|---|---|---|---|---|---|---|---|
| | *Voter Regis-tration* | | *Fund-raising* | | *Getting Out the Vote* | | *Face-to-face Canvassing* | | *Telephone Canvassing* | |
| | *Rep.* | *Dem.* | *Rep.* | *Dem.* | *Rep.* | *Dem.* | *Rep.* | *Dem.* | *Rep.* | *Dem.* |
| Carter | .24 | .27 | .18 | .19 | .23 | .27 | .14 | .18 | .26 | .29 |
| Reagan | .79 | .51 | .70 | .67 | .81 | .67 | .59 | .43 | .84 | .56 |
| Anderson | .26 | .30 | .23 | .30 | .19 | .23 | .20 | .28 | .20 | .25 |
| D. Senate | .13 | .35 | .32 | .48 | .18 | .33 | .10 | .27 | .18 | .29 |
| R. Senate | .38 | .15 | .30 | .24 | .43 | .20 | .25 | .17 | .38 | .15 |
| D. Congress | .66 | .54 | .45 | .55 | .36 | .57 | .35 | .51 | .39 | .56 |
| R. Congress | .64 | .35 | .64 | .50 | .66 | .42 | .58 | .32 | .65 | .51 |
| D. Assembly | .30 | .53 | .48 | .49 | .38 | .53 | .30 | .52 | .34 | .51 |
| R. Assembly | .52 | .34 | .57 | .55 | .56 | .43 | .49 | .36 | .56 | .46 |
| D. Local | .32 | .49 | .33 | .37 | .39 | .47 | .33 | .40 | .35 | .46 |
| D. District | .34 | .49 | .34 | .36 | .39 | .47 | .27 | .33 | .33 | .44 |
| D. County | .28 | .54 | .33 | .40 | .27 | .49 | .18 | .36 | .19 | .42 |
| D. State | .29 | .42 | .38 | .43 | .31 | .36 | .23 | .24 | .32 | .29 |
| R. Local | .80 | .63 | .56 | .64 | .75 | .66 | .59 | .52 | .77 | .58 |
| R. District | .73 | .54 | .59 | .56 | .76 | .59 | .56 | .51 | .74 | .56 |
| R. County | .75 | .56 | .64 | .66 | .71 | .61 | .54 | .44 | .72 | .56 |
| R. State | .65 | .48 | .74 | .66 | .65 | .56 | .46 | .37 | .59 | .42 |
| Labor PAC | .44 | .58 | .52 | .55 | .38 | .59 | .25 | .44 | .28 | .47 |
| Bus. PAC | .21 | .28 | .55 | .57 | .23 | .30 | .17 | .28 | .22 | .33 |
| Prof. PAC | .20 | .26 | .46 | .46 | .22 | .31 | .13 | .25 | .17 | .31 |

Democratic efforts and nearly twice as generous when rating their own party units' prowess, our Democratic informants collectively gave higher ratings *on every count* to Republican campaign efforts than to the work of their own side. A digest of these patterns is given in Table 5.11.

On count after count, roughly half of those party activists who were willing to rate units of their own party were also prepared to make esti-

**Table 5.11.  Campaign Intensity Scores by Informants Assessing Both Sides, Showing Proportions Who See Different Party Rivalry Situations**

| | Democratic Edge* | Matched Efforts* | Republican Edge* | | Cases | Did Not Rate Both Sides* |
|---|---|---|---|---|---|---|
| Voter Registration | | | | | | |
| Republican informants | 1 | 37 | 62 | : 100 | 93 | 66 |
| Democratic informants | 26 | 63 | 11 | : 100 | 83 | 59 |
| Fundraising | | | | | | |
| Republican informants | 3 | 52 | 45 | : 100 | 77 | 68 |
| Democratic informants | 18 | 69 | 13 | : 100 | 76 | 63 |
| Getting Out the Vote | | | | | | |
| Republican informants | 2 | 36 | 62 | : 100 | 83 | 68 |
| Democratic informants | 27 | 60 | 13 | : 100 | 83 | 59 |
| Face-to-Face Canvassing | | | | | | |
| Republican informants | 1 | 58 | 41 | : 100 | 84 | 70 |
| Democratic informants | 22 | 69 | 9 | : 100 | 80 | 61 |
| Telephone Canvassing | | | | | | |
| Republican informants | 1 | 46 | 53 | : 100 | 90 | 69 |
| Democratic informants | 27 | 64 | 9 | : 100 | 90 | 56 |
| Composite of Five Activities | | | | | | |
| Republican informants | 2 | 45 | 53 | : 100 | 85 | 69 |
| Democratic informants | 24 | 65 | 9 | : 100 | 82 | 60 |

*In percent.

mates about the prowess of the rival party's units in their own legislative district. Such a low level of knowledge about the other camp is surprising. If one uses a Schumpeterian (1939) or Downsian (1957) model of the democratic election process as an oligopolistic competition between two or three organized rival camps, each seeking to mobilize its own following and to attract a "floating vote," and each *continuously aware* of the countervailing efforts of its rival, one expects much higher levels than these of knowledge about the campaign efforts of that rival.[5] In practice, it is understandable that those who voluntarily become party activists may often be preoccupied with the difficulties of mounting and coordinating a fundraising or get-out-the-vote project. It is less easily understood that—busy or not with their own side's campaign effort—they seldom try to inform themselves about

**Table 5.12.  Comparative Evaluations by Republican and Democratic Informants of the 1980 Campaign Efforts of Rival Units**

|  | Voter Regis- tration | Fund- raising | Getting to Polls | Face-to- face Canvas- sing | Tele- phone Canvas- sing |
|---|---|---|---|---|---|
| Republican Efforts |  |  |  |  |  |
| Rep. Informants | .66 | .59 | .67 | .51 | .66 |
| Dem. Informants | .46 | .56 | .52 | .39 | .46 |
| Difference (R − D) | +.22 | +.03 | +.15 | +.12 | +.20 |
| Democratic Efforts |  |  |  |  |  |
| Rep. Informants | .28 | .35 | .31 | .24 | .29 |
| Dem. Informants | .45 | .40 | .44 | .35 | .41 |
| Difference (R − D) | −.17 | −.05 | −.13 | −.11 | −.12 |

Note: Campaign effort scores range from −1 to 1.

rival efforts undertaken in their home terrain. To learn that a "sense of rivalry" is not overwhelmingly present among party activists raises basic questions about the widely accepted competitive model of election politics.

It also suggests the fruitfulness of giving special attention to those activists who *did* claim some knowledge about the rival party's efforts as well as their own. Operationally, a measure of campaign advantage can be fashioned by subtracting the campaign intensity score attributed to a specific rival party unit (say, the Carter campaign unit in a given locale) from the score given to one's own party unit (e.g., the Reagan unit in this example). The result is a trichotomous measure, where −1 expresses a belief that the Democratic unit has the edge over its rival, 0 indicates that the party units are seen as well matched, and +1 means that the Republicans are seen as having an effectiveness edge. For Los Angeles County as a whole, table 5.12 shows what such a measure of relative campaign advantage discloses for 1980.

In considering Table 5.12, it should be remembered that sizable majorities in both parties are excluded from it because they did *not* make assessments of both parties' efforts. On average, 60 percent of the Democrats and 69 percent of the Republicans were unwilling or unable to rate both sides.

The table shows quite different patterns characterizing the views of knowledgeable Democrats and Republicans. A full majority of the latter (53 percent) gave their party a definite edge over its rival, while only a quarter of the Democrats (24 percent) saw their party as putting forth a *greater* campaign effort, count for count, than its rival. Moreover, while the Democrats at best saw their party effort *matching* its rival, the Republicans held that their effort *at least equaled* if not surpassed the other side 98 percent of the time.

### The Effects of Partisan Context

One more line of inquiry can be reported — the effect of the partisan character of a locale on these appraisals of campaign advantage made by party activists. Since the UCLA project sampled activists from all assembly districts in the county in proper ratios, it is possible to examine the differences in campaign intensity scores registered by those working in "sure territory," "doubtful areas," or "lost terrain," using the actual 1980 voting behavior for each district to classify it in partisan terms. In Table 5.13, a three-way breakdown treats areas where Republicans won by margins of 17 to 60 percentage points as Republican ground, districts where Democrats prevailed by 11 to 75 points as Democratic terrain, and in-between areas as competitive. It should be noted that, in these same constituencies, quite different margins of victory characterized the presidential, senatorial, and congressional contexts. Because of the way in which California parties are organized, however, there is a strategic importance to the task of capturing and/or holding the state assembly seat, or acknowledging the virtual impossibility of doing so.

Overall, Table 5.13 shows that only in Democratic areas did the Carter campaign effort rate rather high compared with the performance rating of other Democratic units. Reagan's nuclear campaign unit, by contrast, was strong in all kinds of political terrain.

An especially interesting pattern emerges in Table 5.14, where the detailed specifications of rival party workers, claiming knowledgeability about both sides, are merged. A cell-for-cell matchup of rival unit ratings is achieved by subtracting the Democratic effort score from its Republican counterpart. When this is done, the 1980 pattern of rival party efforts is starkly revealed as lopsided.

First, in virtually every kind of terrain, in virtually every contest between rival candidate units, at each level or regular party organizational effort, and on all five kinds of campaign activity, the Republicans outdid the Democrats. Only in Democratic strongholds did Senator Cranston's campaign effort succeed in outstripping Gann's.[6] Only in Democratic strongholds did Democratic party assembly candidates outperform their rivals and its congressional nominees achieve a near standoff.

**Table 5.13.  Comparison of Campaign Intensity Scores by Panels of
Knowledgeable Informants in Contrasting Political Locales**

|  | Republican Districts | Competitive Districts | Democratic Districts | Whole County | N |
|---|---|---|---|---|---|
| *Republican Informants Only* | | | | | |
| Reagan for President unit | .74 | .73 | .73 | .73 | 180 |
| Republican for U. S. Senate | .46 | .33 | .36 | .38 | 144 |
| Republican for Congress | .66 | .75 | .57 | .63 | 160 |
| Republican for State Assembly | .68 | .84 | .39 | .56 | 154 |
| Local Repub. club/committee | .76 | .72 | .64 | .68 | 158 |
| Districtwide Repub. unit | .75 | .69 | .64 | .68 | 149 |
| Countywide Repub. unit | .62 | .62 | .65 | .64 | 141 |
| Statewide Repub. unit | .50 | .55 | .68 | .61 | 133 |
| Voter registration drives | .74 | .71 | .69 | .71 | 185 |
| Fundraising drives | .73 | .66 | .59 | .64 | 177 |
| Getting out the vote | .68 | .74 | .69 | .70 | 179 |
| Face-to-face canvassing | .57 | .57 | .49 | .52 | 172 |
| Telephone canvassing | .75 | .70 | .70 | .71 | 175 |
| Composite Republican Effort | .68 | .66 | .62 | .65 | 167 |
| *Democratic Informants Only* | | | | | |
| Carter for President unit | .14 | .21 | .41 | .28 | 153 |
| Democrat for U.S. Senate | .25 | .28 | .48 | .36 | 125 |
| Democrat for Congress | .53 | .62 | .55 | .57 | 147 |
| Democrat for State Assembly | .27 | .65 | .49 | .51 | 141 |
| Local Dem. club/committee | .22 | .54 | .54 | .46 | 158 |
| Districtwide Dem. unit | .18 | .51 | .56 | .45 | 149 |
| Countywide Dem. unit | .39 | .42 | .60 | .49 | 141 |
| Statewide Dem. unit | .24 | .26 | .51 | .36 | 133 |
| Voter registration drives | .32 | .48 | .58 | .48 | 169 |
| Fundraising drives | .28 | .43 | .46 | .41 | 166 |
| Getting out the vote | .33 | .49 | .56 | .48 | 167 |
| Face-to-face canvassing | .24 | .39 | .46 | .39 | 163 |
| Telephone canvassing | .34 | .46 | .55 | .47 | 163 |
| Composite Democratic Effort | .28 | .42 | .48 | .41 | 157 |

**Table 5.14.  Net Advantage in Campaign Efforts, as Judged by Panels of Knowledgeable Informants in Contrasting Political Locales**

| Cell-for-Cell Matching (Republican score minus Democratic score) | Repub-lican Districts | Competi-tive Districts | Demo-cratic Districts | Whole County | N |
|---|---|---|---|---|---|
| Presidential campaign units | +.60 | +.52 | +.31 | +.34 | 180 |
| Senatorial campaign units | +.21 | +.05 | −.12 | +.02 | 144 |
| Congressional campaign units | +.13 | +.13 | +.02 | +.06 | 160 |
| Assembly campaign units | +.41 | +.19 | −.10 | +.15 | 154 |
| Local party clubs/committees | +.54 | +.18 | +.10 | +.22 | 158 |
| Districtwide party units | +.57 | +.18 | +.08 | +.23 | 149 |
| Countywide party units | +.23 | +.20 | +.05 | +.15 | 141 |
| Statewide party units | +.26 | +.29 | +.17 | +.25 | 133 |
| Voter registration drives | +.42 | +.23 | +.11 | +.23 | 185 |
| Fundraising drives | +.45 | +.23 | +.13 | +.23 | 177 |
| Getting out the vote | +.35 | +.25 | +.13 | +.22 | 179 |
| Face-to-face canvassing | +.33 | +.18 | +.03 | +.13 | 172 |
| Telephone canvassing | +.41 | +.24 | +.15 | +.24 | 175 |
| Composite Partisan Efforts | +.40 | +.24 | +.14 | +.24 | 167 |

Second, it is clear that the nature of each district's political terrain did affect the assessments of rival prowess made by knowledgeable activist-informants in both parties. In Republican areas the composite partisan efforts of the rival sides produced a +.40 advantage for the Republicans on a scale from −1.0 to +1.0. On more competitive ground, the Republicans outmatched their rivals by +.24. Even in Democratic territory, virtually every candidate unit, every organizational level, and every campaign drive found the Republicans outpointing their rivals—on average, the margin was +.14.

It seems fair to claim some discriminatory power for the campaign intensity scores generated by this experimental campaign efforts instrument, first used in the 1980 UCLA project. The complexity of that instrument does not seem to have fazed our informants. In our tables, (1) the replication of patterns disclosed—the persistent contrast between intensity scores registered by Republicans and Democrats, or the consistent diminution of the Republican advantage when attention shifts from that party's sure to doubtful to lost areas of strength—as well as (2) the *prima facie* plausibility of the results themselves—the onesideness of Reagan's race, the relative weakness of Gann's, the closeness of the congressional contests, and the full spectrum of incumbent advantages implicit in the state assembly appraisals—argue that these measures are reflecting political reality quite well. Validity is always threatened when standardized data-gathering methods obtain scores from respondents who vary greatly—some of whom are cautious, realistic, and well informed; while others are careless, fantasy-prone, and poorly informed. Yet clearly we need to develop research tools like this if political scientists are to be able in future election years to base their net assessments of campaign prowess of *differentiated empirical appraisals* made by well-placed and knowledgeable informants, instead of on guesswork.

## Conclusion

These findings about party activists in Los Angeles County range over many topics and touch upon beliefs, mental adjustments, and knowledgeable assessments of the political scene. Three sets of general conclusions seem warranted.

First, party activists are interested in the *substance* of politics, and they continue to work *despite* persistent doubts about the voters, the candidates, and the electoral system. Activists enter politics, stay in politics, discuss political problems with other activists, develop considerable skepticism about what to expect of ordinary voters, and an appreciation of the need to be flexible and to think of politics as "the art of the possible."

Second, the views of activists about public issues need to be appraised in light of how these informants size up the Republican and Democratic voters in their localities. *Preferences are tempered by expectations.* For the party activist, personal policy views are part of an "issue alignment perspective" which reflects her or his sensitivity to voter consensus or to voter cleavage. To an activist who wants to affect policy, have a voice in party affairs, and win elections, personal preferences on public policy issues are not uncritically expressed hopes or wishes. Linked to expectations about what the voters want, some of those policy preferences seem unattainable, while others seem ready for fulfillment. The opinions of voting blocs may change or persist over time; to some extent, too, it may be necessary for an activist to revise her or his own political priorities. Some issues have to be "put on the back burner." Other issues are joined along partisan lines, and their fate is tied closely to the near-term success or failure of one's party. Still other policies are so widely popular that, no matter which party wins, some implementation of such policies seems likely.

Finally, party activists are not necessarily imbued with a *sense of rivalry* toward the other organized contending party in their locality. For most, working for the party is like working for any worthy purpose—organizing joint efforts, generating support, recruiting help—without worrying about the countervailing efforts by rival forces taking place in the same locality.

Still, about a third in each party was sufficiently interested in what the rival camp was doing to claim (and to demonstrate in detail) a differentiated knowledge of how intense a campaign effort was forthcoming from both sides at four organizational levels, in five different kinds of campaign drives, and in contests for four different public offices. On count after count, our informants in the Democratic camp agreed with their Republican counterparts.

These findings provide grounds for holding that political realism at the grassroots level of American politics is not such a scarce commodity, for all the ideological zeal that prompts many activists and sustains their participation, even when they grow discouraged about winning or skeptical about electoral democracy.

## Notes

1. See Dwaine Marvick, "Party Activists in Los Angeles, 1963–78: How Well-Matched Rivals Shape Election Options," in *Political Elites and Social Change: Studies of Elites Roles and Attitudes*, ed. Moshe Czudnowski (DeKalb: Northern Illinois Univ. Press, 1983), 64–101; Marvick, "Political Linkage Functions of Rival Party Activists in the United States: Los Angeles, 1969–74"; and Marvick, "Party Organizational Personnel and Electoral Democracy in Los Angeles, 1964–72."

2. Marvick, "Party Activists in Los Angeles, 1963–78."

3. Ibid.

4. Schumpeter, *Capitalism, Socialism, and Democracy*; Robert Dahl, *A Preface to Democratic Theory* (Chicago: Univ. of Chicago Press, 1956); and Downs, *An Economic Theory of Democracy*.

5. Schumpeter, *Capitalism, Socialism, and Democracy*; and Downs, *An Economic Theory of Democracy*.

6. Paul Gann was the Republican nominee to the U.S. Senate in California in 1980, opposing Democratic incumbent Alan Cranston. Cranston won reelection with 60% of the vote.

CHAPTER 6

# Local Parties in Chicago:
# The Machine in Transition

*William Crotty*

The Chicago party organization is reputed to represent one of the last, if not the last, of the old-time, big-city machines. Some look to it as the embodiment of what political parties should be, in an era in which their role and contributions are undergoing a critical reevaluation. Others see the machine as a curiosity, a holdover from another era, that for reasons peculiar to the demographic and political environment of Chicago has undergone little change. From either perspective, an examination of the operations and personnel of the Chicago parties would appear to offer an unusual opportunity for understanding better the relationship between a party and its environment, and the costs and contributions implicit in the interchange.

## Research Design

With this in mind, the present study was initiated to explore (a) the social and personal characteristics of party leaders; (b) the political background and career pathways of the party leaders; (c) party structure and intraorganizational decision making and interactions; and (d) party operations and activities during an election. The focus of the analysis was on the 160 ward (for Chicago) and township (for Cook County suburbs) committee members. This permitted analytic comparisons among the Chicago Democratic party operation within the city, the Republican city organization and activities, and the suburban operations of both parties.

The 50 ward and 30 township committee members represent the functionally equivalent positions within each of the parties. Together, the ward and township committee members constitute the Cook County central committees for each of the parties.

The fieldwork for the study was done in spring and early summer of 1981. An interview schedule of sixty-five items was administered to the committee members, covering such topics as party activity, organizational structure, operations during the presidential election of 1980, off-year party concerns, political experience and background, perceptions of the constituency, patronage use, political entry, campaign strategy and effectiveness, and policy views. The report that follows examines the data relating to personal characteristics, political experience and motivations, party structure, and party activities.

The questionnaire was administered both through personal interviews conducted by professional interviewers and by mail. The same questionnaire, consisting of mostly closed-ended items, was used in both situations. Of the 157 ward and township committee members (three positions were vacant), returns were received from 89, for a response rate of 57 percent.

### Social Characteristics

Chicago and Cook County committee members of *both* parties had deep roots within their communities. From 80 to 96 percent had lived in their communities for ten years or more. Somewhat surprisingly, the greatest longevity was found among Republican ward committee members in Chicago. Similarly, between 79 and 84 percent of the committee members had lived in their immediate neighborhoods for over ten years (Table 6.1).

If the key to understanding personal political involvement is the political and community activity of the parents—and specifically of the mother—then Chicago represents something of an exception. A majority of the committee members' mothers were not active in community groups, and 80 percent or more were not active in any capacity in party politics.

The socialization pattern for local politics in Chicago may be more typical of that found in another age. Chicago politics is not considered the province of the female. Despite the city's having one of the first, and one of the few, woman mayors governing a large metropolitan area, the party organization—the continuing base of political power—is controlled by men. Of the 157 committee members surveyed, only ten (6 percent of the total) were women (three Democrats and seven Republicans).

Virtually all committee members were married and most had children.

**Table 6.1. Demographic Attributes of Party Committee Members (In Percent)**

| Variable | Democrats All | Democrats Chicago | Democrats Suburbs | Republicans All | Republicans Chicago | Republicans Suburbs | Total (Both Parties) |
|---|---|---|---|---|---|---|---|
| *Lived in Chicago or Area (Years)* | | | | | | | |
| 1 or less | 14 | 12 | 16 | 14 | 0 | 17 | 10 |
| 2–5 | 0 | 0 | 0 | 0 | 0 | 0 | 0 |
| 6–10 | 2 | 0 | 5 | 2 | 4 | 0 | 2 |
| 11 or more | 84 | 88 | 79 | 84 | 96 | 83 | 88 |
| | 100 | 100 | 100 | 100 | 100 | 100 | 100 |
| *Lived in Neighborhood (Years)* | | | | | | | |
| 1 or less | 4 | 8 | 0 | 0 | 0 | 0 | 1 |
| 2–5 | 7 | 0 | 0 | 2 | 4 | 16 | 5 |
| 6–10 | 7 | 8 | 6 | 7 | 7 | 5 | 7 |
| 11 or more | 82 | 84 | 94 | 91 | 89 | 79 | 87 |
| | 100 | 100 | 100 | 100 | 100 | 100 | 100 |
| *Mother Active in Community Affairs* | | | | | | | |
| Very | 18 | 26 | 11 | 20 | 22 | 17 | 19 |
| Somewhat | 21 | 16 | 28 | 24 | 15 | 39 | 23 |
| Not active | 61 | 58 | 61 | 56 | 63 | 44 | 58 |
| | 100 | 100 | 100 | 100 | 100 | 100 | 100 |
| *Mother Active in Party* | | | | | | | |
| Very | 0 | 0 | 0 | 0 | 0 | 0 | 0 |
| Somewhat | 16 | 10 | 22 | 19 | 22 | 17 | 18 |
| Not Active | 84 | 90 | 78 | 81 | 78 | 83 | 82 |
| | 100 | 100 | 100 | 100 | 100 | 100 | 100 |
| *Marital Status* | | | | | | | |
| Now | 88 | 86 | 89 | 79 | 67 | 94 | 83 |
| Once | 12 | 14 | 11 | 18 | 26 | 6 | 15 |
| Never | 0 | 0 | 0 | 4 | 7 | 0 | 2 |
| | 100 | 100 | 100 | 100 | 100 | 100 | 100 |
| *Children (Number)* | | | | | | | |
| 1 | 6 | 10 | 0 | 10 | 14 | 6 | 8 |
| 2 | 28 | 32 | 25 | 15 | 24 | 6 | 21 |
| 3 | 33 | 37 | 31 | 38 | 24 | 55 | 36 |

**Table 6.1. Continued**

| Variable | Democrats | | | Republicans | | | Total (Both Parties) |
|---|---|---|---|---|---|---|---|
| | All | Chicago | Suburbs | All | Chicago | Suburbs | |
| 4 | 19 | 21 | 19 | 21 | 24 | 16 | 20 |
| 5 | 8 | 0 | 19 | 10 | 9 | 11 | 10 |
| 6 | 0 | 0 | 0 | 3 | 0 | 5 | 1 |
| 7 or more | 6 | 0 | 6 | 3 | 5 | 0 | 4 |
| | 100 | 100 | 100 | 100 | 100 | 100 | 100 |
| *Age* | | | | | | | |
| 21 or younger | 17 | 35 | 18 | 15 | 22 | 7 | 1 |
| 21–30 | 30 | 17 | 35 | 47 | 39 | 58 | 12 |
| 31–40 | 33 | 24 | 35 | 27 | 22 | 35 | 28 |
| 41–50 | 20 | 24 | 12 | 8 | 13 | 0 | 38 |
| 51–81 | 0 | 0 | 0 | 3 | 4 | 0 | 21 |
| | 100 | 100 | 100 | 100 | 100 | 100 | 100 |
| *Race* | | | | | | | |
| White | 87 | 82 | 95 | 79 | 64 | 95 | 83 |
| Black | 10 | 13 | 5 | 21 | 36 | 5 | 16 |
| Hispanic | 3 | 5 | 0 | 0 | 0 | 0 | 1 |
| | 100 | 100 | 100 | 100 | 100 | 100 | 100 |
| *Education* | | | | | | | |
| H.S. or less | 21 | 19 | 23 | 11 | 11 | 11 | 15 |
| Some college | 12 | 14 | 11 | 38 | 48 | 23 | 26 |
| Col. grad. | 12 | 10 | 11 | 22 | 11 | 39 | 18 |
| Grad. school | 12 | 14 | 11 | 13 | 11 | 16 | 13 |
| Prof. school | 43 | 43 | 44 | 16 | 19 | 11 | 28 |
| | 100 | 100 | 100 | 100 | 100 | 100 | 100 |
| *Religious Preference* | | | | | | | |
| Protestant | 39 | 16 | 17 | 40 | 42 | 39 | 30 |
| Catholic | 45 | 63 | 65 | 48 | 42 | 56 | 55 |
| Jewish | 11 | 21 | 6 | 12 | 18 | 5 | 13 |
| None | 5 | 0 | 12 | 0 | 0 | 0 | 2 |
| | 100 | 100 | 100 | 100 | 100 | 100 | 100 |
| *Attend Religious Services* | | | | | | | |
| Usually | 50 | 45 | 53 | 40 | 36 | 44 | 44 |
| Sometimes | 42 | 50 | 35 | 58 | 60 | 56 | 51 |
| Never | 8 | 5 | 12 | 2 | 4 | 0 | 5 |
| | 100 | 100 | 100 | 100 | 100 | 100 | 100 |

Many had fairly large families. For example, from two-thirds (for the Democrats) to three-fourths (for the Republicans) had families with three or more children.

Most of the party chairmen—63 percent for the Democrats and 75 percent for the Republicans—were between twenty and forty years of age. The vast majority were white (83 percent). Only 16 percent were black and 1 percent Hispanics. The highest incidence of black committee members, (and this was a surprise) was found in the Republican party in Chicago (36 percent, compared to 13 percent for the Chicago Democrats).

Sixty percent of the Democratic committee members and almost one-half of the Republicans (48 percent) were Catholic. Thirteen percent were Jewish. Virtually all (95 percent) attended religious services, and a sizeable portion (44 percent) did so with some frequency.

Approximately 60 percent of the committee members were college graduates. More than half of the Democrats had attended graduate or professional school, compared with 29 percent of the Republicans.

Ethnically, the Democrats were diverse, with Irish, Poles, Italians, and Greeks counted among their leaders. The same groups were represented in the Republican party leadership, but in lesser numbers. The dominant ethnic and cultural groups among Republicans were blacks (24 percent of the total, entirely in the Chicago Republican party) and those with mixed heritage (22 percent).

As for occupation (Table 6.2), most (70 to 94 percent) of the committee members' jobs involved dealing with the public, coordinating the work of others, persuading and bargaining with others, and working with and through organized groups. The skills developed in such positions would seem relevant and easily transferable to politics. Sixty percent (79 percent of the Chicago Democrats) did business directly with government agencies.

Most committee members (80 percent) were in high-status occupations —some type of professional, technical, or managerial position. This was virtually universally (95 percent) true for the Democrats, who as a group held somewhat higher-status positions than the Republicans.

In income, party committee members did well. More than 80 percent made $25,000 or more. Democrats did particularly well. Ninety-four percent earned over $25,000, and over half (53 percent) had incomes of $50,000 or more.

Most committee members' spouses did not work. Fifty-eight percent listed their spouses as housewives. This figure was particularly high for the Democrats (74 percent), suggesting—in line with other data—a more traditional social and family pattern underlying the Chicago party structure than may be evident in other areas of the country.

**Table 6.2. Occupation of Party Committee Members\* (In Percent)**

| Variable | Democrats | | | Republicans | | | Total (Both Parties) |
|---|---|---|---|---|---|---|---|
| | All | Chicago | Suburbs | All | Chicago | Suburbs | |
| *Committee Member's Occupation* | | | | | | | |
| Professional | 76 | 90 | 57 | 27 | 30 | 23 | 49 |
| Manager (salaried) | 16 | 5 | 31 | 25 | 22 | 29 | 21 |
| Manager (self-employed) | 3 | 0 | 6 | 16 | 15 | 18 | 10 |
| Clerical | 0 | 0 | 0 | 2 | 4 | 0 | 1 |
| Sales worker | 0 | 0 | 0 | 7 | 10 | 0 | 4 |
| Craftsman | 0 | 0 | 0 | 7 | 4 | 12 | 4 |
| Service worker | 0 | 0 | 0 | 2 | 4 | 0 | 1 |
| Housewife | 0 | 0 | 0 | 5 | 4 | 6 | 3 |
| Retired | 5 | 5 | 6 | 9 | 7 | 12 | 7 |
| | 100 | 100 | 100 | 100 | 100 | 100 | 100 |
| *Spouse's Occupation* | | | | | | | |
| Professional | 13 | 27 | 0 | 16 | 20 | 12 | 15 |
| Manager (salaried) | 6 | 13 | 0 | 3 | 0 | 6 | 4 |
| Manager (self-employed) | 3 | 0 | 6 | 5 | 0 | 12 | 4 |
| Clerical | 3 | 0 | 6 | 19 | 10 | 29 | 12 |
| Sales worker | 0 | 0 | 0 | 0 | 0 | 0 | 1 |
| Craftsman | 0 | 0 | 0 | 3 | 5 | 0 | 3 |
| Service worker | 0 | 0 | 0 | 5 | 10 | 0 | 0 |
| Housewife | 75 | 53 | 88 | 46 | 50 | 41 | 60 |
| Retired | 0 | 17 | 0 | 13 | 15 | 0 | 1 |
| | 100 | 100 | 100 | 100 | 100 | 100 | 100 |
| *Occupation Involves\*\** | | | | | | | |
| Dealing with public | 95 | 95 | 94 | 93 | 96 | 88 | 94 |
| Coordinating the work of others | 90 | 90 | 88 | 83 | 84 | 81 | 86 |
| Persuading others and bargaining | 84 | 85 | 81 | 82 | 86 | 75 | 83 |
| Doing business with the gov't | 70 | 79 | 59 | 50 | 46 | 56 | 60 |

**Table 6.2.Continued**

| Variable | Democrats | | | Republicans | | | Total (Both Parties) |
|---|---|---|---|---|---|---|---|
| | All | Chicago | Suburbs | All | Chicago | Suburbs | |
| Working with organized groups | 81 | 84 | 77 | 61 | 64 | 56 | 71 |
| *Income* | | | | | | | |
| Under $4,999 | 0 | 0 | 0 | 3 | 4 | 0 | 1 |
| $5,000–$9,999 | 0 | 0 | 0 | 0 | 0 | 0 | 0 |
| $10,000–$14,999 | 0 | 0 | 0 | 0 | 0 | 0 | 0 |
| $15,000–$19,999 | 2 | 0 | 6 | 13 | 18 | 6 | 8 |
| $20,000–$24,999 | 3 | 0 | 6 | 15 | 18 | 13 | 9 |
| $25,000–$29,999 | 14 | 11 | 12 | 10 | 8 | 13 | 12 |
| $30,000–$49,999 | 28 | 22 | 35 | 28 | 26 | 31 | 28 |
| $50,000 and over | 53 | 67 | 41 | 31 | 26 | 37 | 42 |
| | 100 | 100 | 100 | 100 | 100 | 100 | 100 |
| N | 44 | 24 | 19 | 45 | 27 | 18 | 89 |

\* Figures are rounded.
\*\* Respondents answering "usually" (as against "rarely") are reported in table.

Overall, then, the ward and township committee members tended to have lived in the area for long periods of time. They were mostly men— and family men at that, with good-sized families. Most were religious, the majority Catholics. While most were young, they were well educated; they earned their livelihoods from prestigious occupations; and they earned good salaries. The majority of spouses were housewives.

*Comment*
Ward committee positions appear to be important, high-status positions. Their occupants were generally successful people who had done well in private pursuits. This was particularly true for the Democrats, reinforcing the picture of the Chicago ward committee member as the most powerful and influential figure within the Democratic party organization. In this regard Milton Rakove's depiction seems accurate:

> The most significant of all the party's relationships with any of the constituent parts of the organization are its dealings with ward organizations in the city. Each of Chicago's fifty wards is an entity to itself, a fiefdom ruled in the party's name by a committeeman who is prince of the blood. . . ."[1]

The picture has changed from that reported by Harold Gosnell for ward committee members in 1928 and 1936.[2] At those points, Republicans generally held more prestigious business and professional positions. The modal occupational category for Republicans was lawyers with higher status clientele and prestigious law practices. Ward committee members who were lawyers do ". . . not make a profession out of politics. Their main interest is in the law, and politics is a side line for them." The same could be said for most of the Republican ward committee members in Gosnell's study. They reflected the values and pursuits of their base in the city's electorate and looked on politics as a part-time or civic service.

The Democratic committee members were of a different character and for them politics had greater meaning. As related by Gosnell: ". . . a number of Democratic committeemen who started as clerks or saloon-keepers make politics their profession. Many of these men lack the necessary educational background to go into law. A few of the Democratic ward bosses who are lawyers belong to firms which are notorious for their connections with the big tax-dodgers and the leading figures of the underworld. Several ward committeemen were members of a law firm which had a large criminal practice with prominent gangsters as clients and also a large tax-receivership practice."[3]

## Professional Backgrounds

The political roots of the committee members run deep (Table 6.3). Over half had been in politics for over twenty years, and 90 percent had been politically involved for more than ten years. Seventy percent of the Chicago Democratic committee members had been in politics for over twenty years. The vast majority (71 percent) considered themselves the strongest of partisans.

The respondents' immediate personal environments tend to support their political interests. Almost 90 percent of all the committee members claimed friends who were either "somewhat" or "very" interested in politics. Sixty-five percent of the Democrats (and 68 percent of the Chicago ward committee members) had friends who were very interested in politics. Only 46 percent of all the Republicans had friends this interested. The Republican group with the greatest support from immediate acquaintances were the suburban committee members. Over 70 percent of the party ward and township leaders (led by the Chicago Democrats, with 78 percent) had friends directly active in politics in some capacity.

**Table 6.3. Political Background\* (In Percent)**

| Variable | Democrats | | | Republicans | | | Total (Both Parties) |
|---|---|---|---|---|---|---|---|
| | All | Chicago | Suburbs | All | Chicago | Suburbs | |
| *Years Active in Party* | | | | | | | |
| 1 or less | 4 | 4 | 5 | 5 | 7 | 0 | 5 |
| 2–5 | 5 | 0 | 11 | 0 | 0 | 0 | 2 |
| 6–10 | 2 | 0 | 5 | 2 | 0 | 6 | 2 |
| 11–20 | 34 | 25 | 47 | 33 | 41 | 22 | 34 |
| 21 or more | 55 | 71 | 32 | 60 | 52 | 72 | 57 |
| N = 89 | 100 | 100 | 100 | 100 | 100 | 100 | 100 |
| *Strength of Partnership* | | | | | | | |
| Very Strong 1 | 70 | 70 | 74 | 73 | 70 | 78 | 72 |
| 2 | 11 | 9 | 10 | 13 | 15 | 11 | 12 |
| 3 | 7 | 9 | 5 | 5 | 4 | 6 | 6 |
| 4 | 7 | 12 | 0 | 7 | 7 | 5 | 7 |
| 5 | 0 | 0 | 0 | 0 | 0 | 0 | 0 |
| Very Weak 6 | 5 | 0 | 11 | 2 | 4 | 0 | 3 |
| N = 88 | 100 | 100 | 100 | 100 | 100 | 100 | 100 |
| *Friends Interested in Politics* | | | | | | | |
| Very | 61 | 65 | 53 | 46 | 40 | 56 | 53 |
| Somewhat | 30 | 31 | 31 | 40 | 44 | 33 | 35 |
| Not very | 7 | 0 | 16 | 14 | 16 | 11 | 11 |
| Not at all | 2 | 4 | 0 | 0 | 0 | 0 | 1 |
| N = 86 | 100 | 100 | 100 | 100 | 100 | 100 | 100 |
| *Friends Active in Politics* | | | | | | | |
| Most | 30 | 30 | 26 | 35 | 36 | 33 | 33 |
| About half | 44 | 48 | 42 | 35 | 32 | 39 | 40 |
| Few | 21 | 18 | 26 | 28 | 28 | 28 | 24 |
| None | 5 | 4 | 6 | 2 | 4 | 0 | 3 |
| N = 86 | 100 | 100 | 100 | 100 | 100 | 100 | 100 |

\*Figures are rounded.

Furthermore, most committee members had held, and continued to hold, a variety of positions with political responsibility within the parties (Table 6.4). Seventy percent or more had served as precinct officials or as district-level party officials. Between 50 and 60 percent had attended state conventions and/or national party conventions. One-fifth had served on the state central committee and all, of course, were members of their parties' county committees. In addition, at the time of the study, 30 percent continued to serve as precinct officials (more common in the suburbs) and on city- and district-level party committees. More Republicans than Democrats had actually sought public elective office. Most commonly, these offices were local or county positions, state legislative seats, and (for four Republicans) congressional offices. The level of public office most sought by Democrats was county. Eighty percent of the committee members indicated a willingness to take a position of responsibility within the party, should one become available.

The overall picture that emerged was of a highly committed, well-satisfied cadre of experienced political professionals. This characterization held true for the Chicago Democrats as well. Also striking were the impressive levels of political experience recorded by the suburban Democrats and by the Republican Chicago and suburban committee members. Almost two out of three committee members (and 75 percent of the Chicago Democrats) had held some type of government patronage position.

Most of the committee members were highly active in party affairs and party organizations at various levels (Table 6.4). This was to be expected and reinforces the professional emphasis that has emerged. The committee members were considerably less active in community, interest, social-issue, and single-issue groups. It could have been expected that those groups might provide a breeding ground for political involvement and constitute a

**Table 6.4. Party-Related Positions Sought or Held by Committee Members***
**(In Percent)**

| Variable | Democrats | | | Republicans | | | Total (Both Parties) |
|---|---|---|---|---|---|---|---|
| | All | Chicago | Suburbs | All | Chicago | Suburbs | |
| *Party Positions* have *Held*** | | | | | | | |
| Precinct | 69 | 83 | 50 | 72 | 73 | 71 | 71 |
| Ward | 45 | 54 | 33 | 37 | 46 | 24 | 41 |
| City | 30 | 38 | 18 | 33 | 36 | 29 | 31 |

**Table 6.4.  Continued**

| Variable | Democrats | | | Republicans | | | Total (Both Parties) |
|---|---|---|---|---|---|---|---|
| | All | Chicago | Suburbs | All | Chicago | Suburbs | |
| District | 27 | 35 | 17 | 28 | 20 | 39 | 27 |
| County | 40 | 48 | 29 | 37 | 35 | 41 | 39 |
| State | 33 | 47 | 28 | 10 | 4 | 18 | 21 |
| State convention delegate | 55 | 63 | 44 | 68 | 62 | 78 | 62 |
| National convention delegate | 60 | 71 | 45 | 47 | 40 | 56 | 53 |
| N = 89 | | | | | | | |
| *Party Positions* now *Held*** | | | | | | | |
| Precinct | — | — | — | — | — | — | — |
| Ward | — | — | — | — | — | — | — |
| City | — | — | — | — | — | — | — |
| District | 44 | 44 | 42 | 27 | 19 | 40 | 35 |
| County | 51 | 44 | 58 | 29 | 5 | 50 | 40 |
| State | 21 | 17 | 21 | 16 | 19 | 11 | 18 |
| State convention delegate | 28 | 22 | 32 | 16 | 11 | 22 | 22 |
| National convention delegate | 14 | 9 | 17 | 12 | 47 | 0 | 8 |
| N = 89 | | | | | | | |
| *Patronage (Non-Civil Service) in Government* | | | | | | | |
| Now held | 34 | 29 | 41 | 25 | 30 | 17 | 29 |
| Once held | 37 | 46 | 24 | 33 | 30 | 39 | 35 |
| Never held | 29 | 25 | 35 | 42 | 40 | 44 | 39 |
| N = 86 | 100 | 100 | 100 | 100 | 100 | 100 | 100 |
| *Accept Position of Responsibility in Party* | | | | | | | |
| Definitely, yes | 84 | 74 | 95 | 77 | 76 | 78 | 81 |
| Probably, yes | 11 | 22 | 0 | 16 | 16 | 17 | 14 |
| Probably, no | 0 | 0 | 0 | 2 | 0 | 5 | 1 |
| Definitely, no | 5 | 4 | 5 | 5 | 8 | 0 | 4 |
| N = 86 | 100 | 100 | 100 | 100 | 100 | 100 | 100 |

\* Figures are rounded.
\*\* Multiple entries do not add to 100%.

nucleus of support and a stepping-stone for those wishing to enter political life. This may be true in other communities. It is not the case in Chicago.

Table 6.5 makes the point. The groups with which the committee members were associated are categorized by political, community, interest, and social issues. As can be seen, the differences in levels of involvement are substantial. Almost all committee members were active to some degree at each level of the local party. Three-quarters were also involved with community associations, not as many as worked with the varying levels of the party, but still an impressive figure. Relatively few committee members were directly involved with labor unions or veterans' groups, and even fewer with social issue groups that concern themselves with such things as the Equal Rights Amendment, pollution, the environment, abortion, or nuclear proliferation. Roughly two-thirds to three-quarters of the committee members were *not* members of such organizations, and another 10 to 15 percent hardly ever interacted with these groups or their supporters. The figures are almost a mirror image of the committee members' involvement with the party apparatus.

Issue groups do not appear to be a spawning ground for party activists in Chicago and its suburbs. While there were differences between the parties and between the central city and suburbs in this regard, the major theme is the similarity between the parties. It would appear that Chicago has a relatively traditional, slow-to-change political environment that emphasizes neighborhood and political groups as the basis for building a political career.

*The Present and the Past*
Rising through the ranks has become legendary within the Chicago party organization. Take the testimony of three successful Chicago politicians of different eras, each with impeccable credentials for Chicago politics. First is Jake Arvey, the Cook County chairman—instrumental in promoting Richard J. Daley to mayor and Paul Douglas to the U.S. Senate—and a power in the Democratic National Committee until his death at eighty-two in 1977. Second is George Dunne, sixty-seven, a ward committeeman, successor to Daley as Cook County Democratic chairman and president of the Cook County Board of Commissioners. And third is Edward M. Burke, a rising young (thirty-six) ward committeeman, alderman, and the organization's candidate for state's attorney in 1980. The interviews with these machine leaders were given to Milton L. Rakove and are related in his *We Don't Want Nobody Nobody Sent* (1979).

**Table 6.5.  Involvement in Political, Community, Interest, and
Social Issue Groups (In Percent)**

| Group Category | Democrats | Republicans | Total (Both Parties) |
|---|---|---|---|
| Political Party Organizations (Local, Ward, District, County) | | | |
| Very | 69 | 55 | 62 |
| Somewhat | 29 | 38 | 33 |
| Hardly | 1 | | 3 |
| Not member | 1 | 3 | 2 |
| | 100 | 100 | 100 |
| N | 142 | 158 | 300 |
| Community Groups (Church, School, Civic, Neighborhood) | | | |
| Very | 45 | 35 | 40 |
| Somewhat | 36 | 35 | 36 |
| Hardly | 11 | 19 | 15 |
| Not member | 8 | 11 | 9 |
| | 100 | 100 | 100 |
| N | 132 | 132 | 264 |
| Interest Groups (Labor Union, Veteran's Group) | | | |
| Very | 17 | 8 | 12 |
| Somewhat | 19 | 18 | 19 |
| Hardly | 25 | 28 | 27 |
| Not member | 39 | 46 | 42 |
| | 100 | 100 | 100 |
| N | 52 | 61 | 113 |
| Social Issue Groups (Environmental, Anti-Abortion, Feminist, Anti-Nuclear) | | | |
| Very | 10 | 4 | 15 |
| Somewhat | 17 | 4 | 9 |
| Hardly | 12 | 14 | 12 |
| Not a member | 61 | 78 | 64 |
| | 100 | 100 | 100 |

*Jake Arvey*: Arvey's background is similar to those of many ethnics who formed the base of the machine for generations. According to Arvey's account:

> My father came here in 1892 from Poland, what was then Russia. He then sent for my mother and my four older brothers. She came here in 1894. He had a milk store on Pacifica Avenue, now called LaSalle Street, between Harrison and Polk. On November 3, 1895 . . . I was the first child born to them in America. This made me, in my father's eyes, a symbol of what he had striven for all the years, to come to America and find opportunity here for his children.

Arvey's father died when he was thirteen. The family moved to a new home in the 24th Ward, later to become Arvey's base of power. He left school to help support the family, working days and going to school nights. Eventually, he made up his high school credits and at the age of twenty-one had taken and passed the bar exam.

Before he could vote (in 1914) he began working a precinct in the 24th Ward in support of an anti-machine candidate. Rival political factions wooed him and he joined one and campaigned regularly for mayoral, state legislative, sanitary district and ward committeemen candidates while joining numerous local Jewish and civic groups. In 1923, at the age of twenty-nine he was elected ward alderman and in 1934 ward committeeman, going on from there to play a prominent role in city and state politics and eventually in the national Democratic party.[4]

*George Dunne*: Dunne's story is much like Arvey's. Dunne began his political career in his teens. "I have been active politically since I was about fourteen years old, working in the precincts. I was a precinct captain before I could cast a vote." Dunne grew up in the ward (the 42nd) in which he still lives. His father was a sexton in the local Catholic church for thirty-three years. His father died when Dunne was twelve, and he went to work as the manager of the local playground. He eventually rose through the ranks to become assistant general superintendent of the park district.

Meanwhile, he stayed active in politics. He continued as a precinct captain and in addition was elected to the state legislature. Dunne became Democratic floor leader, subsequently being elected to the Cook County Board, the governing body for the county that includes Chicago, and later serving as its president. The way in which Dunne, a close personal and political ally of the late Mayor Richard J. Daley, was chosen for the county board gives an indication of how things were done when Daley ran the machine.

I didn't want to go on the county board. I was perfectly happy with the park district and in the legislature. I was on the executive committee of the [Democratic party's] central committee. We had a luncheon meeting and Matt Danaher, who was then a kind of a secretary around the central committee, said to me, "George, the mayor wants you to go in as a possible candidate." I said, "Matt, I'm not interested in getting on the county board." He said, "The mayor thinks you ought to present yourself, George."[5]

From here Dunne went on to a long and influential career in Chicago politics, continuing to serve as ward committeeman, president of the county board and, for a period after Daley's death, formal head of the machine (i.e., chair of the Democratic Cook County party). Dunne was one of the few ward committeemen able to adapt gracefully to the changing political climate, remaining on a friendly basis with most of the committeemen representing white ethnic wards as well as those supporting the black mayor, Harold Washington, in the post-1983 period.

*Edward Burke*: Burke is presently an alderman and 14th Ward committeeman with a substantial private law practice. Head of the City Council's finance committee, he is one of the leaders (along with Edward Vrdolyak, alderman, 10th Ward committeeman and present chair of the Cook County Democratic party) of the Majority 29, the anti-Washington faction in the continuing "Council Wars" of the post-1983 period. Burke grew up in his present southside ward and attended Catholic schools there. His father, who "had little formal education," was a machine patronage appointee as a laborer in the city's water department, served as a deputy sheriff and bailiff, and was elected alderman in 1953 and ward committeeman in 1965. "I grew up in politics. The entire family structure revolved around politics. I can remember going to political meetings with my father when I was just a toddler."

Burke's father died in 1968 "and the remains had not even been cold when the political animals of our organization began plotting as to who would become the committeeman, and who would become the alderman. My most vivid recollections of the wake were the little clusters of men around the funeral parlor, discussing who would get what." Burke sought the position and won; at twenty-four he became "the youngest man in Chicago's history to become a ward committeeman."[6]

The cases cited could come from another era fifty to one hundred years ago. They are classic examples of machine politics, the foundation of the present machine. They explain how people rose to positions of power within the machine in the early 1900s (Arvey), during the Depression and the Daley post–World War II political generation (Dunne), and today (Burke). Things have changed little.

With this as background, and based on the returns from the questionnaire, we may sketch the typical Chicago Democratic ward committee member. As noted, most are males with strong ties to their neighborhoods and most often with strong ethnic identifications (Irish, Polish, Italian, or Greek). They tend to be Catholics, attend church services regularly, are married, have children, are well-educated, probably having attended law school. Politically, the ward leaders have been actively involved in politics for over twenty years; have served in a variety of party positions; and continue to be active to some degree in most of these. The horizons are well-defined; they consist of the traditional pathways of advancement within the machine. These pathways are as durable and as rewarding for the newer generation of politicians as they were for the fathers and grandfathers before them.

*Comment*

Many of the trends that have swept national politics and have influenced other localities give no evidence of even beginning to penetrate in any serious manner (see below) the recruitment patterns and career paths that have endured for generations in the Chicago machine. There is turnover in the party organization, but those who come along to fill the vacancies advance by much the same means their predecessors did. They may be better educated and financially more independent, but in other more basic respects differ little from the men they replace.

## Motivational Patterns

My father was honored to be called a politician. The phrase that he used to express his governmental life was, "Good government is good politics and good politics is good government." To some it was a cliche, but to him it was the essence of his life.[7]

State's Attorney and Ward Committeeman
Richard M. Daley commenting on his father.

... I had no ambition of getting a job in politics. I had a job, but we had slow seasons in the heating business, so Alderman [Vito] Marzullo called me in April 1960 and offered me a job at the county hospital as a security officer. It was on the late shift, which would work in very well with my business during the day. I took the job.

I was seven years at the county hospital. When I first started . . . I was paid $264 a month. When I left . . . they were paying me $363 a month. From there, I went to the Port of Chicago, which has now merged with the Department of Public Works, bridge operations. I am a bridge tender. It's about a $15,000-a-year job. . . . And I work the precinct on the side.[8]

> Mid-sixtyish, long-time Polish precinct captain
> Chicago Democratic Organization

Party activists give many reasons for becoming involved politically. These range from ideology and the desire to promote some type of public policy objective to the need of a job or the persuasion of a friend. Two of the answers that can be given—two of the extremes perhaps—are those put forward above by Richard M. Daley in explaining to Milton L. Rakove why his father had remained politically active and by a Polish precinct captain in describing to Rakove how he entered politics and why he continued in it. Most people have several reasons for staying politically active. In Chicago and its suburbs, the principal reasons given by activists are politics as a way of life and the desire to influence policy (Table 6.6). A strong sense of party identification is the third reason.

There emerges a sense that political in-breeding and acculturation runs deep in Chicago. People are brought up in a locality and introduced to politics and political activity at the local level at an early age, and then they continue in it. In many areas, particularly in the city and for Democrats, participation takes on a broader social and economic perspective. A job can be (and often is) dependent on the performance on one's political responsibilities. Politics as a way of life has very real meaning to people so clearly socialized into the prevailing political values. Similarly, influencing the policies of government may take on meaning at the local level, and in such a highly politicized environment, quite different from what respondents, giving the same reason, may mean at the national level. Influencing government policy locally may mean insuring that one's patronage position is continued, that the trash is picked up, that city lights and streets are repaired, and that the police are particularly vigilant in fighting crime in the neighborhood. It is interesting to note that the two groups who most strongly endorse influencing the government, Chicago Democrats and suburban Republicans, are the ones in the best position to do just that.

The reasons *least* often given for staying politically active are also interesting. In order, these were: making business contacts (a sensitive issue in Chicago), 9 percent of those replying; being close to influential people, 11 percent; community recognition, 24 percent; personal career advancement, 28 percent (the Chicago Democrats are something of an exception

**Table 6.6. Motivation for Being Active in Politics\* (In Percent)**

| Variable | Democrats | | | Republicans | | | Total (Both Parties) |
|---|---|---|---|---|---|---|---|
| | All | Chicago | Suburbs | All | Chicago | Suburbs | |
| Personal friendships with candidate | 32 | 35 | 29 | 26 | 27 | 24 | 29 |
| Political work is part of my way of life | 82 | 75 | 90 | 68 | 68 | 72 | 75 |
| Strong party attachment | 68 | 70 | 63 | 71 | 69 | 72 | 69 |
| Friendships and social contacts | 54 | 60 | 47 | 47 | 39 | 59 | 50 |
| Fun and excitement of campaigns | 55 | 53 | 53 | 58 | 64 | 50 | 57 |
| Building a personal career in politics | 40 | 53 | 28 | 19 | 23 | 12 | 28 |
| Influencing policies of government | 72 | 80 | 63 | 80 | 73 | 89 | 76 |
| Being close to influential people | 16 | 15 | 17 | 7 | 12 | 0 | 11 |
| Sense of community obligation | 53 | 53 | 53 | 58 | 68 | 44 | 55 |
| Making business contacts | 14 | 15 | 12 | 5 | 8 | 0 | 9 |
| Recognition in community | 23 | 25 | 22 | 23 | 31 | 12 | 24 |
| N | 41 | 20 | 21 | 45 | 27 | 18 | 86 |

\*Table gives only answers identified as "very important" by respondents. Figures are rounded.

here; half of them gave this reason); and personal friendship with a candidate, 29 percent. No suburban Republican gave either of the first two reasons for political involvement.

Between the extremes, the activists offered such explanations as the fun and excitement of campaigns, 57 percent; a sense of community obligation, 55 percent; and friendships and social contacts with other party workers, 50 percent. Chicago Democrats (60 percent) and suburban Republican leaders (59 percent) found this last reason far more compelling than either the suburban Democrats (47 percent) or the Chicago Republicans (39 percent). Chicago Republican activists were motivated to a far greater degree by such things as the fun of campaigns, the personal satisfaction of the act itself, and a sense of community or ideological obligation than were the other groups of leaders.

Abstract principles and commitments and the "fun" of campaigning may help compensate those with little chance of electoral victory for the hopelessness of the immediate political environment. The winners see politics differently. The two groups who enjoy the most political success, Chicago Democrats and suburban Republicans, displayed several parallels in the reasons offered for their involvement. While there were also similarities, especially in relation to political attachments, between the Chicago activists in the two parties, there were also some striking differences. For example, community obligation and campaign excitement were substantially less important to the Chicago Democrats than to the Chicago Republicans, while friendships and social contacts with other party workers and the opportunity to develop a political career were considerably more important to the Democratic than to the Republican leaders within the city (on the average, 25 percentage points divided the Chicago party activists on these items).

In data not reported in the tables, the party activists claimed as the major reasons for initial political entry the desire to influence government policy (a minor consideration, however, for the group with little real opportunity to do it, the Chicago Republicans), a sense of community obligation, and politics as part of a way of life. The recall data on these items indicated a considerably less intense commitment in explaining entry. In retrospect, many reasons seemed moderately important but few compelling.

Much the same pattern was true for answers given when the party leaders were asked what they would miss most in an immediate political withdrawal. The single biggest item (24 percent of the respondents anticipated that this would be "very important") was the camaraderie of working with other party activists. The only other major consequence (21 percent of the sample volunteered this as "very important") was perhaps guilt—the failure to act on a sense of commitment to the community. Beyond these factors, the party leaders might miss a number of things moderately, but none with a compelling sense of loss.

Overall, then, political in-breeding and a concern with the common welfare appeared to be the reasons most important in sustaining political involvement. There were differences among the subgroups within the population, with the pattern of responses for the Chicago Democrats and suburban Republicans providing some contrasts, both with each other and with those in more frustrating, less electorally satisfying situations (the Chicago Republicans and the suburban Democratic committeemen).

### Party Structure and Decision Making

Judging from the responses in Table 6.7 as to whom they interact with and with what frequency, the Democrats appeared to form a better integrated party than the Republicans. There was more interaction of ward party leaders with those at other levels of the party hierarchy. The differences were particularly noticeable at the precinct and ward levels, where the proportion of Democrats meeting with precinct or other ward leaders was twice that of the Republicans. The Democratic advantage was maintained in the frequency of meetings with the district, county, city, and state party leaders.

By this measure, the most cohesive party group was, predictably, the Chicago Democrats. In fact, they set a pattern that the other party groups might aspire to. Most impressively, and perhaps this tells the whole story, 64 percent of the ward committeemen met with their precinct leaders one or more times a week (the next highest percentage, 41 percent was suburban Republicans), and 59 percent interacted with other ward leaders on a weekly basis. No other party group began to match this. Further, one-third of the ward committee members consulted with city and county party leaders, the next most significant levels of party organization, on a *weekly* basis. The data indicate a highly cohesive, well-organized party structure.

Not surprisingly, the Chicago Democrats were satisfied with their role in running the party (65 percent believed their influence was about right), and half felt they had a great deal of influence in party affairs. Suburban Republican leaders demonstrated the next most cohesive organization, being the group (after the Chicago Democrats) in which most believed they had a great deal of influence in their party and that their role in party decision making was about right (55 percent agreed with this statement).

The least impressive organizations were those of the suburban Democrats and the Chicago Republicans. They met relatively infrequently with leaders at other levels of the party hierarchy. Few (11 percent for the suburban Democrats; 27 percent for the Chicago Republicans) believed they had a great deal of influence within the party, and most (67 percent for the suburban Democrats; 59 percent for the Chicago Republicans) would have liked to see their role within it enhanced.

In this same context, it would appear that the changes that have shaken the national party have had some effect on the parties in the Chicago area. Most party leaders agreed that there had been a change in the kinds of people active in party politics (see Table 6.8 and below). The Democrats

**Table 6.7. Role in the Party Organization\* (In Percent)**

| Variable | Democrats | | | Republicans | | | Total (Both Parties) |
|---|---|---|---|---|---|---|---|
| | All | Chicago | Suburbs | All | Chicago | Suburbs | |
| How often do you meet with: | | | | | | | |
| *Precinct leaders* | | | | | | | |
| Once or twice per week | 53 | 64 | 38 | 31 | 24 | 41 | 41 |
| Once or twice per month | 47 | 36 | 62 | 62 | 64 | 59 | 55 |
| Once or twice per year | 0 | 0 | 0 | 5 | 8 | 0 | 3 |
| Hardly ever | 0 | 0 | 0 | 2 | 4 | 0 | 1 |
| | 100 | 100 | 100 | 100 | 100 | 100 | 100 |
| *Ward Party Leaders* | | | | | | | |
| Once or twice per week | 40 | 59 | 8 | 19 | 18 | 22 | 30 |
| Once or twice per month | 57 | 41 | 84 | 64 | 68 | 57 | 60 |
| Once or twice per year | 3 | 0 | 18 | 11 | 9 | 14 | 7 |
| Hardly ever | 0 | 0 | 0 | 6 | 5 | 7 | 3 |
| | 100 | 100 | 100 | 100 | 100 | 100 | 100 |
| *District-Level Party Leaders* | | | | | | | |
| Once or twice per week | 18 | 29 | 0 | 5 | 0 | 13 | 12 |
| Once or twice per month | 58 | 48 | 75 | 56 | 62 | 47 | 56 |
| Once or twice per year | 21 | 19 | 25 | 36 | 33 | 40 | 29 |
| Hardly ever | 3 | 4 | 0 | 3 | 5 | 0 | 3 |
| | 100 | 100 | 100 | 100 | 100 | 100 | 100 |
| *County-Level Party Leaders* | | | | | | | |
| Once or twice per week | 22 | 35 | 6 | 13 | 14 | 12 | 17 |

**Table 6.7.  Continued**

| Variable | Democrats | | | Republicans | | | Total (Both Parties) |
|---|---|---|---|---|---|---|---|
| | All | Chicago | Suburbs | All | Chicago | Suburbs | |
| Once or twice per month | 59 | 48 | 71 | 56 | 59 | 53 | 58 |
| Once or twice per year | 19 | 17 | 23 | 28 | 23 | 35 | 24 |
| Hardly ever | 0 | 0 | 0 | 3 | 4 | 0 | 1 |
| | 100 | 100 | 100 | 100 | 100 | 100 | 100 |
| *City-Level Party Leaders* | | | | | | | |
| Once or twice per week | 30 | 38 | 18 | 15 | 9 | 23 | 22 |
| Once or twice per month | 58 | 57 | 55 | 37 | 45 | 23 | 47 |
| Once or twice per year | 9 | 5 | 18 | 37 | 32 | 46 | 24 |
| Hardly ever | 3 | 0 | 9 | 11 | 14 | 8 | 7 |
| | 100 | 100 | 100 | 100 | 100 | 100 | 100 |
| *State-Level Party Leaders* | | | | | | | |
| Once or twice per week | 20 | 19 | 23 | 6 | 0 | 13 | 15 |
| Once or twice per month | 31 | 38 | 23 | 28 | 24 | 33 | 30 |
| Once or twice per year | 40 | 38 | 39 | 44 | 43 | 47 | 42 |
| Hardly ever | 9 | 5 | 15 | 22 | 33 | 7 | 15 |
| N = 89 | 100 | 100 | 100 | 100 | 100 | 100 | 100 |
| *Influence in Running the Party* | | | | | | | |
| Very Little | 7 | 5 | 11 | 16 | 23 | 6 | 12 |
| Some | 22 | 18 | 28 | 25 | 27 | 22 | 23 |
| Fair Amount | 37 | 27 | 50 | 25 | 23 | 28 | 31 |
| A Great Deal | 34 | 50 | 11 | 34 | 27 | 44 | 34 |
| N = 85 | 100 | 100 | 100 | 100 | 100 | 100 | 100 |

**Table 6.7. Continued**

| Variable | Democrats | | | Republicans | | | Total (Both Parties) |
|---|---|---|---|---|---|---|---|
| | All | Chicago | Suburbs | All | Chicago | Suburbs | |
| *Assessment of Role in Running the Party* | | | | | | | |
| More | 49 | 35 | 67 | 56 | 59 | 50 | 52 |
| About Right | 51 | 65 | 33 | 44 | 41 | 50 | 48 |
| Less | 0 | 0 | 0 | 0 | 0 | 0 | 0 |
| N = 84 | 100 | 100 | 100 | 100 | 100 | 100 | 100 |

*Figures are rounded.

(including 85 percent of the Chicago committee members polled) felt the changes have had a moderate effect on the party. Republicans were less sure. Fifty percent of the suburban Republican leaders believed the impact had been profound, yet 21 percent of the Chicago Republicans acknowledged that change has taken place but believed it has had little consequential impact.

The suburban party leaders (including 80 percent of the Democrats) believed that the changes have been for the good of the party. The Chicago Republicans were undecided. The Democrats endorsed the changes more generally than did the Republicans, perhaps indicating an ability on the part of the Democrats to adapt successfully to the new developments without weakening their organization.

Republicans were found to rely substantially more on such techniques as polling, television, and direct mail than did the more traditionally-oriented Democrats. Ninety-four percent of the suburban Republicans (and 85 percent of the city Republicans) employed these means to reach voters. Seventy-seven percent of the suburban Democrats did also. The "new politics" of media and mass-mailing techniques had made considerably less headway among Chicago Democrats.

Roughly one-half of the Democrats did not feel that the new developments had seriously weakened the party. The suburban Republicans were divided in their assessments and closer to the Democrats. The group most hurt by increasing reliance on new campaign technologies were the Chicago Republicans, arguably the weakest party unit of the four in the study.

In comparison with ten years ago, three-fourths of the suburban Demo-

**Table 6.8.  Changes in Party Organizations\* (In Percent)**

| Variable | Democrats | | | Republicans | | | Total (Both Parties) |
|---|---|---|---|---|---|---|---|
| | All | Chicago | Suburbs | All | Chicago | Suburbs | |
| *Changes in kinds of people active in the party* | | | | | | | |
| Yes | 85 | 86 | 83 | 82 | 92 | 67 | 84 |
| No | 15 | 16 | 17 | 18 | 8 | 33 | 16 |
| N = 85 | 100 | 100 | 100 | 100 | 100 | 100 | 100 |
| *If yes, have changes been* | | | | | | | |
| Extreme | 22 | 15 | 27 | 33 | 25 | 50 | 28 |
| Moderate | 78 | 85 | 73 | 53 | 54 | 50 | 65 |
| They exist but no direct impact | 0 | 0 | 0 | 14 | 21 | 0 | 7 |
| N = 72 | 100 | 100 | 100 | 100 | 100 | 100 | 100 |
| *Changes have been* | | | | | | | |
| Good for the party | 67 | 55 | 80 | 42 | 33 | 59 | 54 |
| Bad for the party | 25 | 30 | 20 | 33 | 33 | 33 | 29 |
| No difference | 8 | 15 | 0 | 25 | 34 | 8 | 17 |
| | 100 | 100 | 100 | 100 | 100 | 100 | 100 |
| *Is there a reliance in your area on TV, polls, direct mail techniques?* | | | | | | | |
| Somewhat | 63 | 50 | 77 | 89 | 85 | 94 | 77 |
| Not too much | 32 | 41 | 23 | 9 | 11 | 6 | 20 |
| Not at all | 5 | 9 | 0 | 2 | 4 | 0 | 3 |
| N = 85 | 100 | 100 | 100 | 100 | 100 | 100 | 100 |
| *New developments weaken the party* | | | | | | | |
| To a large extent | 7 | 9 | 6 | 24 | 26 | 17 | 16 |
| Somewhat | 42 | 36 | 44 | 45 | 44 | 35 | 43 |
| Not too much | 44 | 41 | 50 | 18 | 19 | 35 | 30 |
| Not at all | 7 | 14 | 0 | 13 | 11 | 13 | 11 |
| N = 86 | 100 | 100 | 100 | 100 | 100 | 100 | 100 |

**Table 6.8.  Continued**

| Variable | Democrats | | | Republicans | | | Total (Both Parties) |
|---|---|---|---|---|---|---|---|
| | All | Chicago | Suburbs | All | Chicago | Suburbs | |
| *Activity of local party compared to 10 years ago* | | | | | | | |
| About the same | 33 | 59 | 11 | 36 | 24 | 44 | 35 |
| More active | 35 | 32 | 78 | 54 | 28 | 44 | 44 |
| Less active | 32 | 9 | 11 | 10 | 48 | 12 | 21 |
| N = 84 | 100 | 100 | 100 | 100 | 100 | 100 | 100 |
| *Political parties stronger or weaker in last 10 years* | | | | | | | |
| About the same | 22 | 27 | 17 | 16 | 17 | 17 | 19 |
| Stronger | 12 | 9 | 11 | 5 | 4 | 5 | 9 |
| Weaker | 66 | 64 | 72 | 79 | 79 | 78 | 72 |
| N = 83 | 100 | 100 | 100 | 100 | 100 | 100 | 100 |

*Figures are rounded.

crats believed their local party organizations were more active than they had been. Most (59 percent) Chicago Democrats felt that they remained as active as they had been previously. To suburban Republicans (88 percent), their local parties were as active as, or more active than, a decade ago. The only falloff occurred among Chicago Republicans. Approximately half (48 percent) felt their party was less active than it had been.

Two-thirds to three-fourths of all the committee members believed, however, that political parties were weaker than they had been a decade earlier. Democrats were less convinced of their party's weakening than Republicans, and Chicago Democrats were least convinced of all the four major groups. Yet, the major finding was that at least six out of ten felt that the changes of the last few years had not helped the parties.

## Comment
The Chicago Democrats appeared substantially better organized and more confident of their role than the other party units. The suburban Republicans again appeared to be the second-best party unit organizationally.

The Chicago Democrats were the least affected by the new developments, although they, like the other groups, believe that the recent developments in campaign technology have served to weaken the party's control over its electorate and its influence in governmental policy making.

Decision-making and influence patterns within the party structures were difficult to pin down. The Chicago Democrats did interact on an impressively regular basis with party workers and leaders within the organization. This may serve as a model of intraorganizational coherence for other parties. It is difficult to believe that it is repeated with any frequency in other localities.

Decision making is another matter. In Chicago power is centralized in the city and county leadership and in the ward leaders. The committee members appeared to find the relationship acceptable. There was no great dissatisfaction with the distribution of power nor any movement for change. Intraparty democracy, per se a movement of force in the national parties and in presidential selection, is not a factor at the local level in Chicago politics. The explanation may be simple enough. As the Jewish ward leader of a black machine ward told interviewer Milton Rakove, "I do run a tough ward and demand an awful lot from people. It's predominately black, but I've never had any problems in all the years I've been here. I've threatened to throw a few from the window, from the twentieth floor here in my office, but aside from that, it's been very quiet."[9]

## Party Activities

The essence of party politics and the key to effective party organization is service—or so the party leaders would have you believe. For example, in explaining what they give constituents in return for their vote and why the voter should support the party organization and its candidates, Democratic party leaders in the city, in particular, offered an impressive list of services and engaged in a full range of activities designed to hold their supporters' loyalty.

> My job as a precinct captain, in the last twenty years, I devoted 365 days a year to politics. My telephone number is given to everybody in the precinct, and I told them, "No matter what time of the day or night, you call me if you need me." ... You have to know your people. You have to be there for their wants and needs. Communication and service is the success of a precinct captain.[10]
>
> Sixtyish Italian precinct captain, state representative and,
> for twenty-five years, patronage worker in the
> Department of Streets and Sanitation

I spend tremendous hours, about seventy hours a week, being a ward commit-teeman. Practically most of the time, when I'm not doing anything here in the county building, is spent doing things related to the ward and my responsibility as a committeeman. I'm always going to parties and affairs, and getting all kinds of calls, usually complaints. The job of committeeman is non-paying, but if you really want to work at it, it takes a lot of time. . . .

You have to deliver services. That's the thing I do. When it's election time, we debate issues. After the people have made a decision, I just get out there and start working until another election comes along.[11]

Fifty-one year old black ward leader
and Democratic county commissioner

Before the election, I'll spot-check half the precincts in the ward myself. We're on the phones every night, calling people in every precinct. I call them myself, personally. "How many times has the [precinct] captain been around? What did he say?" We also have a sign check. I want signs up in the windows. That means people have been around and are committed. We get good results.[12]

Up-and-coming young (41) white
Democratic committeeman and alderman

We did things to stimulate interest [in the election] and we spend a lot of time with people. We gave parties, helped the children, and ran social and cultural and athletic events. You can't carry a precinct or a ward by going out two weeks before an election and talking to people. It's a day-to-day activity where you are with people, where you help them from day to day. When a precinct captain does his job well, people vote for him, not the candidate. Sometimes people wouldn't care who the candidate was, as long as they felt they were going to continue to get good service.[13]

Established black ward leader, former state senator,
city commissioner, and present city clerk

The very first thing I do each morning, I get my car out of the garage and I take a ride through the alleys. Many of the people . . . have a piece of furniture to throw out in the alley, or a mattress, and I'm afraid that punks will set a match to it and set a garage on fire. I make a list. I stop at the [Streets and Sanitation] ward yard . . . and give it to the superintendent . . . . And they'll pick it up. I also see when a man needs a garbage can. . . . If a fella really needs one, I'll tell him "Look, when you get home from work, come over and pick one up." They're happy to get them. Also, the Latinos ask questions or explanations of some of the papers they get. Many times, if they have a traffic violation, we have a lawyer in the organization who goes and represents these lads in court for no fee to them. That's a free service that the organization provides if a fella gets a ticket.[14]

Late sixtyish, Polish precinct captain
and long-time ward worker

**Table 6.9.  Committee Members' Party Activities\* (In Percent)**

| Variable | Democrats | | | Republicans | | | Total (Both Parties) |
|---|---|---|---|---|---|---|---|
| | All | Chicago | Suburbs | All | Chicago | Suburbs | |
| *Hours per week worked in campaign* | | | | | | | |
| 5 | 0 | 0 | 0 | 2 | 0 | 6 | 1 |
| 10 | 2 | 0 | 5 | 2 | 4 | 0 | 2 |
| 15 | 5 | 0 | 5 | 5 | 4 | 6 | 5 |
| 20 | 18 | 9 | 32 | 9 | 11 | 6 | 14 |
| 25 | 5 | 0 | 11 | 16 | 11 | 22 | 10 |
| 30 | 14 | 13 | 16 | 20 | 19 | 22 | 17 |
| 35 | 2 | 4 | 0 | 4 | 4 | 5 | 3 |
| 40 | 14 | 22 | 5 | 7 | 7 | 5 | 10 |
| 45 | 5 | 9 | 0 | 11 | 7 | 17 | 9 |
| 50 | 33 | 43 | 21 | 24 | 33 | 11 | 28 |
| Over 50 | 2 | 0 | 5 | 0 | 0 | 0 | 0 |
| N = 88 | 100 | 100 | 100 | 100 | 100 | 100 | 100 |
| *Did you work for* | | | | | | | |
| One candidate | 2 | 4 | 0 | 5 | 4 | 6 | 3 |
| Party ticket | 98 | 96 | 100 | 95 | 96 | 94 | 97 |
| N = 85 | 100 | 100 | 100 | 100 | 100 | 100 | 100 |
| *How active do you expect to be in the next year* | | | | | | | |
| Very active | 98 | 96 | 100 | 86 | 89 | 82 | 92 |
| Sporadically active | 2 | 4 | 0 | 12 | 8 | 18 | 7 |
| Not active | 0 | 0 | 0 | 2 | 3 | 0 | 1 |
| N = 84 | 100 | 100 | 100 | 100 | 100 | 100 | 100 |

\*Figures are rounded.

By all accounts, the job of party leader is a demanding one. This was borne out by the data (Table 6.9). Most worked long hours. The city committee members put in longer hours than their suburban counterparts, and the Chicago Democrats put in the longest of all. In Table 6.9, if we consider only forty hours and above, the equivalent of a full-time job plus overtime, the dedication of the city Democrats is readily apparent. Seventy-two percent of the Chicago Democrats worked forty or more hours, compared to

47 percent of the Chicago Republicans and one-third of the suburban party committee members (31 percent of the Democrats and 33 percent of the Republicans). Furthermore, virtually all the respondents (98 percent of the Democrats and 86 percent of the Republicans) expected to be "very" busy in the coming year, an interim nonelection period but apparently one of continuing importance for the parties. The level of commitment is impressive.

Virtually all of the ward and township committee members (97 percent) worked for the entire party ticket rather than concentrating their energies on any one candidate or office.

Also, virtually all of the party leaders (96 percent) placed the greatest faith in face-to-face contact for mobilizing voters behind party candidates (Table 6.10). The Democrats—more than the Republicans (80 percent to 60 percent)—and the Chicago Democrats most of all (91 percent), also placed great faith in appearances before groups as a way to reach and motivate voters. The leaders of both parties had less confidence in telephone canvassing, mailed campaign literature, billboards, and posters as methods of influencing voters.

There were exceptions to the general pattern. The suburban Republican committee members placed substantially more faith in media advertising than the other party units, and they were more inclined to favor mailed campaign literature. The suburban Republicans and the Chicago Demo-

**Table 6.10. Effectiveness of Party Activities\* (In Percent)**

| Variable | Democrats | | | Republicans | | | Total (Both Parties) |
|---|---|---|---|---|---|---|---|
| | All | Chicago | Suburbs | All | Chicago | Suburbs | |
| *Face-to-face canvassing* | | | | | | | |
| Very | 95 | 96 | 94 | 98 | 100 | 94 | 96 |
| Not very | 5 | 4 | 6 | 2 | 0 | 6 | 4 |
| Don't know | 0 | 0 | 0 | 0 | 0 | 0 | 0 |
| N = 84 | 100 | 100 | 100 | 100 | 100 | 100 | 100 |
| *Telephone canvassing* | | | | | | | |
| Very | 35 | 32 | 41 | 39 | 36 | 44 | 37 |
| Not very | 60 | 58 | 59 | 51 | 52 | 50 | 55 |
| Don't know | 5 | 10 | 0 | 10 | 12 | 6 | 8 |
| N = 78 | 100 | 100 | 100 | 100 | 100 | 100 | 100 |

**Table 6.10.  Continued**

| Variable | Democrats | | | Republicans | | | Total (Both Parties) |
|---|---|---|---|---|---|---|---|
| | All | Chicago | Suburbs | All | Chicago | Suburbs | |
| *Appearances before groups* | | | | | | | |
| Very | 80 | 91 | 71 | 60 | 62 | 56 | 70 |
| Not very | 18 | 9 | 23 | 31 | 23 | 44 | 24 |
| Don't know | 2 | 0 | 6 | 9 | 15 | 0 | 6 |
| N = 82 | 100 | 100 | 100 | 100 | 100 | 100 | 100 |
| *Mail campaign literature* | | | | | | | |
| Very | 39 | 30 | 50 | 45 | 38 | 56 | 42 |
| Not very | 61 | 70 | 50 | 50 | 54 | 44 | 56 |
| Don't know | 0 | 0 | 0 | 5 | 8 | 0 | 2 |
| N = 79 | 100 | 100 | 100 | 100 | 100 | 100 | 100 |
| *Radio or TV ads* | | | | | | | |
| Very | 54 | 53 | 59 | 56 | 50 | 65 | 55 |
| Not very | 41 | 37 | 41 | 32 | 38 | 23 | 36 |
| Don't know | 5 | 10 | 0 | 12 | 12 | 12 | 9 |
| N = 78 | 100 | 100 | 100 | 100 | 100 | 100 | 100 |
| *Billboards and posters* | | | | | | | |
| Very | 39 | 43 | 35 | 21 | 25 | 14 | 30 |
| Not very | 56 | 52 | 59 | 66 | 67 | 64 | 61 |
| Don't know | 5 | 5 | 6 | 13 | 8 | 22 | 9 |
| N = 77 | 100 | 100 | 100 | 100 | 100 | 100 | 100 |

\*Figures are rounded.

crats offered a series of contrasts. The city Democrats relied less on television and radio advertising and had little confidence in mail or telephone canvassing—all techniques favored more by the suburban Republicans. The Chicago Democrats placed somewhat more emphasis on posters and billboards and strongly approved of personal appearances before groups, appeals the suburban Republicans found far less useful.

In data not reported in the tables, on the activities engaged in by the party organizations at various levels, a related emphasis was found. *All* of the local Democratic organizations in the city of Chicago engaged in extensive voter-registration drives, face-to-face canvassing, and get-out-the-vote campaigns on election day. Two out of three engaged in fundraising and only one in four in telephone canvassing. The pattern among suburban Democrats was similar but the effort less extensive (on the average, 13 percent fewer local organizations invested heavily in this activity), except for telephone canvassing (one-half, or twice as many, suburban Democratic organizations employed this extensively). The suburban Republican organizations heavily invested in: fundraising (93 percent), get-out-the-vote campaigns (88 percent), voter registration (77 percent), and face-to-face canvassing (75 percent). The city Republican wards fell well below the other groups in the extent of the activities (on the average, 25 percentage points per item below the suburban Republicans), although the emphases on personal and traditional machine priorities (face-to-face canvassing, voter registration, and get-out-the-vote efforts) more resembled the city Democrats than either of the suburban parties. Finally, a concern with all phases of campaigning characterized the Democratic party hierarchy (district, city, and county organizations) more than it did the Republicans. The Democrats appeared to be more consistently and intensively organized at all levels than the Republicans.

Data unreported in the tables suggested that the only other party of candidate organizations sufficiently strong to involve themselves actively in campaigning were, for the Democrats, the Carter-for-President committees and, for the Republicans, the Reagan-for-President committees. Groups organized by congressional candidates also supplemented the work of three of the regular party organizations, but not that of the Chicago Republicans.

More surprisingly, labor and business-related and single-issue PACs appeared to have little direct impact on the campaign. At least party leaders were unaware of substantial activity by such groups being conducted outside of normal party channels in their areas.

*Comment*
It would appear that the "new politics" of saturation media campaigns, impersonal electronic and telephonic campaigning, and heavy emphasis on raising large sums of money to support these activities has not penetrated the Chicago area to a substantial degree. The basic emphasis—particularly for the city parties—remains old-fashioned, people-to-people campaigning. The problems the Chicago Republicans, short of manpower and the normal prerequisites of a traditional organization, have in competing with the entrenched Democratic organization are substantial. Without access to

modern technology and the funds to employ it extensively, their position must be (as it is) untenable. It may be also that an emphasis on depersonalized electronic campaigning, however well funded, would be inadequate in the face of a well-mobilized, year-round operation of the sort maintained by the Chicago Democrats. The "old politics," at least as practiced in Chicago, appears little threatened by the new campaign emphases or by the appeal of television. The Republicans within the city offer little real challenge, and those in the suburbs do not compete directly with the Chicago organization for control over the urban vote. As a consequence, they can be tolerated. Even so, in recent elections the city Democrats have begun efforts to extend their influence, and their organization, to the working-class, blue-collar suburbs that border the city.

**Summary**

The principal findings of the study of local party organization in Chicago and Cook County during the 1980 presidential election included the following.

*Concerning party personnel:*
1. Both Democratic and Republican party committee members in Chicago and Cook County have deep roots within their communities. Most have lived in their city and in their immediate neighborhood for at least ten years.
2. Almost all of the party committee are men (94 %).
3. Almost all of the party committee members are family men, long married; between two-thirds (for the Democrats) and three-fourths (for the Republicans) have families with three or more children.
4. Most party committee members are at midlife or older; about half are Catholic; virtually all are church members; 60 percent are college graduates; most are in occupations that deal with the public.

In short, ward and township committee positions appear to be high-visibility positions within the political parties that attract well-established citizens with solid community roots and familiarity.

*Concerning professionalism*
1. Party committee members have extensive political experience. Ninety percent have been active in politics for better than a decade, and one-half have twenty or more years of experience.

2. Most committee members have friends and associates actively involved in politics, although this is truer for Chicago Democrats and suburban Republicans than for the other groups.
3. Most party committee members have held a wide variety of positions within the political party, reinforcing the impression of an experienced and professional group of party leaders.
4. Most party committee members appear satisfied with their positions, although a good number would like more say in the way the parties run campaigns.
5. Most party committee members are, or have been, involved in neighborhood and local community groups. They are not active in social issue and policy groups, spawning grounds of many party activists in other urban areas.

Party committee members, in sum, tend to be highly experienced and knowledgeable party members with many years of service within the party.

*Concerning party operations:*
1. Chicago and Cook County political parties tend to be better organized and more active than political parties in other urban areas, although the degree of organization and electoral activity of political parties in all of the urban areas studied is considerably greater than one would have been led by previous studies to expect.
2. Party committee members interact and meet with party members and those seeking elective office with a good deal of frequency. Again, the degree of contact is greater than some studies have suggested, indicating a degree of cohesion to, and communication within, the parties that is greater than had been anticipated. This may mean that parties at the local level are more cohesive and representative than previous studies indicated. The most cohesive of the groups studied is the Chicago Democrats.
3. The groups most satisfied with their role within the party and with their responsibilities are, first, Chicago Democrats, and second, suburban Republicans.
4. While the "new politics" of the media, PACs, and the like have had a major impact on the national parties, their impact on the local parties is less certain and less clear. Party committee members in Chicago and Cook County rely more on established organizational means to reach voters, such as face-to-face canvassing, telephone contact, registration efforts, and get-out-the-vote drives on election day, which most engage in extensively. The impact of PACs, in particular, in funding races and supplanting the party organization in efforts on behalf of candidates, appears minimal.
5. Most party committee members, while they have observed the new reliance on television, polling, and PAC funding, and the "new politics" emphasis in general, do not feel that these developments have seriously weakened their local parties.

6. The Chicago Democrats believe that their party is as active now as it was ten years ago. Most suburban Republicans and Democrats feel that their parties are now more active than they were ten years ago, and Chicago Republicans believe that their party is somewhat less active than a decade ago.
7. Most party committee members engage in a wide range of campaign and election day activity, an indication of a vital party system.

The Chicago and Cook County political parties, then, are active in all phases of the election. Although there are differences among the city and suburban parties and between Democrats and Republicans in organization and activity levels, the party organizations are more cohesive than expected. Although there are differences among party groups in Chicago and Cook County, in general, political parties at the local level appear to be in good condition and actively concerned with and involved in the local electoral process.

## Conclusion

It is difficult to assess the Chicago Democratic organization through any conventional measures of party organization or through ones that gauge the extensiveness and penetration of campaign activities. The pervasiveness of its organization and the year-round services it provides to constituents take it beyond the range of the sporadically organized and intermittently active party organizations, with their amateur leadership, found in other areas. The Chicago machine is both rare and impressive in the range of services offered, the cohesiveness and permanence of its structure, the professionalism and experience of its members at all levels, and, of course, its electoral successes. The difficulties the opposition party faces make its position virtually hopeless.

There is little likelihood that the situation will change substantially. The greatest Republican strength is found in the suburban parties. Here it is impressive, although it seems to have little carry-over or relationship to the city party. The suburban Democrats, who have a working alliance, uneasy at times, with the Chicago Democrats, do appear reasonably well organized and electorally active (although, of course, they are not nearly as cohesively structured or as impressive campaign instruments as their city counterparts).

It is not difficult to demonstrate the strength of the Chicago Democratic organization. But it is harder to explain why the Chicago machine has continued to exist and even to prosper at a time when, nationwide, the urban machine is—and for decades has been—in decline. The Chicago

Democratic machine—in the folklore of American politics, everything a political party could be or could aspire to become—seems like a vestige of another age. Why has it survived? Tradition, able leadership, patronage and a personalized reward system, and impressive service delivery to its constituents—all these are partial answers. The Democratic organization also exists in an environment hospitable to its continued functioning (Table 6.11). The political environment is basically noncompetitive, Democratic, and nonideological. The machine is supported by the business community ("If you objectively analyze the assets and advantages of Chicago, you will come to one conclusion. It is simply one of the best cities in the world for business," says the former president of Continental Bank[15]) and has old-line labor leaders tied into its leadership.[16] It can call on the support of blue-collar and white-collar voters and is strong among those with low to moderate incomes. It has a traditional ethnic, Catholic base, still culturally alive and important in Chicago. And the majority of Chicago wards (85 percent) is changing slowly if at all. The "building blocs" of the machine should remain in place for the foreseeable future. The basis of Republican strength in the suburbs is equally predictable, the reverse of that found for Democrats in the city. It also should remain stable.

Table 6.11. Nature of the Districts* (In Percent)

| Variable | Democrats | | | Republicans | | | Total (Both Parties) |
|---|---|---|---|---|---|---|---|
| | All | Chicago | Suburbs | All | Chicago | Suburbs | |
| *Party Division* | | | | | | | |
| Republican | 27 | 5 | 53 | 41 | 12 | 82 | 34 |
| Competitive | 11 | 11 | 12 | 14 | 16 | 12 | 13 |
| Democratic | 62 | 84 | 35 | 45 | 72 | 6 | 53 |
| N = 79 | 100 | 100 | 100 | 100 | 100 | 100 | 100 |
| *Party Orientation* | | | | | | | |
| Conservative | 31 | 29 | 36 | 32 | 15 | 57 | 32 |
| Moderate | 54 | 50 | 64 | 56 | 65 | 43 | 55 |
| Liberal | 15 | 21 | 0 | 12 | 20 | 0 | 13 |
| N = 79 | 100 | 100 | 100 | 100 | 100 | 100 | 100 |
| *Income Level* | | | | | | | |
| High income | 14 | 11 | 20 | 15 | 8 | 25 | 15 |
| Middle income | 72 | 63 | 80 | 65 | 58 | 75 | 68 |
| Low income | 14 | 26 | 0 | 20 | 34 | 0 | 17 |
| N = 71 | 100 | 100 | 100 | 100 | 100 | 100 | 100 |

**Table 6.11.  Continued**

| Variable | Democrats | | | Republicans | | | Total (Both Parties) |
|---|---|---|---|---|---|---|---|
| | All | Chicago | Suburbs | All | Chicago | Suburbs | |
| *Racial Composition* | | | | | | | |
| Mostly white | 68 | 61 | 83 | 58 | 33 | 94 | 62 |
| Mixed | 16 | 17 | 17 | 22 | 34 | 6 | 20 |
| Mostly black | 16 | 23 | 0 | 20 | 33 | 0 | 18 |
| N = 71 | 100 | 100 | 100 | 100 | 100 | 100 | 100 |
| *Occupational Status* | | | | | | | |
| Mostly prof./bus. | 25 | 13 | 33 | 22 | 20 | 24 | 23 |
| Mostly other | | | | | | | |
| White-collar | 13 | 6 | 20 | 24 | 25 | 24 | 19 |
| Mixed | 56 | 69 | 47 | 30 | 35 | 24 | 42 |
| Other | 6 | 12 | 0 | 24 | 20 | 28 | 16 |
| N = 71 | 100 | 100 | 100 | 100 | 100 | 100 | 100 |
| *Religious Affiliation* | | | | | | | |
| Mostly Catholic | 41 | 53 | 29 | 35 | 38 | 31 | 38 |
| Mostly Protestant | 9 | 5 | 7 | 19 | 21 | 15 | 14 |
| Mostly Jewish | 9 | 5 | 14 | 3 | 4 | 0 | 6 |
| Different religions | 41 | 37 | 50 | 43 | 38 | 54 | 42 |
| N = 71 | 100 | 100 | 100 | 100 | 100 | 100 | 100 |
| *Degree of Change in Districts* | | | | | | | |
| Rapidly changing | 11 | 15 | 8 | 12 | 15 | 8 | 12 |
| Slowly changing | 56 | 71 | 42 | 41 | 35 | 50 | 47 |
| Not changing | 33 | 14 | 50 | 47 | 50 | 42 | 41 |
| N = 59 | 100 | 100 | 100 | 100 | 100 | 100 | 100 |

*Figures are rounded.

The machine is predominantly white. The minorities (blacks and to a lesser extent Hispanics) have been organized within the machine. The major potential problem area for the machine is, and has been, blacks. Blacks have been incorporated into the machine since the early days of U.S. Rep. William Dawson. Black "plantation wards" have been bought off, and at a relatively cheap price; some black wards are still led, this study indicated, by white ethnic machine politicians. The black leaders are divided.[17] Some have cast their lot with the machine; others align themselves with the more activist and outspoken black community organizations; and still other drift between the two poles, attempting to alienate as few people as possible. With 40 percent of the city's population black (in the 1980 census), blacks (as they have historically) represent an uneasy junior partner in the machine alliance—exploited, under-rewarded, poorly represented, yet politically docile. The 1983 mayoral candidacy and the eventual election as mayor of U.S. Rep. Harold Washington may have laid the basis for a more politically assertive black constituency.

Problems remain, however. Washington won in a divided Democratic primary against two white opponents (incumbent Mayor Jane Byrne and Richard M. Daley, the late mayor's son). He won a general election race with clear racial overtones ("Epton For Mayor. Before It's Too Late.")[18] against a Republican opponent (Bernard Epton) who had at least the tacit support of the Cook County Democratic chairman, Edward Vrdolyak, and many regular Democrats. Washington will have to repeat his electoral successes to continue in office and to begin to exercise political power commensurate with that enjoyed by his two post-Daley predecessors as mayor. Once elected, Washington faced new difficulties, the so-called "Council Wars." A bloc of twenty-nine machine aldermen (the "Majority 29"), led by Vrdolyak, has consistently and angrily opposed Washington and his "Minority 21" aldermen, registering a succession of impressive victories and claiming for the city council a voice in city government unparalleled in recent history. The eventual resolution of the continuing "Council Wars" is likely to be decided only in future elections.

The black leaders remain divided. Not all support Washington, although few publicly oppose him. The ward organizations have changed little. Whites still retain control of the Chicago power structure. The black constituency will have to reassert itself at successive elections to begin to claim the political rewards its numbers would warrant.[19]

The Chicago machine has had its problems. The machine of the 1980s is not the monolithic force of the Daley years. Nonetheless, despite constant internal bickering and feuding, despite divisions and racial polarization, the machine survives. Whether seen on the ward level or viewed as a collection of political warlords, each with his own organization and ends, the machine continues to function with little apparent change from a decade ago. Whatever the trends in the rest of the nation, the Chicago Democratic party remains healthy; politically dominant, if divided; well organized at the ward and local levels, its leadership little changed; and still capable of providing to its supporters a range of services unlikely to be matched elsewhere.

**Notes**

1. Quoted in Rakove, *Don't Make No Waves*, 106. A considerable number of books deals with the recent Chicago machine. Among these would be: Royko, *Boss*; Eugene Kennedy, *Himself*; O'Connor, *Clout*; O'Connor, *Requiem*; and Ward Heeler [pseud.], *The Election: Chicago Style* (Chicago: Feature Group, 1977).

2. Gosnell, *Machine Politics*, 47.

3. Ibid., 47-48.

4. Rakove, *We Don't Want Nobody Nobody Sent*, 3-4.

5. Ibid., 76-77.

6. Ibid., 139-40.

7. Ibid., viii.

8. Ibid., 113.

9. Ibid., 67.

10. Ibid., 97.

11. Ibid., 197-98.

12. Ibid., 34.

13. Ibid., 158.

14. Ibid., 108.

15. Quoted in Gregory D. Squires, Kathleen McCourt, Larry Bennett, and Philip Nyden, "Chicago: The City That Works, For Less" (Paper presented at Annual Meeting of the Midwest Political Science Association, Chicago, April 1985), 12-13. The report critically assesses Chicago's economic planning and priorities. For other discussions of resource allocations, see: Kenneth R. Mladenka, "The Urban Bureaucracy and the Chicago Political Machine: Who Gets What and the Limits to Political Control," in Gove and Masotti, *After Daley*, 146-58; Donald H. Haider, "Capital Budgeting and Planning in the Post-Daley Era," Gove and Masotti, *After Daley*, 159-74; Martin Meyerson and Edward C. Banfield, *Politics, Planning, and the Public Interest* (Glencoe, Ill.: Free Press, 1955); and Banfield, *Political Influence*.

16. On the role of labor unions in Chicago politics, see: William J. Grimshaw, *Union Rule in the Schools: Big-City Politics in Transformation* (Lexington, Mass.: Lexington Books, 1979); and Grimshaw, "The Daley Legacy: A Declining Politics of Party, Race, and Public Unions," in Gove and Masotti, *After Daley*, 57-87.

17. These developments are discussed in: Harold F. Gosnell, *Negro Politicians: The Rise of Negro Politics in Chicago* (Chicago: Univ. of Chicago Press, 1935); James Q. Wilson, *Negro Politics: The Search for Leadership* (New York: Free Press, 1960); William J. Grimshaw, *Black Politics in Chicago: The Quest for Leadership, 1929-1979* (Chicago: Loyola University Center for Urban Policy, 1980); Michael B. Preston, "Black Politics in the Post-Daley Era," in Gove and Masotti, *After Daley*; and Grimshaw, "The Daley Legacy."

18. Paul Kleppner, *Chicago Divided: The Making of a Black Mayor* (DeKalb: Northern Illinois Univ. Press, 1985), 210. Also on the elections, see: Paul Kleppner

and Stephen C. Baker, "Electoral Revolution Chicago Style: The Democratic Primary, February 1983" (Paper presented at Annual Meeting of the Midwest Political Science Association, Chicago, April 1983); and Doris A. Graber, "Candidate Images in a Mayoral Race of Racism, Feminism, and Ghosts of the Past" (Paper presented at Annual Meeting of the American Political Science Association, Chicago, Sept. 1983).

19. A court-mandated redistricting of 7 wards in order to more equitably represent Hispanic voters resulted in special aldermanic elections in these wards in 1986. In a series of acrimonious and bitterly contested races in which the formal leadership of the Cook County Democratic Party, under its chairman, Edward Vrdolyak, also the leader of the City Council's "Majority 29" and himself a ward leader, supported candidates opposed to those backed by the Democratic Mayor, Harold Washington. In several close votes, the Washington forces picked up four seats, realigning the City Council 25–25 and giving the Mayor the decisive vote in case of a tie. For the first time since his election in 1983, Washington began to exercise control of the Council and of various city-related agencies, in the process replacing long-entrenched machine leaders and cutting the patronage resources available to the white Democratic bloc. Curiously, the Democratic organization felt its next best chance to defeat Washington was to introduce a non-partisan electoral system to Chicago, although the maneuver to put it into effect before the February primary and the April, 1987 general election appeared thwarted. These developments provided the context for the 1987 mayoral election, the next step in the fight for the control of Chicago and the future of the machine.

# Appendix:
# Examples of Questionnaires Used in the Studies

## Questionnaire 1

Local Party Organizational Study
Harris County Texas

This questionnaire is part of a study of party organizations in several cities. In addition to Houston, party activists in Los Angeles, Chicago, and Nashville, Tennessee are being asked these or similar questions. We are interested in how you evaluate the problems of party organization and campaign coordination in your local area. We also want your estimates of how much campaign activity different kinds of party units and campaign committees engaged in during the fall election campaign in 1980. And we want to learn how you view the issues emphasized in the 1980 campaigns, and the changing role of organized political parties in recent election years.

All answers to this survey will be kept entirely confidential. They will be tabulated and analyzed in statistical form, solely for scholarly purposes. Questions about the nature of the study can be referred to Richard Murray, Assoc. Professor of Political Science at the University of Houston, or to Tom Pardue, Ph.D. candidate in Political Science at the University of Houston. Both can be reached at 749-4885.

To begin with, we'd like to ask you a few questions about your own political experience.

1. First, how long have you been active in party politics?
_____ years.

2. How strong a party supporter would you say you were? On an eight point scale with one being a very strong party supporter and eight a very weak party supporter, where would you place yourself? (RECORD RESPONSE)_____

3. We are interested in how active precinct committee members are in other organizations. Would you say you were very active in, somewhat active in, hardly active at all, or not a member of (READ LIST, CIRCLE RESPONSE)

|  | Very | Somewhat | Hardly | NonMember | Not Sure |
|---|---|---|---|---|---|
| A Local party club | ____ | ____ | ____ | ____ | ____ |
| A church related group | ____ | ____ | ____ | ____ | ____ |
| A school related group | ____ | ____ | ____ | ____ | ____ |
| A Community service group | ____ | ____ | ____ | ____ | ____ |
| A labor union | ____ | ____ | ____ | ____ | ____ |
| An environmental protection organization | ____ | ____ | ____ | ____ | ____ |
| An anti-abortion group | ____ | ____ | ____ | ____ | ____ |
| A feminist movement group | ____ | ____ | ____ | ____ | ____ |
| Another political action group (HAVE SPECIFY) | ____ | ____ | ____ | ____ | ____ |

4.  Which of the following party positions have you ever held?  (IF ANY, ASK WHEN)

    Local party club officer     No \_\_\_\_     Yes \_\_\_\_    When _____

    Senate district level post   No \_\_\_\_     Yes \_\_\_\_    When _____

    County level position     No \_\_\_\_     Yes \_\_\_\_    When _____

    State executive committee   No \_\_\_\_     Yes \_\_\_\_    When _____

    State convention delegate   No \_\_\_\_     Yes \_\_\_\_    When _____

    National convention delegate No \_\_\_\_     Yes \_\_\_\_    When _____

5.  Have you ever held an appointive political or a non-civil-service position in government?  No \_\_\_\_   Once \_\_\_\_   Now \_\_\_\_  (IF EVER DID, ASK) Were you paid? \_\_\_\_\_

6.  Have you ever sought or held any of the following public offices?

    Civil or municipal office    Sought \_\_\_    Held \_\_\_    (IF HELD) When \_\_\_\_\_

    School Board             Sought \_\_\_    Held \_\_\_    (IF HELD) When \_\_\_\_\_

    State Legislature        Sought \_\_\_    Held \_\_\_    (IF HELD) When \_\_\_\_\_

    Other Local office       Sought \_\_\_    Held \_\_\_    (IF HELD) When \_\_\_\_\_

    State or national office    Sought \_\_\_    Held \_\_\_    (IF HELD) When \_\_\_\_\_

7.  Politically, how would you rate yourself on a 7 point liberal to conservative scale, with one being very liberal, four being moderate or middle of the road, and 7 very conservative? _____

8.  In explaining why you yourself have been active in organized politics in recent years, how important are these reasons.  Would you say that personal friendship for a candidate was a very important, somewhat important, or not important reason for your being active in organized politics?  What about (READ REST OF LIST, RECORD)

|  | Very Important | Somewhat | Not Important |
|---|---|---|---|
| My personal friendship for a candidate | \_\_\_\_ | \_\_\_\_ | \_\_\_\_ |
| Active political work is part of my way of life | \_\_\_\_ | \_\_\_\_ | \_\_\_\_ |
| I am strongly attached to my political party | \_\_\_\_ | \_\_\_\_ | \_\_\_\_ |
| I enjoy the friendships and social contacts I have with other party workers | \_\_\_\_ | \_\_\_\_ | \_\_\_\_ |
| I like the fun and excitement of campaigns | \_\_\_\_ | \_\_\_\_ | \_\_\_\_ |
| I am trying to build a personal career in politics | \_\_\_\_ | \_\_\_\_ | \_\_\_\_ |
| I see campaign work as a way of influencing the politics of government | \_\_\_\_ | \_\_\_\_ | \_\_\_\_ |
| I like the feeling of being close to influential people | \_\_\_\_ | \_\_\_\_ | \_\_\_\_ |
| Party work helps me make business contacts | \_\_\_\_ | \_\_\_\_ | \_\_\_\_ |
| Party work helps me fulfill my sense of community obligation | \_\_\_\_ | \_\_\_\_ | \_\_\_\_ |
| Party work gives me a feeling of recognition in my community | \_\_\_\_ | \_\_\_\_ | \_\_\_\_ |

9.  Next, I'd like to read you some positions that might be taken by public officials.  Could you please tell me if you strongly favor each position, somewhat favor it, somewhat oppose it, or strongly oppose it.  The first position is a constitutional amendment to make abortion illegal.  Do you strongly favor such an amendment, somewhat favor it, somewhat oppose it, or strongly oppose a constitutional amendment to make abortion illegal?  (READ OTHER STATEMENTS, RECORD CORRECT RESPONSE)

| | Strongly Favor | Somewhat Favor | Somewhat Oppose | Strongly Oppose | Not Sure |
|---|---|---|---|---|---|
| A constitutional amendment making abortion illegal | ___ | ___ | ___ | ___ | ___ |
| Repealing the windfall profits tax on oil and gas | ___ | ___ | ___ | ___ | ___ |
| Increasing military spending | ___ | ___ | ___ | ___ | ___ |
| Repealing the 55 mile an hour speed limit | ___ | ___ | ___ | ___ | ___ |
| Ratifying the Equal Rights Amendment | ___ | ___ | ___ | ___ | ___ |

10. I'd now like to read you some alternative or opposing positions on public issues and ask where you would place yourself on a seven point scale that ranges between strong support for one position and strong support for the other. The first choice is: The United States should continue to rely on a volunteer army for its defense needs OR Registration and the draft should be reinstated. With a rating of one being strong support for the volunteer army and seven strong support for the draft. where would you place yourself on a seven point scale? (REPEAT LAST SENTENCE IF PERSON IS CONFUSED ABOUT WHAT SCALE MEANS -- CIRCLE OPTION CHOSEN)

1      2      3      4      5      6      7
Rely on vol. army                   Reinstate draft

11. The second choice is between: The building of nuclear power plants should continue to be part of our national energy policy OR Construction of nuclear power plants should be stopped and reliance placed on conservation and alternate sources of energy. With one being strong support for building more nuclear plants and seven for conservation and alternative energy sources, where would you place yourself?

1      2      3      4      5      6      7
Continue building                Conserve and rely on
nuclear plants                  alternative energy sources

12. To meet Soviet challenges the U.S. should increase its military presence around the world and support countries threatened by the Soviets even if they have authoritarian governments. OR the U.S. should maintain a course of nonintervention and support for human rights. (REPEAT WHAT ONE AND SEVEN MEAN ON SCALE)

1      2      3      4      5      6      7
Inc. Military presence          Maintain nonintervention, human
and aid                        rights

13. The next choice is between: There should be a government insurance plan which would cover all medical expenses, OR Medical expenses should be paid by individuals and through private insurance. One means strong support for government medical insurance, seven strong support for private insurance.

1      2      3      4      5      6      7
Government insurance               Private insurance

14. Everything possible should be done to protect the legal rights of those accused of committing crimes. OR It is more important to stop criminal activity even at the risk of reducing the rights of the accused.

1      2      3      4      5      6      7
Protect rights of accused          Stop criminal activity

15. The government should spend a lot less money even if it means reducing services in such areas as health and education. OR The government should continue to provide such services even if it means no reduction in government.

1      2      3      4      5      6      7
Decrease spending, reduce services      Continue spending, services

16. We are interested in how party workers view working within the party. For each of the following statements about party matters, could you please indicate whether you strongly agree, agree, disagree, or strongly disagree with the point of view stated. (CIRCLE CHOICE)

| | Strongly Agree | Agree | Disagree | Strongly Disagree | Not Sure |
|---|---|---|---|---|---|
| Controversial positions should be avoided in a party platform in order to insure party unity | ___ | ___ | ___ | ___ | ___ |
| Local party activities should be conducted free of state party direction | ___ | ___ | ___ | ___ | ___ |

| | Strongly Agree | Agree | Disagree | Strongly Disagree | Not Sure |
|---|---|---|---|---|---|
| Good precinct chairs at my level must support any candidate nominated by the party even if they basically disagree strongly with the candidate's views | ____ | ____ | ____ | ____ | ____ |
| Except under unusual circumstances, a precinct committeeman should remain officially and unofficially neutral in primary contests, even when I have a personal preference | ____ | ____ | ____ | ____ | ____ |
| Party organization and unity are more important than free and total discussion of issues which may divide the party | ____ | ____ | ____ | ____ | ____ |
| Candidates should not compromise their basic values even if such compromise is necessary to win | ____ | ____ | ____ | ____ | ____ |

17.  In the fall 1980 campaign, which of the following did you participate in within your precinct? (READ LIST, CHECK OFF ACTIVITIES ENGAGED IN)

    Voter registration____                Putting up signs, posters____
    Door to door canvassing____           Fundraising____
    Telephone canvassing____              Working the polls on election day____
    Distributing literature____           Getting out the vote on election day____
    Recruiting volunteers____             Other (HAVE SPECIFY)_____

18.  What was the most important activity your local precinct organization engaged in during the 1980 campaign? (RECORD COMMENTS)

19.  About how many people actively worked for your local party organization in your precinct during the last campaign?  (RECORD COMMENTS)

20.  Which of the following 3 statements do you feel most accurately reflected the condition of your local precinct organization in the last campaign? (READ STATEMENTS, CHECK RESPONSE)

    It made a maximum effort to win the election for the party candidates___

    It could have been better organized and done more to help party candidates___

    Local precinct organization was pretty much nonexistent___

20a. About how many hours per week did you spend on party work during the 1980 campaign?
    _____

21.  From your experience, how would you evaluate the strength of your precinct organization compared to 5-10 years ago?  Is it:

    Significantly stronger___     Somewhat stronger___     There's been little change___
    It is somewhat weaker___      It is significantly weaker___         I can't say___

22.  A lot of work on behalf of candidates is done outside the local precinct organizations by other party groups, candidate organizations, interest groups and others.  In the 1980 campaign which of the following statements best describes the relative role your local precinct organization played in working for the party's candidates in your neighborhood? (READ, CHECK RESPONSE)

    The precinct organization was the most important group working for the party's candidates___

    The precinct organization was one of several important groups working for the party's candidates___

    The precinct organization was not a very important factor in local campaigning___

    The precinct organization was inactive in the 1980 campaign___

23. We are interested in how much activity some of these non-precinct groups engaged in within your area in the 1980 campaign. Specifically, we'd like to know the extent to which they registered voters, raised money, worked to get out the vote, and engaged in face to face or telephone canvassing. I'd like to read you a list of several of these organizations and ask you whether they did much, or not much, in your precinct in each of these activities.

First, what about your party's presidential organization? Would you say it did much with regard to voter registration in your precinct? What about fund raising? Getting out the vote? Face to face canvassing? Telephone canvassing? (RECORD BELOW, THEN READ REST OF LIST OF ORGANIZATIONS, AND THE ACTIVITY LIST)

| Campaigning units | Voter Registration | | Fund Raising | | Getting out The Vote | | Face to Face Canvassing | | Telephone Canvassing | |
|---|---|---|---|---|---|---|---|---|---|---|
| | Much | Little | Much | Little | Much | Little | Much | Little | Much | Little |
| The presidential organization | ___ | ___ | ___ | ___ | ___ | ___ | ___ | ___ | ___ | ___ |
| The Harris County party orgn. | ___ | ___ | ___ | ___ | ___ | ___ | ___ | ___ | ___ | ___ |
| Congressional candidate orgn. | ___ | ___ | ___ | ___ | ___ | ___ | ___ | ___ | ___ | ___ |
| State legislative candidate orgns. | ___ | ___ | ___ | ___ | ___ | ___ | ___ | ___ | ___ | ___ |
| Labor unions (For your party's candidates only) | ___ | ___ | ___ | ___ | ___ | ___ | ___ | ___ | ___ | ___ |
| Other non-party groups | ___ | ___ | ___ | ___ | ___ | ___ | ___ | ___ | ___ | ___ |

24. We would like to conclude with a few questions about your background. First, in which of the following age categories do you fall?

Under 30_____   30 - 39_____   40 - 49_____   50 - 59_____   60 or over_____

25. What is your race or ethnicity?_____

26. What is your principal occupation or profession?_____

27. Are you married? Yes_____   No_____
(IF YES) What is your spouse's occupation?_____

28. What is the highest level of formal education you completed?_____

29. In what state and community were you brought up?_____

30. How long have you lived in the Houston area?_____

31. And what, if any, is your religious preference?_____

32. One final question. In which of the following categories would you estimate your family income fell last year? (READ LIST, CHECK RESPONSE)

Under $10,000_____   $10-20,000_____   $20-30,000_____   $30-40,000_____
$40-50,000_____   $Over $50,000_____   Refused_____

Thank you very much for your cooperation
--------------------------------------------------------------------------------
Sex of Respondent:   Male_____   Female_____

## Questionnaire 2

Dear Party Leader:

This brief questionnaire is part of a scientific inquiry into Tennessee political life being conducted by the University of Tennessee, Knoxville.

We are mainly interested in how you evaluate the problems of party organization and campaign coordination in your area. We also want your estimates of how much campaign activity different kinds of party units and campaign committees engaged in during the fall campaign weeks of 1980 in your district. And we want to learn how you view the issues emphasized in the 1980 campaigns, the strategies of rival candidates and the changing role of organized political parties in recent election years.

No more than a few minutes are needed to complete this questionnaire. Your answers will be kept entirely confidential. They will be tabulated and analyzed in quantitative form, solely for scholarly purposes. Thank you for your cooperation in helping us to study the actual workings of grassroots party politics in 1980.

Professor Anne Hopkins
Department of Political Science
University of Tennessee
Knoxville, TN 37916

POLITICAL EXPERIENCE

How long have you been active in party politics? _____ years

Which political party do you support? _____ Repub. _____ Democ. _____ Other

How strong a partisan would you rate yourself?

very strong *_____*_____*_____*_____*_____*_____*_____* very weak
          1     2     3     4     5     6     7     8

How much time per week this fall did you give to party organizational work and campaign activities?

hours  *_____*_____*_____*_____*_____*_____*_____*_____*_____*_____*
      50   45   40   35   30   25   20   15   10   5   0

Are you active in any of these organizations?

| | Very | Somewhat | Hardly | Non-member |
|---|---|---|---|---|
| *Council District Committee | _____ | _____ | _____ | _____ |
| *Countywide party unit | _____ | _____ | _____ | _____ |
| *Other level party unit (specify) | _____ | _____ | _____ | _____ |
| _____ | | | | |
| *Church-related group | _____ | _____ | _____ | _____ |
| *School-related group | _____ | _____ | _____ | _____ |
| *Civic group | _____ | _____ | _____ | _____ |
| *Neighborhood Association/group | _____ | _____ | _____ | _____ |
| *Labor union | _____ | _____ | _____ | _____ |
| *Veteran's group | _____ | _____ | _____ | _____ |
| *Environmental protection group | _____ | _____ | _____ | _____ |
| *Anti-abortion group | _____ | _____ | _____ | _____ |
| *Feminist Movement group | _____ | _____ | _____ | _____ |
| *Anti-nuclear group | _____ | _____ | _____ | _____ |
| *Civil rights group | _____ | _____ | _____ | _____ |
| *Other group (specify) _____ | _____ | _____ | _____ | _____ |
| _____ | | | | |

Which of the following <u>party</u> positions have you ever held?

|  | have held | now hold |
|---|---|---|
| *Council district committee/official | _____ | _____ |
| *County party committee/official | _____ | _____ |
| *Congressional district committee/ official | _____ | _____ |
| *State central committee/official | _____ | _____ |
| *County convention delegate | _____ | _____ |
| *State convention delegate | _____ | _____ |
| *National convention delegate | _____ | _____ |

Are you in charge of the work for your party in the 1980 campaign in your council district?

_____yes _____ no   If no, who is the leader in charge?

Name _____

Address _____

Have you ever held an appointive (non-civil service) position in government?

_____ now _____once _____ never

Which of the following elected <u>public</u> offices have you sought?

|  | sought | held | when held? |
|---|---|---|---|
| *County level official? | _____ | _____ | _____ |
| *School Board member | _____ | _____ | _____ |
| *Other local official? | _____ | _____ | _____ |
| *State legislator? | _____ | _____ | _____ |
| *Other state-level official? | _____ | _____ | _____ |
| *Congress? | _____ | _____ | _____ |

If you had the opportunity to take a position of responsibility in the party organization this coming year, would you do so?

_____Definitely yes _____probably yes _____probably no _____Definitely no

How interested in political developments are most of your personal friends?

_____Very _____Somewhat _____Not very _____Not at all

How many of your personal friends are active in organized politics?

_____Most _____About half _____Few _____None

Was there ever a time when you thought your party's supporters would have been justified in splitting their ballots?

_____Yes _____No

BACKGROUND INFORMATION

During the years you were growing up, where did you live?

_____Big city _____Suburb _____Small city _____Town _____Rural area

_____South _____East _____Midwest _____West _____Abroad

How long have you lived in Nashville/Davidson County? _____years

How long have you lived in your present neighborhood? _____years

When you were growing up, how active was your mother:

| *in community affairs? | _____Very | _____Somewhat | _____Not active |
| *in party politics? | _____Very | _____Somewhat | _____Not active |

And how active was your father:

| *in community affairs? | _____Very | _____Somewhat | _____Not active |
| *in party politics? | _____Very | _____Somewhat | _____Not active |

What are your family's national or ethnic origins? _____

Are your married? _____Now _____Once _____Never

How many children? _____

Spouse's main occupation? _____

Your main occupation? _____

Does your occupation involve:

    *Dealing with the public? _____Usually _____Rarely
    *Coordinating the work of others? _____Usually _____Rarely
    *Persuading others and bargaining? _____Usually _____Rarely
    *Doing business with the government? _____Usually _____Rarely
    *Working with organized groups? _____Usually _____Rarely

What was your approximate family income in 1980 before taxes?

    _____Under $4999 _____$5000 - $9999 _____$10,000 - 14,999 _____$15,000 - $19,999

    _____$20,000 - 24,999 _____$25,000 - 29,999 _____$30,000 - 49,999

    _____$50,000 and over

Year of birth _____ Sex _____ Race _____

Education: _____High school or less _____Some college _____College graduate

    _____Graduate school _____Professional

Religious preference? _____Protestant _____Catholic _____Jewish _____None

    _____Other (specify) _____

    What denomination? _____

How often do you attend religious services?

    _____Usually _____Sometimes _____Never

In general terms, how would you describe your council district?

| | | | |
|---|---|---|---|
| _____Republican | _____Conservative | _____Urban | _____High Income |
| _____Competitive | _____Moderate | _____Suburban | _____Middle Income |
| _____Democratic | _____Liberal | _____Rural | _____Low Income |

| | | |
|---|---|---|
| _____Mostly White | _____Mostly Professional/Business | _____Mostly Catholic |
| _____Mixed | _____Mostly other white collar | _____Mostly Protestant |
| _____Mostly Black | _____Mostly working class | _____Mostly Jewish |
| | _____Mixed | _____Different Religions |

_____Rapidly Changing

_____Slowly Changing

_____Not Changing

People have different ideas about the effectiveness and fairness of modern campaign tactics.  In the 1980 campaign in your Council district how would you rate each of these tactics:

| | HOW EFFECTIVE? | | | | HOW FAIR? | | |
|---|---|---|---|---|---|---|---|
| | Very | Somewhat | Not at all | | Okay | Doubtful | Bad |
| *Stress a candidates's personality rather than his (or her) stand on issues | ____ | ____ | ____ | | ____ | ____ | ____ |
| *Stir up controversy rather than be restrained | ____ | ____ | ____ | | ____ | ____ | ____ |
| *Meet smear attacks with counter charges rather than ignore them | ____ | ____ | ____ | | ____ | ____ | ____ |
| *Stress self interest rather than community wide consequences | ____ | ____ | ____ | | ____ | ____ | ____ |
| *Stress rival's bad record rather than own performance and plans | ____ | ____ | ____ | | ____ | ____ | ____ |
| *Be specific on issues rather than be vague on issues | ____ | ____ | ____ | | ____ | ____ | ____ |

In general, do you consider yourself

_____a liberal  _____a moderate  _____a conservative  _____other (specify)_____

Compared with each of the following:

| | ON MOST ISSUES, ARE YOU | | |
|---|---|---|---|
| | more liberal | the same | more conservative |
| *your personal friends? | ____ | ____ | ____ |
| *your neighbors? | ____ | ____ | ____ |
| *other members of your family? | ____ | ____ | ____ |
| *most people where your work? | ____ | ____ | ____ |
| *Democratic party workers you know? | ____ | ____ | ____ |
| *Republican party workers you know? | ____ | ____ | ____ |
| *most Democratic voters in your Council district? | ____ | ____ | ____ |
| *most Republican voters in your Council district? | ____ | ____ | ____ |

In examining why YOU have been active in organized politics in recent years, how important are these reasons?

| | Very Important | Somewhat Important | Not Important |
|---|---|---|---|
| *My personal friendship with a candidate | ____ | ____ | ____ |
| *Active political work is part of my way of life | ____ | ____ | ____ |
| *I am strongly attached to my party | ____ | ____ | ____ |
| *I enjoy the friendships and social contacts I have with other party workers | ____ | ____ | ____ |
| *I like the fun and excitement of campaigns | ____ | ____ | ____ |
| *I am trying to build a personal career in politics | ____ | ____ | ____ |
| *I see campaign work as influencing the policies of government | ____ | ____ | ____ |
| *I like the feeling of being close to influential people | ____ | ____ | ____ |
| *Party work helps me fulfill my sense of community obligation | ____ | ____ | ____ |
| *Party work helps me make business contacts | ____ | ____ | ____ |
| *Party work gives me a feeling of recognition in my community | ____ | ____ | ____ |

Which one of these reasons best explains why you became active? _____

SELECTED PUBLIC ISSUES

YOUR OWN PERSONAL VIEW
In this field the federal government should do:

| | more | same | less | no opinion |
|---|---|---|---|---|
| *Work for nuclear disarmament | ____ | ____ | ____ | ____ |
| *Control the cost of living | ____ | ____ | ____ | ____ |
| *Cut defense spending | ____ | ____ | ____ | ____ |
| *Expand opportunities for the poor | ____ | ____ | ____ | ____ |
| *Get tough with urban violence | ____ | ____ | ____ | ____ |
| *Stop air and water pollution | ____ | ____ | ____ | ____ |
| *Desegregate housing | ____ | ____ | ____ | ____ |
| *Desegregate schools | ____ | ____ | ____ | ____ |
| *Require energy saving practices | ____ | ____ | ____ | ____ |
| *Increase America's military strength | ____ | ____ | ____ | ____ |
| *Help Third World countries | ____ | ____ | ____ | ____ |
| *Cut government payrolls | ____ | ____ | ____ | ____ |
| *Revitalize America's cities | ____ | ____ | ____ | ____ |

YOUR ADVICE FOR CAMPAIGN STRATEGY
To run for office in this area, a
candidate should:

| | stress | mention | ignore |
|---|---|---|---|
| *Work for nuclear disarmament | ____ | ____ | ____ |
| *Control the cost of living | ____ | ____ | ____ |
| *Cut defense spending | ____ | ____ | ____ |
| *Expand opportunities for the poor | ____ | ____ | ____ |
| *Get tough with urban violence | ____ | ____ | ____ |
| *Stop air and water pollution | ____ | ____ | ____ |
| *Desegregate housing | ____ | ____ | ____ |
| *Desegregate schools | ____ | ____ | ____ |
| *Require energy saving practices | ____ | ____ | ____ |
| *Increase America's military strength | ____ | ____ | ____ |
| *Help Third World countries | ____ | ____ | ____ |
| *Cut government payrolls | ____ | ____ | ____ |
| *Revitalize America's cities | ____ | ____ | ____ |

In my precinct probably most
Democratic voters want the federal
government to do:

| | stress | mention | ignore |
|---|---|---|---|
| *Work for nuclear disarmament | ____ | ____ | ____ |
| *Control the cost of living | ____ | ____ | ____ |
| *Cut defense spending | ____ | ____ | ____ |
| *Expand opportunities for the poor | ____ | ____ | ____ |
| *Get rough with urban violence | ____ | ____ | ____ |
| *Stop air and water pollution | ____ | ____ | ____ |
| *Desegregate housing | ____ | ____ | ____ |
| *Desegregate schools | ____ | ____ | ____ |
| *Require energy saving practices | ____ | ____ | ____ |
| *Increase America's military strength | ____ | ____ | ____ |
| *Help Third World countries | ____ | ____ | ____ |
| *Cut government payrolls | ____ | ____ | ____ |
| *Revitalize America's cities | ____ | ____ | ____ |

In my precinct probably most Republican
voters want the federal government to do:

| | stress | mention | ignore |
|---|---|---|---|
| *Work for nuclear disarmament | ____ | ____ | ____ |
| *Control the cost of living | ____ | ____ | ____ |
| *Cut defense spending | ____ | ____ | ____ |
| *Expand opportunities for the poor | ____ | ____ | ____ |
| *Get rough with urban violence | ____ | ____ | ____ |
| *Stop air and water pollution | ____ | ____ | ____ |
| *Desegregate housing | ____ | ____ | ____ |
| *Desegregate schools | ____ | ____ | ____ |
| *Require energy saving practices | ____ | ____ | ____ |
| *Increase America's military strength | ____ | ____ | ____ |
| *Help Third World countries | ____ | ____ | ____ |
| *Cut government payrolls | ____ | ____ | ____ |
| *Revitalize America's cities | ____ | ____ | ____ |

During the weeks of the 1980 campaign this fall, which of these activities:

|  | did you personally engage in? | were you personally responsible for? | how many helpers worked with you? |
|---|---|---|---|
| *Voter Registration | _____ | _____ | _____ |
| *Fund Raising | _____ | _____ | _____ |
| *Getting out the vote (on election day) | _____ | _____ | _____ |
| *Face-to-face canvassing | _____ | _____ | _____ |
| *Telephone canvassing | _____ | _____ | _____ |
| *Literature distribution | _____ | _____ | _____ |
| *Other (specify) _____ | _____ | _____ | _____ |

In your canvassing in this district what percentage of the voters did you reach?
_____%

In you activity in the campaign this fall did you work specifically
for one candidate _____
for the party ticket _____

(If for one candidate) For which office?
_____

Between the 1978 election and the 1980 campaign how active were you in party work?
_____ very active    _____ sporadically    _____ not active

How active do you expect to be during the coming year?
_____ very active    _____ sporadically    _____ not active

Here are a few commonly heard statements.
Do you agree of disagree with them?

|  | PERSONALLY, DO YOU | | | |
|---|---|---|---|---|
|  | Strongly agree | agree | disagree | Strongl disagre |
| *Campaign appeals should be vague enough to attract a broad spectrum of voters. | _____ | _____ | _____ | _____ |
| *Only party organization run by a few leaders is really effective. | _____ | _____ | _____ | _____ |
| *Elected public official should be kept strictly accountable to the party organization. | _____ | _____ | _____ | _____ |
| *Parties should try to reconcile conflicting views rather than take controversial stands. | _____ | _____ | _____ | _____ |
| *Parties should play down some issues if it will alter the chances of winning. | _____ | _____ | _____ | _____ |
| *Widespread participation should be encouraged in making most party decisions. | _____ | _____ | _____ | _____ |
| *Stronger state wide parties are necessary even if local units must be overruled. | _____ | _____ | _____ | _____ |
| *Part-time volunteers play a more important role in the party's campaign than any other segment of a party. | _____ | _____ | _____ | _____ |
| *Parties should see to it that those who work for the party get help in the form of jobs and other things if they need it. | _____ | _____ | _____ | _____ |
| *In selecting its candidates, years of work for the party should count heavily. | _____ | _____ | _____ | _____ |
| *If you disagree with a major stand of your party, stop working for it. | _____ | _____ | _____ | _____ |
| *A good party worker must support any candidate nominated by the party even if he or she basically disagrees with that candidate. | _____ | _____ | _____ | _____ |
| *In order to be an effective political force, a party must maintain good working relationships with local interest groups. | _____ | _____ | _____ | _____ |
| *The most important function of a political party is nominating candidates for office. | _____ | _____ | _____ | _____ |
| *Most officeholders are thinking only of what is in it for them. | _____ | _____ | _____ | _____ |
| *Too few good people run for office any more. | _____ | _____ | _____ | _____ |
| *Few people know what is in their own best interest in the long run. | _____ | _____ | _____ | _____ |
| *Arguments about policy are beyond the grasp of most voters. | _____ | _____ | _____ | _____ |
| *Recent national party reforms have had a good effect on the workings of my party | _____ | _____ | _____ | _____ |

ESTIMATED LEVELS OF VARIOUS CAMPAIGN ACTIVITIES IN YOUR PRECINCT DURING THE FALL CAMPAIGN

| CAMPAIGN ACTIVITIES CARRIED OUT BY | Please leave items blank if unknown | VOTER REGISTRATION | | FUND RAISING | | GETTING OUT THE VOTE | | FACE-TO-FACE CANVASSING | | TELEPHONE CANVASSING | |
|---|---|---|---|---|---|---|---|---|---|---|---|
| | | Much | Not Much | Much | Not Much | Much | Not Much | Much | Not Much | Much | Not Much |
| Regular Party Organizational Units | | | | | | | | | | | |
| *Sub-Council District Democ. Committees | | | | | | | | | | | |
| *Sub-Council District Repub. Committees | | | | | | | | | | | |
| *Council District Democ. Organization | | | | | | | | | | | |
| *Council District Repub. Organization | | | | | | | | | | | |
| *Countywide Democ. Organization | | | | | | | | | | | |
| *Countywide Repub. Organization | | | | | | | | | | | |
| Candidate Campaign Units | | | | | | | | | | | |
| *Carter for President Organizations | | | | | | | | | | | |
| *Reagan for President Organizations | | | | | | | | | | | |
| *Anderson for President Organizations | | | | | | | | | | | |
| *Democrat for Congress | | | | | | | | | | | |
| *Republican for Congress | | | | | | | | | | | |
| *Democrat for State Legislature | | | | | | | | | | | |
| *Republican for State Legislature | | | | | | | | | | | |
| Political Action Committees | | | | | | | | | | | |
| *Labor Union PACs | | | | | | | | | | | |
| *Business-based PACs | | | | | | | | | | | |
| *Profession-based PACs | | | | | | | | | | | |
| *Other PACs:  A. _____ | | | | | | | | | | | |
| (specify)    B. _____ | | | | | | | | | | | |

How often do you get to meet with:

|  | Once or Twice a Week | Once or Twice a Month | Once or Twice a Year | Hardly Ever |
|---|---|---|---|---|
| *Council District level party leaders |  |  |  |  |
| *County level party leaders |  |  |  |  |
| *State level party leaders |  |  |  |  |

What is the best way to become active in politics around here?  Should you begin by working for a
_____ candidate? _____ an incumbent official? _____ become active in the local
or what? (specify) _____.          party organization?

In this area, how effective would you say these ways to persuade voters are:

|  | Very | Not Very | Don't Know |
|---|---|---|---|
| *Face to Face Canvassing? |  |  |  |
| *Telephone Canvassing? |  |  |  |
| *Appearances before groups? |  |  |  |
| *Mailout Campaign literature? |  |  |  |
| *Radio or TV ads? |  |  |  |
| *Billboards and Posters |  |  |  |

How much say do district leaders like you generally have in running your party's district organization?

_____very little   _____some   _____fair amount   _____a great deal

Have you personally observed changes in the kinds of people who give time and effort to party affairs, in the last 10 years?
_____yes   _____no
What changes?_____
_____
_____

In recent years in Tennessee, including 1980, a heavy reliance has been placed on radio and TV "spot" commercials, on private opinion polls, on fund raising and electioneering by computerized mailing techniques, and on campaign management firms.  Has this occurred in your area here?

_____yes, to a large extent _____somewhat _____not too much _____no, not at all

These newer methods are said to weaken the major role of organized political parties and to discourage people from becoming active in party affairs.  Has this happened in your case?

_____yes, to a large extent _____somewhat _____not too much _____no, not at all

How important is the work of your party's local organization today compared to 10 years ago

_____about the same _____stronger _____weaker

Additional Comments:

## Questionnaire 3

NON-PROFIT
ORGANIZATION
U.S. POSTAGE
PAID
ANN ARBOR, MICH
PERMIT NO. 144

ADDRESS CORRECTION REQUESTED

PROFESSOR SAM ELDERSVELD
INSTITUTE FOR SOCIAL RESEARCH — RM 4055
P.O. BOX 1248
ANN ARBOR, MI 48106

POLITICAL EXPERIENCE

How long have you been active in party politics? _____ years
Which political party do you support? _____ Repub. _____ Democ ___ Other
How strong a partisan would you rate yourself?

very strong •—•—•—•—•—•—•—• very weak
     1    2    3    4    5    6    7    8

How much time per week this fall did you give to party organizational work and campaign
activities?

Hours •—•—•—•—•—•—•—•—•—• •
    50  45  40  35  30  25  20  15  10  5  0

Are you active in any of these organizations?

| | Very | Somewhat | Hardly | Nonmember |
|---|---|---|---|---|
| • Ward Committee | ☐ | ☐ | ☐ | ☐ |
| • Districtwide party unit | ☐ | ☐ | ☐ | ☐ |
| • Countywide party unit | ☐ | ☐ | ☐ | ☐ |
| • Other level party unit (specify) | ☐ | ☐ | ☐ | ☐ |
| • Church-related group | ☐ | ☐ | ☐ | ☐ |
| • School-related group | ☐ | ☐ | ☐ | ☐ |
| • Civic group | ☐ | ☐ | ☐ | ☐ |
| • Neighborhood Association/group | ☐ | ☐ | ☐ | ☐ |
| • Labor union | ☐ | ☐ | ☐ | ☐ |
| • Veterans' group | ☐ | ☐ | ☐ | ☐ |
| • Environmental protection group | ☐ | ☐ | ☐ | ☐ |
| • Anti-Abortion group | ☐ | ☐ | ☐ | ☐ |
| • Feminist Movement group | ☐ | ☐ | ☐ | ☐ |
| • Anti-Nuclear group | ☐ | ☐ | ☐ | ☐ |
| • Other group (specify) | ☐ | ☐ | ☐ | ☐ |

### Precinct Leader Interview

Dear Party Leader:

This brief questionnaire is part of a scientific inquiry into Michigan political life being conducted by The University of Michigan.

We are mainly interested in how you evaluate the problems of party organization and campaign coordination in your area. We also want your estimates of how much campaign activity different kinds of party units and campaign committees engaged in during the fall campaign weeks of 1980 in your district. And we want to learn how you view the issues emphasized in the 1980 campaigns, the strategies of rival candidates and the changing role of organized political parties in recent election years.

No more than a few minutes are needed to complete this questionnaire. Your answers will be kept entirely confidential. They will be tabulated and analyzed in quantitative form, solely for scholarly purposes. Thank you for your cooperation in helping us to study the actual workings of grassroots party politics in 1980.

Professor Samuel Eldersveld
Department of Political Science
The University of Michigan
Ann Arbor, Michigan 48109

PROFESSOR SAM ELDERSVELD
ROOM 4055

Please fold Questionnaire Firmly with THIS SIDE OUT

NO POSTAGE
NECESSARY
IF MAILED
IN THE
UNITED STATES

**BUSINESS REPLY MAIL**

FIRST CLASS     PERMIT NO. 1100     ANN ARBOR, MI.

POSTAGE WILL BE PAID BY ADDRESSEE

INSTITUTE FOR SOCIAL RESEARCH
P.O. Box 1248
ANN ARBOR, MICHIGAN 48106

Which of the following **party** positions have you held?

|  | have held | now hold |
|---|---|---|
| • Ward committee or official | ☐ | ☐ |
| • City party committee or official | ☐ | ☐ |
| • District committee or official | ☐ | ☐ |
| • County committee or official | ☐ | ☐ |
| • State central committee or official | ☐ | ☐ |
| • State convention delegate | ☐ | ☐ |
| • National convention delegate | ☐ | ☐ |

Are you in charge of the precinct work for your party in the 1980 campaign?
___yes  ___no  If not, who is the precinct leader in charge?
Name_____
Address_____

Have you ever held an appointive (non-civil-service) position in government?
___now  ___once  ___never

Which of the following **public** offices have you sought?

|  | sought | held | when held? |
|---|---|---|---|
| • City level official? | ☐ | ☐ | _____ |
| • County level official? | ☐ | ☐ | _____ |
| • School Board member? | ☐ | ☐ | _____ |
| • Other local official? | ☐ | ☐ | _____ |
| • State legislator? | ☐ | ☐ | _____ |
| • Other state-level official? | ☐ | ☐ | _____ |
| • Congress? | ☐ | ☐ | _____ |

If you had the opportunity to take a position in the party organization this coming year, would you do so?
___Definitely yes  ___probably yes
___Definitely no  ___probably no

How interested in political developments are most of your personal friends?
___Very  ___Somewhat  ___Not very  ___Not at all

How many of your personal friends are active in organized politics?
___Most  ___About half  ___Few  ___None

Was there ever a time when you thought your party's supporters would have been justified in splitting their ballots?
___yes            ___no

BACKGROUND INFORMATION

During the years you were growing up, where did you live?
___Big city  ___Suburb  ___Small city  ___Town  ___Rural Area
___South  ___East  ___Midwest  ___West  ___Abroad
How long have you lived in Detroit?  ___years
How long have you lived in your present neighborhood?  ___years
When you were growing up, how active was your mother:
• in community affairs?  ___Very  ___Somewhat  ___Not active
• in party politics?  ___Very  ___Somewhat  ___Not active

And how active was your father:
• in community affairs?  ___Very  ___Somewhat  ___Not active
• in party politics?  ___Very  ___Somewhat  ___Not active

What are your family's national or ethnic origins?  _____
Are you married?  ___Now  ___Once  ___Never
How many children?  _____
Spouse's main occupation?  _____
Your main occupation?  _____

Does your occupation involve:

| | | |
|---|---|---|
| • Dealing with the public? | ☐ Usually | ☐ Rarely |
| • Coordinating the work of others? | ☐ Usually | ☐ Rarely |
| • Persuading others and bargaining? | ☐ Usually | ☐ Rarely |
| • Doing business with the government? | ☐ Usually | ☐ Rarely |
| • Working with organized groups? | ☐ Usually | ☐ Rarely |

What was your approximate family income in 1980 before taxes?
___Under $4999  ___$5000-$9999
___$10,000-$14,999  ___$15,000-$19,999
___$20,000-$24,999  ___$25,000-$29,999
___$30,000-$49,999  ___$50,000 and over

Year of birth _____  Sex _____  Race _____

Education  ___High school or less  ___Some college  ___College graduate
___Graduate school  ___Professional school

Religious preference?  ___Protestant  ___Catholic  ___Jewish
___Other _____  ___None
What denomination?  _____

How often do you attend religious services?
___Usually  ___Sometimes  ___Never

In general terms, how would you describe your precinct?
___Republican  ___Conservative  ___Urban
___Competitive  ___Moderate  ___Suburban
___Democratic  ___Liberal  ___Rural

___High Income  ___Mostly White  ___Mostly Prof/Business
___Middle Income  ___Mixed  ___Mostly other white collar
___Low Income  ___Mostly Black  ___Mostly working class
  ___Mixed

___Mostly Catholic  ___Rapidly Changing
___Mostly Protestant  ___Slowly Changing
___Mostly Jewish  ___Not Changing
___Different Religions

People have different ideas about the effectiveness and fairness of modern campaign tactics. In the 1980 campaign in your precinct how would you rate each of these tactics?

|  | HOW EFFECTIVE? | | | HOW FAIR? | | |
|---|---|---|---|---|---|---|
|  | Very | Somewhat | Not at all | Okay | Doubtful | Bad |
| • Stress a candidate's personality rather than his (or her) stand on issues. | ☐ | ☐ | ☐ | ☐ | ☐ | ☐ |
| • Stir up controversy rather than be restrained | ☐ | ☐ | ☐ | ☐ | ☐ | ☐ |
| • Meet smear attacks with counter charges rather than ignore them. | ☐ | ☐ | ☐ | ☐ | ☐ | ☐ |
| • Stress self interest rather than community wide consequences | ☐ | ☐ | ☐ | ☐ | ☐ | ☐ |
| • Stress rival's bad record rather than own performance and plans | ☐ | ☐ | ☐ | ☐ | ☐ | ☐ |
| • Be specific on issues rather than be vague on issues | ☐ | ☐ | ☐ | ☐ | ☐ | ☐ |

In general, do you consider yourself
☐ a liberal,
☐ a moderate,
☐ a conservative?
☐ other: _____

Compared with:

| | ON MOST ISSUES, ARE YOU | | |
|---|---|---|---|
|  | more liberal | the same | more conservative |
| • your personal friends? | ☐ | ☐ | ☐ |
| • your neighbors? | ☐ | ☐ | ☐ |
| • other members of your family? | ☐ | ☐ | ☐ |
| • most people where you work? | ☐ | ☐ | ☐ |
| • Democratic party workers you know? | ☐ | ☐ | ☐ |
| • Republican party workers you know? | ☐ | ☐ | ☐ |
| • most Democratic voters in your precinct? | ☐ | ☐ | ☐ |
| • most Republican voters in your precinct? | ☐ | ☐ | ☐ |

If you had to drop out of political activity tomorrow, what things would you miss from such work?  _____

|  | Strongly agree | Agree | Disagree | Strongly disagree |
|---|---|---|---|---|
| • Arguments about policy are beyond the grasp of most voters | ☐ | ☐ | ☐ | ☐ |
| • My national party should adopt policies to ensure better representation of women and minorities | ☐ | ☐ | ☐ | ☐ |
| • Primaries are better than caucuses or conventions for the selection of Presidential candidates | ☐ | ☐ | ☐ | ☐ |
| • Recent national party reforms have had a good effect on the workings of my party | ☐ | ☐ | ☐ | ☐ |

During the weeks of the 1980 campaign this fall, which of these activities:

|  | did you personally engage in? | were you personally responsible for? | how many helpers worked with you |
|---|---|---|---|
| • Voter Registration | ☐ | ☐ | _____ |
| • Fund Raising | ☐ | ☐ | _____ |
| • Getting out the vote (on election day) | ☐ | ☐ | _____ |
| • Face-to-face canvassing | ☐ | ☐ | _____ |
| • Telephone canvassing | ☐ | ☐ | _____ |
| • Literature distribution | ☐ | ☐ | _____ |
| • Other (specify) _____ _____ | ☐ | ☐ | _____ |

In your canvassing in this precinct what percentage of the voters did you reach? _____
Your activity in the campaign this fall did you work specifically **for one candidate**, ☐ or **for the party ticket**, ☐.
(for one candidate) For which office? _____

ESTIMATED LEVELS OF VARIOUS CAMPAIGN ACTIVITIES
IN YOUR PRECINCT DURING THE FALL CAMPAIGN
Please leave items blank if unknown

| CAMPAIGN ACTIVITIES: CARRIED OUT BY | Voter Registration | | Fund raising | | Getting out the vote | | Face-to-face Canvassing | | Telephone Canvassing | |
|---|---|---|---|---|---|---|---|---|---|---|
|  | Much | Not Much | Much | Not Much | Much | Not Much | Much | Not Much | Much | Not Much |
| **Regular Party Organizational Units** | | | | | | | | | | |
| • Local Democ committees | ☐ | ☐ | ☐ | ☐ | ☐ | ☐ | ☐ | ☐ | ☐ | ☐ |
| • Local Repub. committees | ☐ | ☐ | ☐ | ☐ | ☐ | ☐ | ☐ | ☐ | ☐ | ☐ |
| • Districtwide Democ. organization | ☐ | ☐ | ☐ | ☐ | ☐ | ☐ | ☐ | ☐ | ☐ | ☐ |
| • Districtwide Repub organization | ☐ | ☐ | ☐ | ☐ | ☐ | ☐ | ☐ | ☐ | ☐ | ☐ |
| • Countywide Democ. organization | ☐ | ☐ | ☐ | ☐ | ☐ | ☐ | ☐ | ☐ | ☐ | ☐ |
| • Countywide Repub organization | ☐ | ☐ | ☐ | ☐ | ☐ | ☐ | ☐ | ☐ | ☐ | ☐ |
| **Candidate Campaign Units** | | | | | | | | | | |
| • Carter for President organizations | ☐ | ☐ | ☐ | ☐ | ☐ | ☐ | ☐ | ☐ | ☐ | ☐ |
| • Reagan for President organizations | ☐ | ☐ | ☐ | ☐ | ☐ | ☐ | ☐ | ☐ | ☐ | ☐ |
| • Anderson for President organizations | ☐ | ☐ | ☐ | ☐ | ☐ | ☐ | ☐ | ☐ | ☐ | ☐ |
| • Democrat for Congress | ☐ | ☐ | ☐ | ☐ | ☐ | ☐ | ☐ | ☐ | ☐ | ☐ |
| • Republican for Congress | ☐ | ☐ | ☐ | ☐ | ☐ | ☐ | ☐ | ☐ | ☐ | ☐ |
| • Democrat for State Legislature | ☐ | ☐ | ☐ | ☐ | ☐ | ☐ | ☐ | ☐ | ☐ | ☐ |
| • Republican for State Legislature | ☐ | ☐ | ☐ | ☐ | ☐ | ☐ | ☐ | ☐ | ☐ | ☐ |

**Political Action Committees**

| • Labor Union PACs | ☐ | ☐ | ☐ | ☐ | ☐ | ☐ | ☐ | ☐ | ☐ | ☐ |
|---|---|---|---|---|---|---|---|---|---|---|
| • Business-based PACs | ☐ | ☐ | ☐ | ☐ | ☐ | ☐ | ☐ | ☐ | ☐ | ☐ |
| • Profession-based PACs | ☐ | ☐ | ☐ | ☐ | ☐ | ☐ | ☐ | ☐ | ☐ | ☐ |
| • Other PACs (specify) | | | | | | | | | | |
| A _____ | ☐ | ☐ | ☐ | ☐ | ☐ | ☐ | ☐ | ☐ | ☐ | ☐ |
| B _____ | ☐ | ☐ | ☐ | ☐ | ☐ | ☐ | ☐ | ☐ | ☐ | ☐ |

Between the 1978 election and this 1980 campaign how active were you in party work?
☐ very active   ☐ sporadically   ☐ not active

How active do you expect to be during the coming year?
☐ very active   ☐ sporadically   ☐ not active

How often do you get to meet with:

|  | Once or Twice a week | Once or Twice a month | Once or Twice a year | Hardly Ever |
|---|---|---|---|---|
| Other precinct leaders | ☐ | ☐ | ☐ | ☐ |
| District level party leaders | ☐ | ☐ | ☐ | ☐ |
| County level party leaders | ☐ | ☐ | ☐ | ☐ |
| City level party leaders | ☐ | ☐ | ☐ | ☐ |
| State level party leaders | ☐ | ☐ | ☐ | ☐ |

What is the best way to become active in politics around here? Should you begin working for a ☐ candidate? ☐ an incumbent official? ☐ become active in the local party organization or what?_____

In this area, how effective would you say these ways to persuade voters are:

|  | Very | Not Very | Don't Know |
|---|---|---|---|
| Face to Face Canvassing? | ☐ | ☐ | ☐ |
| Telephone Canvassing? | ☐ | ☐ | ☐ |
| Appearances before groups? | ☐ | ☐ | ☐ |
| Mailout Campaign literature? | ☐ | ☐ | ☐ |
| Radio or TV ads? | ☐ | ☐ | ☐ |
| Billboards and Posters? | ☐ | ☐ | ☐ |

How much say do precinct leaders like you generally have in running your party's dist organization? ☐ very little   ☐ some   ☐ fair amount   ☐ a great deal

Do you think that precinct leaders generally should have **more say** in running the dist organization, is it **about right now**, or should they have **less say**?
☐ more   ☐ about right   ☐ less

Have you personally observed changes in the kinds of people who give time and effort party affairs, in the last 10 years?   ☐ yes   ☐ no

What changes? _____

In American politics, many people often characterize an issue position in ideolog terms. From your experience what do active partisans mean by "conservative"?

by "Moderate"?

By "Liberal"?

In recent years in Michigan, including 1980, a heavy reliance has been placed on ra and TV "spot" commercials, on private opinion polls, on fundraising and electioneer by computerized mailing techniques, and on campaign management firms. Has th occurred in your area here?  ☐ yes, to a large extent   ☐ somewhat   ☐ not too mu ☐ no, not at all

These newer methods are said to weaken the major role of organized political parties an to discourage people from becoming active in party affairs. Has this happened in you case?
☐ yes, to a large extent   ☐ somewhat   ☐ not too much   ☐ no, not at all

How important is the work of your party's local organization today compared to 10 ye ago?
☐ about the same   ☐ stronger   ☐ weaker

What should be done to make the party organization more effective?
_____
_____
_____

In examining why you yourself have been active in organized politics in recent years, how important are these reasons?

|  | Very Important | Somewhat Important | Not Important |
|---|---|---|---|
| • My personal friendship with a candidate | ☐ | ☐ | ☐ |
| • Active political work is part of my way of life | ☐ | ☐ | ☐ |
| • I am strongly attached to my party | ☐ | ☐ | ☐ |
| • I enjoy the friendships and social contacts I have with other party workers | ☐ | ☐ | ☐ |
| • I like the fun and excitement of campaigns | ☐ | ☐ | ☐ |
| • I am trying to build a personal career in politics | ☐ | ☐ | ☐ |
| • I see campaign work as influencing the policies of government | ☐ | ☐ | ☐ |
| • I like the feeling of being close to influential people | ☐ | ☐ | ☐ |
| • Party work helps me fulfill my sense of community obligation | ☐ | ☐ | ☐ |
| • Party work helps me make business contacts | ☐ | ☐ | ☐ |
| • Party work gives me a feeling of recognition in my community | ☐ | ☐ | ☐ |

Which one of these reasons best explains why **you** became active?

_____

How do you stand on these current policy issues:
Strict import quotas on foreign automobiles
☐ Favor  ☐ Oppose  ☐ No opinion

Cutting Property Taxes
☐ Favor  ☐ Oppose  ☐ No opinion

Passage of Equal Rights Amendment
☐ Favor  ☐ Oppose  ☐ No opinion

With respect to your general viewpoint on current issues, how do you feel about the statement that "The government ought to help people get doctors and hospital care at low cost. Should the government do this or not?
☐ Agree Strongly  ☐ Agree  ☐ Not Sure  ☐ Disagree  ☐ Disagree Strongly

To run for office in this area a candidate should use what strategy?
On Strict Quotas on Foreign automobiles  ☐ Stress  ☐ Mention  ☐ Ignore
On Cutting Property Taxes  ☐ Stress  ☐ Mention  ☐ Ignore
On Passage of ERA  ☐ Stress  ☐ Mention  ☐ Ignore

SELECTED POLITICAL ISSUES

**YOUR OWN PERSONAL VIEW**
In this field the federal government should do:

|  | more | same | less | no opinion |
|---|---|---|---|---|
| • Work for nuclear disarmament | ☐ | ☐ | ☐ | ☐ |
| • Control the cost of living | ☐ | ☐ | ☐ | ☐ |
| • Cut defense spending | ☐ | ☐ | ☐ | ☐ |
| • Expand opportunities for the poor | ☐ | ☐ | ☐ | ☐ |
| • Get tough with urban violence | ☐ | ☐ | ☐ | ☐ |
| • Stop air and water pollution | ☐ | ☐ | ☐ | ☐ |
| • Desegregate housing | ☐ | ☐ | ☐ | ☐ |
| • Desegregate schools | ☐ | ☐ | ☐ | ☐ |
| • Require energy saving practices | ☐ | ☐ | ☐ | ☐ |
| • Increase America's military strength | ☐ | ☐ | ☐ | ☐ |
| • Help Third World countries | ☐ | ☐ | ☐ | ☐ |
| • Cut government payrolls | ☐ | ☐ | ☐ | ☐ |
| • Revitalize America's cities | ☐ | ☐ | ☐ | ☐ |

**YOUR ADVICE FOR CAMPAIGN STRATEGY**
To run for office in this area, a candidate should:

|  | stress | mention | ignore |
|---|---|---|---|
| • Work for nuclear disarmament | ☐ | ☐ | ☐ |
| • Control the cost of living | ☐ | ☐ | ☐ |
| • Cut defense spending | ☐ | ☐ | ☐ |
| • Expand opportunities for the poor | ☐ | ☐ | ☐ |
| • Get tough with urban violence | ☐ | ☐ | ☐ |
| • Stop air and water pollution | ☐ | ☐ | ☐ |
| • Desegregate housing | ☐ | ☐ | ☐ |
| • Desegregate schools | ☐ | ☐ | ☐ |
| • Require energy saving practices | ☐ | ☐ | ☐ |
| • Increase America's military strength | ☐ | ☐ | ☐ |
| • Help Third World countries | ☐ | ☐ | ☐ |
| • Cut government payrolls | ☐ | ☐ | ☐ |
| • Revitalize America's cities | ☐ | ☐ | ☐ |

In my precinct probably **most** Democratic voters want the federal government to do:

|  | more | the same | less |
|---|---|---|---|
| • Work for nuclear disarmament | ☐ | ☐ | ☐ |
| • Control the cost of living | ☐ | ☐ | ☐ |
| • Cut defense spending | ☐ | ☐ | ☐ |
| • Expand opportunities for the poor | ☐ | ☐ | ☐ |
| • Get tough with urban violence | ☐ | ☐ | ☐ |
| • Stop air and water pollution | ☐ | ☐ | ☐ |
| • Desegregate housing | ☐ | ☐ | ☐ |
| • Desegregate schools | ☐ | ☐ | ☐ |
| • Require energy saving practices | ☐ | ☐ | ☐ |
| • Increase America's military strength | ☐ | ☐ | ☐ |
| • Help Third World countries | ☐ | ☐ | ☐ |
| • Cut government payrolls | ☐ | ☐ | ☐ |
| • Revitalize America's cities | ☐ | ☐ | ☐ |

In my precinct probably **most** Republican voters want the Federal government to do:

|  | more | the same | less |
|---|---|---|---|
| • Work for nuclear disarmament | ☐ | ☐ | ☐ |
| • Control the cost of living | ☐ | ☐ | ☐ |
| • Cut defense spending | ☐ | ☐ | ☐ |
| • Expand opportunities for the poor | ☐ | ☐ | ☐ |
| • Get tough with urban violence | ☐ | ☐ | ☐ |
| • Stop air and water pollution | ☐ | ☐ | ☐ |
| • Desegregate housing | ☐ | ☐ | ☐ |
| • Desegregate schools | ☐ | ☐ | ☐ |
| • Require energy saving practices | ☐ | ☐ | ☐ |
| • Increase America's military strength | ☐ | ☐ | ☐ |
| • Help Third World countries | ☐ | ☐ | ☐ |
| • Cut government payrolls | ☐ | ☐ | ☐ |
| • Revitalize America's cities | ☐ | ☐ | ☐ |

Here are a few commonly heard statements. Do you agree or disagree with them?

PERSONALLY, DO YOU

|  | Strongly agree | agree | disagree | Strongly disagree |
|---|---|---|---|---|
| • Campaign appeals should be vague enough to attract a broad spectrum of voters | ☐ | ☐ | ☐ | ☐ |
| • Only party organizations run by a few leaders are really effective | ☐ | ☐ | ☐ | ☐ |
| • Elected public officials should be kept strictly accountable to the party organization | ☐ | ☐ | ☐ | ☐ |
| • Parties should try to reconcile conflicting views rather than take controversial stands | ☐ | ☐ | ☐ | ☐ |
| • Parties should play down some issues if they will alter the chances of winning | ☐ | ☐ | ☐ | ☐ |
| • Widespread participation should be encouraged in making most party decisions | ☐ | ☐ | ☐ | ☐ |
| • Stronger state and national parties are necessary, even if local units must be overruled | ☐ | ☐ | ☐ | ☐ |
| • Part-time volunteers play a more important role in the party's campaign than any other segment of a party | ☐ | ☐ | ☐ | ☐ |
| • Parties should see to it that those who work for the party get help in the form of jobs and other things if they need it | ☐ | ☐ | ☐ | ☐ |
| • In selecting its candidates, years of work for the party should count heavily | ☐ | ☐ | ☐ | ☐ |
| • If you disagree with a major stand of your party, stop working for it | ☐ | ☐ | ☐ | ☐ |
| • A good party worker must support any candidate nominated by the party even if he or she basically disagrees with that candidate | ☐ | ☐ | ☐ | ☐ |
| • In order to be an effective political force, a party must maintain good working relationships with local interest groups | ☐ | ☐ | ☐ | ☐ |
| • The most important function of a political party is nominating candidates for office | ☐ | ☐ | ☐ | ☐ |
| • Most officeholders are thinking only of what is in it for them | ☐ | ☐ | ☐ | ☐ |
| • Too few good people run for office any more | ☐ | ☐ | | ☐ |
| • Few people know what is in their own best interest in the long run | ☐ | ☐ | ☐ | ☐ |

## Questionnaire 4*

Dear California Party Leader:

This brief questionnaire is part of a scientific inquiry into California political life being conducted at the University of California, Los Angeles. In addition to learning how you view the issues emphasized in the 1980 campaign, we are interested in how you evaluate the problems of party organization and campaign coordination in California.

No more than a few minutes are needed to complete this questionnaire. Your answers will be kept entirely confidential. They will be tabulated and analyzed in quantitative form, solely for scholarly purposes. Thank you for your cooperation in helping us to study the actual workings of California party politics in 1980.

Professor Dwaine Marvick,
Department of Political Science,
University of California, Los Angeles

BACKGROUND

Where were you brought up?

|⎯| Big city |⎯| Suburbs |⎯| Small City |⎯| Village/Farm

|⎯| East |⎯| Midwest |⎯| West |⎯| South |⎯| Abroad

When you were growing up, how active were your parents in community affairs?

|⎯| Very |⎯| Somewhat |⎯| Not active

How strong is your family tradition of being politically active?

|⎯| Strong |⎯| Moderate |⎯| Not at all strong

What are your family's national or ethnic origins? _____

Are you married? _____ How many children? _____

Your main occupation _____ Other _____

Spouse's main occupation _____ Other _____

1980 Family income? _____ Age ____ Sex ____ Race _____

Religious preference? |⎯| Protestant |⎯| Catholic |⎯| Jewish

|⎯| None |⎯| Other

Education: |⎯| No college |⎯| Some college |⎯| Full college

|⎯| Graduate School |⎯| Professional School

Length of California residence: _____ years.

How long lived at present address _____ years.

How long have you been active in party politics? _____ years.

Which political party do you support?

|⎯| Republicans |⎯| Democrats |⎯| Other

*Questionnaire 4 (Los Angeles) is represented here in a slightly modified form from that originally used in the study. Questionnaire 4 was administered as an economical two page, mailed questionnaire version of 8 1/2" by 13", with printing on both sides. The format facilitated easy mailing and return. It was reformatted in this appendix for production purposes. Copies of it in the original format may be obtained from Professor Dwaine Marvick, Department of Political Science, University of California, Los Angeles, Los Angeles, CA 90024.

How strong a partisan would you rate yourself?

Very strong  |__|__|__|__|__|__|__|  Very weak

How much time per week do your currently give to party organization work?

Hours   |__|__|__|__|__|__|__|__|__|__|
       50    40   30   20   10   0

How active are you in voluntary party organizations?

|__| Very active          |__| Somewhat active          |__| Not active

Which _____

Which of the following public offices have you ever sought?

|  | Sought | Held | If successful, when held? |
|---|---|---|---|
| . City-level official? | |__| | |__| | _____ |
| . School board member? | |__| | |__| | _____ |
| . County-level official? | |__| | |__| | _____ |
| . State legislator? | |__| | |__| | _____ |
| . Congressional office | |__| | |__| | _____ |
| . Other? _____ | |__| | |__| | _____ |

Have you ever held an appointive political (non-civil-service) position in

government?    |__| Yes    |__| No

Which of the following party positions have you ever held?

|  |  | WHEN HELD (Years) |
|---|---|---|
| . Local club official | |__| | _____ |
| . District-level official? | |__| | _____ |
| . County central committee? | |__| | _____ |
| . County-level official? | |__| | _____ |
| . State central committee? | |__| | _____ |
| . State-level official? | |__| | _____ |
| . National convention delegate? | |__| | _____ |

If you had the opportunity to take a position of responsibility in the party organization next year, would you do so?

|__| Definitely     |__| Probably     |__| Probably     |__| Definitely
    Yes                                     Not                 Not

How interested in political developments are most of your personal friends?

|__| Very     |__| Somewhat     |__| Not very

How many of your good friends are active in organized politics?

|__| Most     |__| About half     |__| Few

In general terms, how would you describe your assembly district?

- [ ] Republican
- [ ] Competitive
- [ ] Democratic

- [ ] Conservative
- [ ] Moderate
- [ ] Liberal

- [ ] Urban
- [ ] Suburban
- [ ] Rural

- [ ] High income
- [ ] Middle income
- [ ] Low income

- [ ] Large minority blocs
- [ ] Small minority blocs
- [ ] No minority blocs

VARIOUS MODERN CAMPAIGN TACTICS ARE CONTROVERSIAL.
In the 1980 campaign in your assembly district how would you rate each of these tactics?

|  | Good | Fair | Poor |
|---|---|---|---|
| Stress a candidate's personality rather than his stand on issues: | [ ] | [ ] | [ ] |
| Stir up strong emotions rather than be restrained: | [ ] | [ ] | [ ] |
| Meet smear attacks with counter-charges rather than ignore them: | [ ] | [ ] | [ ] |
| Stress group effects rather than community-wide consequences: | [ ] | [ ] | [ ] |
| Stress rival's bad record rather than own performance and plans: | [ ] | [ ] | [ ] |

Financing American campaign activity is increasingly difficult. Which of these methods seems preferable to you? (Please rank from 1 to 4)

- ___ Give parties limited free radio and TV time and mailing privileges
- ___ Rely on large voluntary contributions
- ___ Give parties regular grants from tax money
- ___ Rely on drives for many small contributions

Have you been involved in fund-raising efforts in your district?

[ ] Regularly  [ ] Occasionally  [ ] Never

In efforts to get large contributions?  [ ] Now  [ ] Formerly

To get small donations?  [ ] Now  [ ] Formerly

Thinking only of party workers active in this 1980 campaign, how often in your discussions with them has each of these topics come up:

| | Frequently | Occasionally | Seldom | Never |
|---|---|---|---|---|
| Criticism of a leader in your own party: | [ ] | [ ] | [ ] | [ ] |
| Criticism of a key figure in the rival party: | [ ] | [ ] | [ ] | [ ] |
| Arguments about a public policy: | [ ] | [ ] | [ ] | [ ] |
| Judgments about a fellow campaign worker: | [ ] | [ ] | [ ] | [ ] |
| Know-how for organizing party activities: | [ ] | [ ] | [ ] | [ ] |
| Leads for raising party funds: | [ ] | [ ] | [ ] | [ ] |
| Doubts about a campaign strategy: | [ ] | [ ] | [ ] | [ ] |

Thinking of PEOPLE LIKE YOURSELF who have been ACTIVE IN ORGANIZED POLITICS IN RECENT YEARS, how important is each of these reasons in explaining ...

WHY HAVE THEY BEEN ACTIVE

|  | Very important | Somewhat important | Not important |
|---|---|---|---|
| Influence election results | |_| | |_| | |_| |
| Make social contacts | |_| | |_| | |_| |
| Shape public policies | |_| | |_| | |_| |
| Achieve community recognition | |_| | |_| | |_| |
| Build own political career | |_| | |_| | |_| |
| Gain voice in party affairs | |_| | |_| | |_| |

WHY THEY HAVE STOPPED BEING ACTIVE

|  | Very important | Somewhat important | Not important |
|---|---|---|---|
| No time to spare | |_| | |_| | |_| |
| Other groups take up time | |_| | |_| | |_| |
| Prefer private way of life | |_| | |_| | |_| |
| Tired of campaign work | |_| | |_| | |_| |
| Disillusioned about elections | |_| | |_| | |_| |
| Don´t seem to fit in any more | |_| | |_| | |_| |

Here are some commonly heard statements.

| | strongly agree | agree | disagree | strongly disagree |
|---|---|---|---|---|
| Few people know what is in their own best interest in the long run: | ☐ | ☐ | ☐ | ☐ |
| Elections just don't produce enough good leaders any more: | ☐ | ☐ | ☐ | ☐ |
| Most officeholders are thinking only of what's in it for them: | ☐ | ☐ | ☐ | ☐ |
| To get nominated, most officeseekers make bad commitments: | ☐ | ☐ | ☐ | ☐ |
| A few strong leaders will always run any organization: | ☐ | ☐ | ☐ | ☐ |
| Arguments about policy are beyond the grasp of most voters: | ☐ | ☐ | ☐ | ☐ |
| People are often manipulated by politicians: | ☐ | ☐ | ☐ | ☐ |
| At least half of those active in American political life are corrupt: | ☐ | ☐ | ☐ | ☐ |

Selected Public Issues:

YOUR PERSONAL VIEW:
In this field, the federal government should do:

more    same    less

YOUR FEELING THAT IN THIS ASSEMBLY DISTRICT
probably most DEMOCRATIC VOTERS want the federal government to do:

more    same    less

probably most REPUBLICAN VOTERS want the federal government to do:

more    same    less

Work for nuclear disarmament
Control the cost of living
Cut defense spending
Expand opportunities for poor
Get tough with urban violence
Stop air and water pollution
Desegregate housing and schools
Control illegal traffic in drugs
Eliminate sex discrimination
Achieve workable gun-control laws

In general, do you consider yourself

☐ a radical,
☐ a liberal,
☐ a moderate, or
☐ a conservative?

ON MOST ISSUES, ARE YOU

more liberal    about the same    more conservative

Compared with ...

your close friends?
your neighbors?
other members of your family?
most people where you work?
Democratic party workers you know?
Republican party workers you know?
most people under 30 you know?
most people over 50 you know?
most Democratic voters in this A.D.?
most Republican voters in this A.D.?

# Questionnaire 5

No. _____

Ward Leader Interviews

Dear Ward Leader:

This brief questionnaire is part of scientific inquiry into political party organization in urban areas being conducted by Northwestern University.

We are mainly interested in how you evaluate the problems of party organization and campaign coordination in your area. We also want your estimates of how much you engaged in campaign activity, different kinds of party units and campaign committees during the fall weeks of the 1984 campaign in your district. We also want to learn how you view the issues emphasized in the 1984 campaigns, the strategies of rival candidates and the changing role of organized political parties in recent election years.

No more than a few minutes are needed to complete this questionnaire. Your answers will be kept entirely confidential. They will be tabulated and analyzed in quantitative form, solely for scholarly purposes. Thank you for your cooperation in helping us to study the actual workings of grassroots party politics in 1984.

Professor William Crotty
Department of Political Science
Northwestern University
Evanston, Illinois 60201

Q-1    How long have you lived in Chicago?

_____ YEARS

Q-2    How long have you lived in your present neighborhood?

_____ YEARS

Q-3    How long have you been active in party politics?

_____ YEARS

Q-4    Which political party do you support?  (Circle number)

1.   REPUBLICAN
2.   DEMOCRATIC
3.   OTHER

Q-5    How strong of a partisan are you?  (Circle number)

1.   VERY STRONG
2.   STRONG
3.   MODERATE
4.   WEAK
5.   VERY WEAK

Q-6    How many hours each weak do you give to party organizational work and campaign activities?  (Circle number)

1.   MORE THAN 45 HOURS
2.   35 TO 44 HOURS
3.   25 TO 34 HOURS
4.   15 TO 24 HOURS
5.    5 TO 14 HOURS
6.   LESS THAN 5 HOURS

Q-7    How active are you (if at all) in the following organizations?

|  | Organization Activity (circle best answer for each activity) | | |
|---|---|---|---|
| Precinct committee organization.......VERY | SOMEWHAT | HARDLY | NON-MEMBER |
| Ward committee........................VERY | SOMEWHAT | HARDLY | NON-MEMBER |
| Districtwide party unit...............VERY | SOMEWHAT | HARDLY | NON-MEMBER |
| Countywide party unit.................VERY | SOMEWHAT | HARDLY | NON-MEMBER |
| Other level party unit................VERY | SOMEWHAT | HARDLY | NON-MEMBER |
| (Specify level in margin) | | | |
| Church-related group..................VERY | SOMEWHAT | HARDLY | NON-MEMBER |
| School-related group..................VERY | SOMEWHAT | HARDLY | NON-MEMBER |
| Civic group...........................VERY | SOMEWHAT | HARDLY | NON-MEMBER |
| Neighborhood association/group.......VERY | SOMEWHAT | HARDLY | NON-MEMBER |
| Labor union...........................VERY | SOMEWHAT | HARDLY | NON-MEMBER |
| Veteran's group.......................VERY | SOMEWHAT | HARDLY | NON-MEMBER |
| Environmental protection group.......VERY | SOMEWHAT | HARDLY | NON-MEMBER |
| Anti-abortion group...................VERY | SOMEWHAT | HARDLY | NON-MEMBER |
| Feminist movement group...............VERY | SOMEWHAT | HARDLY | NON-MEMBER |
| Anti-nuclear group....................VERY | SOMEWHAT | HARDLY | NON-MEMBER |
| Other group...........................VERY | SOMEWHAT | HARDLY | NON-MEMBER |
| (Specify group in margin) | | | |

Q-8    Have you ever held any of the following party positions?

|  | Party positions (Circle appropriate answer) | | |
|---|---|---|---|
| Precinct committee or official..........NOW HOLD | HELD IN PAST | NEVER HELD |
| Ward committee or official..............NOW HOLD | HELD IN PAST | NEVER HELD |
| City party committee or official........NOW HOLD | HELD IN PAST | NEVER HELD |
| District committee or official..........NOW HOLD | HELD IN PAST | NEVER HELD |
| County committee or official............NOW HOLD | HELD IN PAST | NEVER HELD |
| State central committee or official.....NOW HOLD | HELD IN PAST | NEVER HELD |
| State convention delegate...............NOW HOLD | HELD IN PAST | NEVER HELD |
| National convention delegate............NOW HOLD | HELD IN PAST | NEVER HELD |

Q-9    Were you in charge of the ward work for your party in the 198  campaign?  (Circle number)

      1.  YES
      2.  NO

Q-10   Have you ever held an appointive (non-civil service) position in government?  (Circle number)

      1.  YES
      2.  NO

Q-11   Have you ever sought any of the following public offices?

|  | Public offices (Circle appropriate answer) | |
|---|---|---|
| City level official...........................YES | NO |
| County level official.........................YES | NO |
| Other local official..........................YES | NO |
| State legislator..............................YES | NO |
| Other state-level office......................YES | NO |
| Congress......................................YES | NO |

Q-12   If you have held any of the following <u>public</u> offices during
       what years did you hold the office?  (Leave blank if office not held)

1.  City level official          _____  TO  _____
2.  County level official        _____  TO  _____
3.  Other local official         _____  TO  _____
4.  State legislator             _____  TO  _____
5.  Other state-level office     _____  TO  _____
6.  Congress                     _____  TO  _____


Q-13   If you had the opportunity to take a position of responsibility in the
       party organization this coming year, would you do so?  (Circle number)

                    1.  DEFIN TELY YES
                    2.  PROBABLY YES
                    3.  PROBABLY NOT
                    4.  DEFIN ELY NOT


Q-14   How interested in political developments are most of your personal
       friends?  (Circle number)

                    1.  VERY INTERESTED
                    2.  SOMEWHAT INTERESTED
                    3.  NOT VERY INTERESTED
                    4.  NOT AT ALL INTERESTED


Q-15   How many of your personal friends are active in organized politics?
       (Circle number)

                    1.  MOST
                    2.  ABOUT HALF
                    3.  FEW
                    4.  NONE


Q-16   Was there ever a time when you thought your party's supporters would
       have been justified in splitting their ballots?  (Circle number)

                    1.  YES
                    2.  NO

Q-17   During the weeks of the 198  campaign this fall, which of the
       following activities did you personally engage in?

|  | Activities engaged in (Circle appropriate answer) | |
|---|---|---|
| Voter registration........................................ | YES | NO |
| Fund raising.............................................. | YES | NO |
| Getting out the vote (election day)...................... | YES | NO |
| Face-to-face canvassing.................................. | YES | NO |
| Telephone canvassing..................................... | YES | NO |
| Literature distribution................................. | YES | NO |
| Other (specify in margin)............................... | YES | NO |

Q-18    During the weeks of the 198  campaign this fall, which of the
following activities were you personally responsible for?

|----------------------------|
| Activities responsible for |
| (Circle appropriate answer) |

Voter registration......................................YES    NO

Fund raising............................................YES    NO

Getting out the vote (election day).....................YES    NO

Face-to-face canvassing.................................YES    NO

Telephone canvassing....................................YES    NO

Literature distribution.................................YES    NO

Other (specify in margin)...............................YES    NO

Q-19    How many co-workers (if any) helped you in the following activities?

Number of helpers

1.   Voter registration                    _____

2.   Fund raising                          _____

3.   Getting out the vote (election day)   _____

4.   Face-to-face canvassing               _____

5.   Telephone canvassing                  _____

6.   Literature distribution               _____

7.   Other (specify in margin)             _____

Q-20    In your ward canvassing activities how many of the voters did
you reach?  (Circle number)

1.   MORE THAN 90%
2.   80% TO 89%
3.   70% TO 79%
4.   60% TO 69%
5.   50% TO 59%
6.   40% TO 49%
7.   30% TO 39%
8.   20% TO 29%
9.   10% TO 19%
10.   LESS THAN 10%

Q-21    In your activity in the campaign this fall did you work specifically
for one candidate?  (Circle number)

1.   YES
2.   NO

Q-22    In you activity in the campaign this fall did you work for the entire
party ticket?  (Circle number)

1.   YES
2.   NO

Q-23    Between the 1978 election and this 198  campaign, how active were
you in party work?  (Circle number)

1.   VERY ACTIVE
2.   SPORADICALLY ACTIVE
3.   NOT ACTIVE

Q-24    How active in party work do expect to be during the coming year?
(Circle number)

1. VERY ACTIVE
2. SPORADICALLY ACTIVE
3. NOT ACTIVE

Q-25    How often do you meet with the following party leaders?

| | Frequency of meetings (Circle appropriate answer) | | |
|---|---|---|---|
| Other ward leaders.....................WEEKLY | MONTHLY | YEARLY | NEVER |
| Precinct party leaders.................WEEKLY | MONTHLY | YEARLY | NEVER |
| District level party leaders...........WEEKLY | MONTHLY | YEARLY | NEVER |
| County level party leaders.............WEEKLY | MONTHLY | YEARLY | NEVER |
| City level party leaders...............WEEKLY | MONTHLY | YEARLY | NEVER |
| State level party leaders..............WEEKLY | MONTHLY | YEARLY | NEVER |

Q-26    What is the best way to become active in politics around here?
(Circle number)

1. WORK FOR A CANDIDATE
2. WORK FOR AN INCUMBENT OFFICIAL
3. BECOME ACTIVE IN LOCAL PARTY ORGANIZATION
4. OTHER (SPECIFY IN MARGIN)

Q-27    In this area, how effective would you say are these ways to persuade
voters?

| | Activity Effectiveness (Circle appropriate answer) | | |
|---|---|---|---|
| Face-to-face canvassing..................VERY | NOT VERY | DON'T KNOW | |
| Telephone canvassing..,.,.,,,...........VERY | NOT VERY | DON'T KNOW | |
| Appearance before groups.................VERY | NOT VERY | DON'T KNOW | |
| Mailout campaign literature..............VERY | NOT VERY | DON'T KNOW | |
| Radio or T.V. ad  ......................VERY | NOT VERY | DON'T KNOW | |
| Billboards and posters...................VERY | NOT VERY | DON'T KNOW | |

Q-28    How much say do ward leaders like you generally have in running your
party's county organization?  (Circle number)

1. A GREAT DEAL
2. A FAIR AMOUNT
3. SOME
4. VERY LITTLE

Q-29    Do you think that ward leaders generally should have more say in
running the county organization, is it about right, or should
they have less say?  (Circle number)

1. MORE SAY
2. ABOUT RIGHT
3. LESS SAY

Q-30    In the last ten years have you personally observed changes in the kinds
of people who give time and effort to party affairs?  (Circle number)

1. YES
2. NO (PLEASE SKIP TO QUESTION 33)

Q-31    If you have observed changes in the kinds of people who give time and effort to party affairs, how extensive have these changes been? (Circle number)

      1. EXTENSIVE
      2. MODERATE
      3. EXIST, BUT HAVE NO DIRECT IMPACT

Q-32    If you have observed changes in the kinds of people who give time and effort to party affairs how beneficial for the party have these changes been? (Circle number)

      1. GOOD FOR THE PARTY
      2. BAD FOR THE PARTY
      3. NO DIFFERENCE EITHER WAY

Q-33    In recent years in Illinois, including 198 , a heavy reliance has been placed on radio and TV "spot" commercials, private opinion polls, fundraising and electioneering by computerized mailing techniques, and campaign management firms.  To what extent have these techniques been utilized in your area?  (Circle number)

      1. TO A LARGE EXTENT
      2. SOMEWHAT
      3. NOT TOO MUCH
      4. NOT AT ALL

Q-34    These newer campaign methods are said to weaken the major role of organized political parties and to discourage people from becomming active in party affairs.  To what extent has this happened in your case?  (Circle number)

      1. TO A LARGE EXTENT
      2. SOMEWHAT
      3. NOT TOO MUCH
      4. NOT AT ALL

Q-35    How active is your party's local organization today compared to ten years ago?  (Circle number)

      1. MORE ACTIVE
      2. ABOUT THE SAME
      3. LESS ACTIVE
      4. DON'T KNOW

Q-36    In general, do you think political parties are stronger, or weaker, today than they were in the past?  (Circle number)

      1. STRONGER
      2. ABOUT THE SAME
      3. WEAKER
      4. DON'T KNOW

Q-37    Here are a few commonly heard statements.  Do you agree or disagree with them?

| | Statement Agreement/Disagreement (Circle appropriate answer) | | |
|---|---|---|---|
| Campaign appeals should be vague enough to attract a broad spectrum of voters...... | STRONGLY AGREE | AGREE | DISAGREE | STRONGLY DISAGREE |
| Only party organization run by a few leaders is really effective............... | STRONGLY AGREE | AGREE | DISAGREE | STRONGLY DISAGREE |
| Elected public officials should be kept strictly accountable to party organization............................. | STRONGLY AGREE | AGREE | DISAGREE | STRONGLY DISAGREE |
| Parties should try to reconcile conflicting views rather than take controversial stands...................... | STRONGLY AGREE | AGREE | DISAGREE | STRONGLY DISAGREE |

Parties should play down some issues if   STRONGLY                              STRONGLY
it will alter their chances of winning.....AGREE   AGREE   DISAGREE   DISAGREE

Widespread participation should be en-      STRONGLY                             STRONGLY
couraged in making most party decisions....AGREE   AGREE   DISAGREE   DISAGREE

Stronger state and national parties are
necessary, even if local units must be     STRONGLY                             STRONGLY
overruled..................................AGREE   AGREE   DISAGREE   DISAGREE

Part-time volunteers play a more
important role in the party's campaign     STRONGLY                             STRONGLY
than any other segment of a party..........AGREE   AGREE   DISAGREE   DISAGREE

Parties should see to it that those who
work for the party get help in the form    STRONGLY                             STRONGLY
of jobs and other things if they need it...AGREE   AGREE   DISAGREE   DISAGREE

In selecting candidates, years of work     STRONGLY                             STRONGLY
for the party should count heavily.........AGREE   AGREE   DISAGREE   DISAGREE

If you disagree with a major stand of      STRONGLY                             STRONGLY
your party, stop working for it............AGREE   AGREE   DISAGREE   DISAGREE

A good party worker must support any
candidate nominated by the party, even
if he or she basically disagrees with      STRONGLY                             STRONGLY
that candidate.............................AGREE   AGREE   DISAGREE   DISAGREE

To be an effective political force, a
party must maintain good working rela-     STRONGLY                             STRONGLY
tionships with local interest groups.......AGREE   AGREE   DISAGREE   DISAGREE

The most important function of a           STRONGLY                             STRONGLY
political party is nominating candidate....AGREE   AGREE   DISAGREE   DISAGREE

Most officeholders are thinking only       STRONGLY                             STRONGLY
of what is in it for them..................AGREE   AGREE   DISAGREE   DISAGREE

Too few good people run for                STRONGLY                             STRONGLY
office any more............................AGREE   AGREE   DISAGREE   DISAGREE

Few people know what is in their own       STRONGLY                             STRONGLY
best interest in the long run..............AGREE   AGREE   DISAGREE   DISAGREE

Arguments about policy are beyond          STRONGLY                             STRONGLY
the grasp of most voters...................AGREE   AGREE   DISAGREE   DISAGREE

My national party should adopt policies to
ensure better representation of women      STRONGLY                             STRONGLY
and minorities.............................AGREE   AGREE   DISAGREE   DISAGREE

Primaries are better than caucuses or
conventions for the selection             STRONGLY                             STRONGLY
of Presidential candidates.................AGREE   AGREE   DISAGREE   DISAGREE

Recent national party reforms have had a   STRONGLY                             STRONGLY
good effect on the workings of my party....AGREE   AGREE   DISAGREE   DISAGREE


BACKGROUND INFORMATION

Q-38    During the years you were growing up, where did you live?  (Circle
        number)

                1.  BIG CITY
                2.  SUBURB
                3.  SMALL CITY
                4.  TOWN
                5.  RURAL AREA

Q-39    In what area of the country did you live?  (Circle number)

            1.  NORTH
            2.  SOUTH
            3.  EAST
            4.  WEST
            5.  MIDWEST
            6.  SOUTHWEST
            7.  NORTHEAST
            8.  ABROAD

Q-40    When you were growing up, how active was your mother in community affairs?  (Circle number)

            1.  VERY
            2.  SOMEWHAT
            3.  NOT AT ALL

Q-41    When you were growing up, how active was your mother in party politics (Circle number)

            1.  VERY
            2.  SOMEWHAT
            3.  NOT AT ALL

Q-42    What is your family's national or ethnic background?

            _____

Q-43    What is your marital status?  (Circle number)

            1.  MARRIED
            2.  DIVORCED
            3.  WIDOW/WIDOWER
            4.  NEVER MARRIED

Q-44    How many children do you have?

            _____

Q-45    What is your spouse's main occupation?

            _____

Q-46    What is your main occupation?

            _____

Q-47    Does your occupation involve any of the following?

| | Occupation Activities (Circle appropriate answer) | | |
|---|---|---|---|
| Dealing with the public | USUALLY SOMETIMES | RARELY | NEVER |
| Coordinating the work of others | USUALLY SOMETIMES | RARELY | NEVER |
| Persuading others and bargaining | USUALLY SOMETIMES | RARELY | NEVER |
| Doing business with the government | USUALLY SOMETIMES | RARELY | NEVER |
| Working with organized groups | USUALLY SOMETIMES | RARELY | NEVER |

Q-48    What was your approximate family income in 1984 before taxes?  (Circle number)

1.  UNDER $4,999
2.  $ 5,000 - $ 9,999
3.  $10,000 - $14,999
4.  $15,000 - $19,999
5.  $20,000 - $24,999
6.  $25,000 - $29,999
7.  $30,000 - $34,999
8.  $35,000 - $39,999
9.  $40,000 - $44,999
10.  $45,000 - $49,999
11.  OVER $50,000

Q-49    In what year were you born?

_____

Q-50    What is your sex?  (Circle number)

1.  MALE
2.  FEMALE

Q-51    What is your race?

_____

Q-52    What is the highest level of education you have achieved? (Circle number)

1.  LESS THAN HIGH SCHOOL
2.  SOME HIGH SCHOOL
3.  HIGH SCHOOL GRADUATE
4.  SOME COLLEGE
5.  COLLEGE GRADUATE
6.  GRADUATE SCHOOL
7.  PROFESSIONAL SCHOOL

Q-53    Religious preference.  (Circle number)

1.  PROTESTANT
2.  CATHOLIC
3.  JEWISH
4.  OTHER _____
5.  NONE

Q-54    How often do you attend religious services?

1.  FREQUENTLY
2.  OCCAS
3.  RARELY
4.  NEVER

Q-55    In general terms how would you describe your ward?  (Circle number in each section)

1.  REPUBLICAN
2.  COMPETITIVE
3.  DEMOCRATIC

1.  CONSERVATIVE
2.  MODERATE
3.  LIBERAL

1.  HIGH INCOME
2.  MIDDLE INCOME
3.  LOW INCOME

Q-55 (continued)

1. MOSTLY WHITE
2. MIXED
3. MOSTLY BLACK

1. MOSTLY PROFESSIONAL/BUSINESS
2. MOSTLY OTHER WHITE COLLAR
3. MIXED
4. MOSTLY BLUE COLLAR

1. MOSTLY PROTESTANT
2. MOSTLY CATHOLIC
3. MOSTLY JEWISH
4. MIXED

1. RAPIDLY CHANGING
2. SLOWLY CHANGING
3. NOT CHANGING

Q-56    People have different ideas about the effectiveness and fairness of modern campaign tactics.  In the 198  campaign in your ward how effective do you feel each of the following tactics were?

|  |
| --- |
| Tactic effectiveness |
| (Circle appropriate answer) |

Stress a candidates personality rather than
his/her stand on issues.........................VERY  SOMEWHAT  NOT AT ALL

Stir up controversy rather than
be restrained..................................VERY  SOMEWHAT  NOT AT ALL

Meet smear attacks with counter charges rather
than ignoring them.............................VERY  SOMEWHAT  NOT AT ALL

Stress self interest rather than community
wide consequences..............................VERY  SOMEWHAT  NOT AT ALL

Stress rival's bad record rather than own
performance and plans..........................VERY  SOMEWHAT  NOT AT ALL

Be specific on issues rather than being
vague on issues................................VERY  SOMEWHAT  NOT AT ALL

Q-57    People have different ideas about the effectiveness and fairness of modern campaign tactics.  In the 198  campaign in your ward how fair do you feel each of the following tactics were?

|  |
| --- |
| Tactic fairness |
| (Circle appropriate answer) |

Stress a candidates personality rather than
his/her stand on issues.........................FAIR  DOUBTFUL  NOT FAIR

Stir up controversy rather than
be restrained..................................FAIR  DOUBTFUL  NOT FAIR

Meet smear attacks with counter charges rather
than ignoring them.............................FAIR  DOUBTFUL  NOT FAIR

Stress self interest rather than community
wide consequences..............................FAIR  DOUBTFUL  NOT FAIR

Stress rival's bad record rather than own
performance and plans..........................FAIR  DOUBTFUL  NOT FAIR

Be specific on issues rather than being
vague on issues................................FAIR  DOUBTFUL  NOT FAIR

Q-58    In general, how liberal or conservative are you?  (Circle number)

1. LIBERAL
2. MODERATE
3. CONSERVATIVE

Q-59    In comparison to the following individuals how liberal or conservative
        are you?

|-------------------------------------------|
|          Liberal/Conservative comparison  |
|             (Circle appropriate answer)   |

your personal friends................MORE LIBERAL   THE SAME   MORE CONSERVATIVE
your neighbors.......................MORE LIBERAL   THE SAME   MORE CONSERVATIVE
other members of your family.........MORE LIBERAL   THE SAME   MORE CONSERVATIVE
most people where you work...........MORE LIBERAL   THE SAME   MORE CONSERVATIVE
Democratic party workers you know....MORE LIBERAL   THE SAME   MORE CONSERVATIVE
Republican party workers you know....MORE LIBERAL   THE SAME   MORE CONSERVATIVE
most Democratic voters in your ward..MORE LIBERAL   THE SAME   MORE CONSERVATIVE
most Republic voters in your ward....MORE LIBERAL   THE SAME   MORE CONSERVATIVE


Q-60    In examining why you yourself have been active in organized politics
        in recent years, how important are the following reasons?

|-------------------------------|
|        Importance of reasons  |
|     (Circle appropriate answer) |

Personal friendship with a candidate.............VERY     SOMEWHAT     NOT AT ALL
A part of my way of life.........................VERY     SOMEWHAT     NOT AT ALL
Strong attachment to my party....................VERY     SOMEWHAT     NOT AT ALL
Friendships & social contact with other workers..VERY     SOMEWHAT     NOT AT ALL
Fun and excitment of campaigns...................VERY     SOMEWHAT     NOT AT ALL
Trying to build a personal career in politics....VERY     SOMEWHAT     NOT AT ALL
Campaign work influences government policies.....VERY     SOMEWHAT     NOT AT ALL
Feeling close to influential people..............VERY     SOMEWHAT     NOT AT ALL
Fulfillment of sense of community obligation.....VERY     SOMEWHAT     NOT AT ALL
Party work helps make business contacts..........VERY     SOMEWHAT     NOT AT ALL
Feeling of recognition in my community...........VERY     SOMEWHAT     NOT AT ALL


Q-61    Which of the above listed reasons best explains why you became
        active in politics?

        _____


Q-62    If you had to drop out of political activity tomorrow, what things
        would you miss most from such work?

        _____
        _____

Q-63    In your opinion, should the federal government do more, the same
        amount or less in each of the following fields?

|  | Government Activity (Circle appropriate answer) | | |
|---|---|---|---|
| Work for nuclear disarmament...............MORE | SAME | LESS | NO OPINION |
| Control the cost of living.................MORE | SAME | LESS | NO OPINION |
| Cut defense spending.......................MORE | SAME | LESS | NO OPINION |
| Expand opportunities for the poor..........MORE | SAME | LESS | NO OPINION |
| Get tough with urban violence..............MORE | SAME | LESS | NO OPINION |
| Stop air and water pollution...............MORE | SAME | LESS | NO OPINION |
| Desegregate housing........................MORE | SAME | LESS | NO OPINION |
| Desegregate schools........................MORE | SAME | LESS | NO OPINION |
| Require energy saving practices............MORE | SAME | LESS | NO OPINION |
| Increase America's military strength........MORE | SAME | LESS | NO OPINION |
| Help Third World countries.................MORE | SAME | LESS | NO OPINION |
| Cut government payrolls....................MORE | SAME | LESS | NO OPINION |
| Push adoption of the ERA ammendment........MORE | SAME | LESS | NO OPINION |
| Cut property taxes.........................MORE | SAME | LESS | NO OPINION |
| Limit imports from other countries.........MORE | SAME | LESS | NO OPINION |

Q-64    How do you feel about the statement that: "The government ought to
        help people get doctors and hospital care at low cost." Should the
        government do this or not?  (Circle number)

            1.  AGREE STRONGLY
            2.  AGREE
            3.  NOT SURE
            4.  DISAGREE
            5.  DISAGREE STRONGLY

Q-65    In your opinion, to run for office in your area, what positions
        should a candidate take regarding government activity in the
        following areas?

|  | Candidate's best stand on government activity (Circle appropriate answer) | | |
|---|---|---|---|
| Work for nuclear disarmament...............MORE | SAME | LESS | NO OPINION |
| Control the cost of living.................MORE | SAME | LESS | NO OPINION |
| Cut defense spending.......................MORE | SAME | LESS | NO OPINION |
| Expand opportunities for the poor..........MORE | SAME | LESS | NO OPINION |
| Get tough with urban violence..............MORE | SAME | LESS | NO OPINION |
| Stop air and water pollution...............MORE | SAME | LESS | NO OPINION |
| Desegregate housing........................MORE | SAME | LESS | NO OPINION |
| Desegregate schools........................MORE | SAME | LESS | NO OPINION |
| Require energy saving practices............MORE | SAME | LESS | NO OPINION |
| Increase America's military strength........MORE | SAME | LESS | NO OPINION |
| Help Third World countries.................MORE | SAME | LESS | NO OPINION |
| Cut government payrolls....................MORE | SAME | LESS | NO OPINION |
| Push adoption of the ERA ammendment........MORE | SAME | LESS | NO OPINION |
| Cut property taxes.........................MORE | SAME | LESS | NO OPINION |
| Limit imports from other countries.........MORE | SAME | LESS | NO OPINION |

Q-66    In my ward, probably <u>most</u> Democratic voters want the federal
        government to do more, <u>less</u> or the same on the following issues.

|---------------------------------------|
| Most Democract voters' position |
| on government activity |
| (Circle appropriate answer) |

| | | | |
|---|---|---|---|
| Work for nuclear disarmament................MORE | SAME | LESS | NO OPINION |
| Control the cost of living.................MORE | SAME | LESS | NO OPINION |
| Cut defense spending.......................MORE | SAME | LESS | NO OPINION |
| Expand opportunities for the poor...........MORE | SAME | LESS | NO OPINION |
| Get tough with urban violence..............MORE | SAME | LESS | NO OPINION |
| Stop air and water pollution...............MORE | SAME | LESS | NO OPINION |
| Desegregate housing........................MORE | SAME | LESS | NO OPINION |
| Desegregate schools........................MORE | SAME | LESS | NO OPINION |
| Require energy saving practices.............MORE | SAME | LESS | NO OPINION |
| Increase America's military strength........MORE | SAME | LESS | NO OPINION |
| Help Third World countries.................MORE | SAME | LESS | NO OPINION |
| Cut government payrolls.....................MORE | SAME | LESS | NO OPINION |
| Push adoption of the ERA ammendment.........MORE | SAME | LESS | NO OPINION |
| Cut property taxes.........................MORE | SAME | LESS | NO OPINION |
| Limit imports from other countries.........MORE | SAME | LESS | NO OPINION |

Q-67    In my ward, probably <u>most</u> Republican voters want the federal
        government to do more, <u>less</u> or the same on the following issues.

|---------------------------------------|
| Most Republican voters' position |
| on government activity |
| (Circle appropriate answer) |

| | | | |
|---|---|---|---|
| Work for nuclear disarmament................MORE | SAME | LESS | NO OPINION |
| Control the cost of living.................MORE | SAME | LESS | NO OPINION |
| Cut defense spending.......................MORE | SAME | LESS | NO OPINION |
| Expand opportunities for the poor...........MORE | SAME | LESS | NO OPINION |
| Get tough with urban violence..............MORE | SAME | LESS | NO OPINION |
| Stop air and water pollution...............MORE | SAME | LESS | NO OPINION |
| Desegregate housing........................MORE | SAME | LESS | NO OPINION |
| Desegregate schools........................MORE | SAME | LESS | NO OPINION |
| Require energy saving practices.............MORE | SAME | LESS | NO OPINION |
| Increase America's military strength........MORE | SAME | LESS | NO OPINION |
| Help Third World countries.................MORE | SAME | LESS | NO OPINION |
| Cut government payrolls.....................MORE | SAME | LESS | NO OPINION |
| Push adoption of the ERA ammendment.........MORE | SAME | LESS | NO OPINION |
| Cut property taxes.........................MORE | SAME | LESS | NO OPINION |
| Limit imports from other countries.........MORE | SAME | LESS | NO OPINION |

# Bibliography:
# Local Political Parties

Adrian, Charles R. "Some General Characteristics of Nonpartisan Elections." *American Political Science Review* 46 (Sept. 1952), 766–76.

———. "A Typology for Nonpartisan Elections." *Western Political Quarterly* 12 (June 1959), 449–58.

Adrian, Charles R., and Oliver Williams. "The Insulation of Local Politics Under the Nonpartisan Ballot." *American Political Science Review* 53 (Dec. 1959), 1052–63.

Allswang, John M. *Bosses, Machines, and Urban Voters*. Port Washington, N.Y.: Kennikat Press/National Univ. Publications, 1977.

Althoff, Phillip, and Samuel C. Patterson. "Political Activism in a Rural County." *Midwest Journal of Political Science* 10 (Feb. 1966), 39–51.

American Political Science Association. *Toward A More Responsible Two-Party System*. New York: Rinehart, 1950.

Arterton, F. Christopher. *Media Politics*. Lexington, Mass.: Lexington Books/D.C. Heath, 1984.

Banfield, Edward C. *Big City Politics*. New York: Random House, 1965.

———. *Political Influence*. New York: Free Press, 1961.

Banfield, Edward C., and James Q. Wilson. *City Politics*. New York: Vintage, 1963.

Beck, Paul A., "Environment and Party: The Impact of Political and Demographic County Characteristics on Party Behavior." *American Political Science Review* 68 (Sept. 1974), 1229–44.

Berelson, Bernard R., Paul F. Lazarsfeld, and William McPhee. *Voting*. Chicago: Univ. of Chicago Press, 1954.

Bibby, John F. "Party Renewal in the National Republican Party." In *Party Renewal in America*, ed. Gerald M. Pomper, pp. 102–15. New York: Praeger, 1980.

Biles, Roger. *Big City Boss*. DeKalb: Northern Illinois Univ. Press, 1984.

Bledsoe, Timothy, and Susan Welch. "Patterns of Political Party Activity Among

U.S. Cities." Paper prepared for Annual Meeting of Midwest Political Science Association, Chicago, April 1985.

Bone, Hugh A. *Grass Roots Party Leadership*. Seattle: Bureau of Governmental Research and Services, Univ. of Washington, 1952.

Bowman, Lewis, and G.R. Boynton. "Activities and Role Definitions of Grass Roots Party Officials." *Journal of Politics* 28 (Feb. 1966), 121–43.

Bowman, Lewis, Dennis Ippolito, and William Donaldson. "Incentives for the Maintenance of Grassroots Political Activism." *Midwest Journal of Political Science* 13 (Feb. 1969), 126–39.

Bridges, Amy. *A City in the Republic*. Cambridge: Cambridge University Press, 1984.

Broder, David S. *The Party's Over*. New York: Harper and Row, 1971.

Browder, Glen, and Dennis Ippolito. "The Suburban Party Activist: The Case of Southern Amateurs." *Social Science Quarterly* 53 (June 1972), 168–75.

Bryce, James. *The American Commonwealth*. New York: Macmillan, 1888.

Burnham, Walter Dean. *Critical Elections and the Mainsprings of American Politics*. New York: Norton, 1970.

————. *The Current Crisis in American Politics*. New York: Oxford Univ. Press, 1982.

————. "Revitalization and Decay: Looking Toward the Third Century of American Electoral Politics." *Journal of Politics* 38 (1976), 146–72.

Burrell, Barbara. "Local Party Officials in Connecticut and Michigan." Ph.D. diss. University of Michigan, 1982.

Carney, Francis. *The Rise of the Democratic Clubs in California*. New Brunswick, N.J.: Eagleton Foundation, 1958.

Clark, Peter, and James Q. Wilson. "Incentive Systems: A Theory of Organization." *Administrative Quarterly* 6 (1961), 136–46.

Constantini, Edward, and Kenneth Craik. "Competing Elites Within a Political Party: A Study of Republican Leadership." *Western Political Quarterly* 22 (Dec. 1969), 879–903.

Conway, M. Margaret, and Frank B. Feigert. "Motivation, Incentive Systems, and the Political Organization." *American Political Science Review* 62 (Dec. 1968), 1159–73.

————. "Incentives and Task Performance of Party Precinct Workers." *Western Political Quarterly* 27 (Dec. 1974), 693–709.

Cornwell, Elmer C. "Bosses, Machines, and Ethnic Groups." *Annals of the American Academy of Political and Social Science* 353 (May 1964), 27–39.

Costikyan, Edward. *Behind Closed Doors*. New York: Harcourt, Brace, 1966.

Cotter, Cornelius P., and John F. Bibby. "Institutional Development of Parties and the Thesis of Party Decline." *Political Science Quarterly* 95 (Spring 1980), 1–27.

Cotter, Cornelius P., James L. Gibson, John F. Bibby, and Robert J. Huckshorn. *Party Organizations in American Politics*. New York: Praeger, 1984.

Cotter, Cornelius P., James L. Gibson, Robert J. Huckshorn, and John F. Bibby. "The Condition of the Party Organizations at the State Level: State-Local Party

Integration." Paper prepared for Annual Meeting of the Southern Political Science Association, Savannah, Nov. 1984.

Crotty, William. *American Parties in Decline*, 2d ed. Boston: Little, Brown, 1984.

————."Party Effort and Its Impact on the Vote." *American Political Science Review* 65 (June 1971), 439–50.

————. *The Party Game*. New York: W.H. Freeman, 1985.

————. "The Party Organization and Its Activities." In *Approaches to the Study of Party Organization*, ed. William Crotty, 247–306. Boston: Allyn and Bacon, 1968.

————. *Party Reform*. New York: Longman, 1983.

————, ed. *Paths to Political Reform*. Lexington, Mass.: Lexington Books/D.C. Heath, 1980.

————. *Political Reform and the American Experiment*. New York: Thomas Y. Crowell, 1977.

Crotty, William, and John S. Jackson, III. *Presidential Primaries and Nominations*. Washington, D.C.: CQ Press, 1985.

Curley, James M. *I'd Do It Again*. Englewood Cliffs, N.J.: Prentice-Hall, 1957.

Cutright, Phillips. "Activities of Precinct Committeemen in Partisan and Nonpartisan Communities." *Western Political Quarterly* 17 (March 1964), 93–108.

————. "Measuring the Impact of Local Party Activity in the General Election Vote." *Public Opinion Quarterly* 27 (Fall 1963), 372–86.

————. "Nonpartisan Electoral Systems in American Cities." *Comparative Studies in Society and History* 5 (Jan. 1963), 212–26.

Cutright, Phillips, and Peter H. Rossi. "Grass Roots Politicians and the Vote." *American Sociological Review* 23 (April 1958), 171–79.

Czudnowski, Moshe M. "Introduction: A Statement of the Issues." In *Does Who Governs Matter?*, ed. Moshe Czudnowski, pp. 3–12. DeKalb: Northern Illinois Univ. Press, 1982.

————. "Political Recruitment." In *Handbook of Political Science, Volume 2: Micropolitical Theory*, ed. Fred I. Greenstein and Nelson W. Polsby, pp. 155–242. Reading, Mass.: Addison-Wesley, 1975.

————. "Toward a Second Generation of Empirical Elite and Leadership Studies." In *Political Elites and Social Change*, ed. Moshe Czudnowski, pp. 243–55. De Kalb: Northern Illinois Univ. Press, 1983.

Dahl, Robert. *Who Governs?* New Haven: Yale Univ. Press, 1961.

David, Paul T. *Party Strength in the United States, 1790–1971*. Charlottesville: Univ. of Virginia Press, 1972.

Dennis, Jack. "Changing Public Support for the American Party System." In *Paths to Political Reform*, ed. William Crotty, pp. 35–66. Lexington, Mass.: Lexington Books/D.C. Heath, 1980.

Dorsett, Lyle W. *Franklin D. Roosevelt and the City Bosses*. Port Washington, N.Y.: Kennikat Press/National Univ. Publications, 1977.

————. *The Pendergast Machine*. Cambridge: Oxford Univ. Press, 1968.

Downs, Anthony. *An Economic Theory of Democracy*. New York: Harper, 1957.

Dudley, Robert L. and Alan R. Gitelson. "Alternative Models of Party Organization." Paper prepared for Annual Meeting of the Southern Political Science Association, Savannah, Nov. 1984.

Duverger, Maurice. *Political Parties*. New York: Wiley, 1954.

Ebner, Michael H., and Eugene M. Tobin, eds. *The Age of Urban Reform*. Port Washington, N.Y.: Kennikat Press/National Univ. Publications, 1977.

Eckstein, Harry. "Party Systems." In *International Encyclopedia of the Social Sciences*, pp. 436–453. New York: Macmillan, 1968.

Eldersveld, Samuel J. "Changes in Elite Composition and the Survival of Party Systems: The German Case." In *Does Who Governs Matter?*, ed. Moshe Czudnowski, pp. 68–89. DeKalb: Northern Illinois Univ. Press, 1982.

————. "The Condition of Party Organization at the Local Level." Paper prepared for Annual Meeting of the Southern Political Science Association, Savannah, Nov. 1984.

————. "Motivations for Party Activism: Multi-National Uniformities and Differences." *International Political Science Review* 4 (1983), 57–70.

————. "Political Elite Linkages in the Dutch Consociational System." In *Linkage and Political Parties*, ed. Kay Lawson, pp. 157–82. New Haven: Yale Univ. Press, 1979.

————. *Political Parties: A Behavioral Analysis*. Chicago: Rand McNally, 1964.

————. *Political Parties in American Society*. New York: Basic, 1982.

Eldersveld, Samuel J., and Bashiruddin Ahmed. *Citizen and Politics: Mass Political Behavior in India*. Chicago: Univ. of Chicago Press, 1978.

Eldersveld, Samuel J., Jan Kooiman, and Theo van der Tak. *Elite Images of Dutch Politics*. Ann Arbor: Univ. of Michigan Press, 1981.

Eldersveld, Samuel J., and Dwaine Marvick. "Work on the Origins, Activities, and Attitudes of Party Activists." *International Political Science Review* 4 (1983), 11–12.

Epstein, Leon. "Political Parties." In *Handbook of Political Science, Volume 4: Nongovernmental Politics*, ed. Fred I. Greenstein and Nelson W. Polsby, pp. 229–77. Reading, Mass.: Addison-Wesley, 1975.

————. *Political Parties in Western Democracies*. New York: Praeger, 1967.

————. "The Scholarly Commitment to Parties." In *Political Science: The State of the Discipline*, ed. Ada Finifter, pp. 127–54. Washington, D.C.: American Political Science Association, 1983.

Forthal, Sonya. *Cogwheels of Democracy*. New York: William-Frederick Press, 1946.

Frost, Richard T. "Stability and Change in Local Party Politics." *Public Opinion Quarterly* 25 (Summer 1961), 221–35.

Fuchs, Ester R. "Mayor Daley and the 'City That Works'?" Paper prepared for Annual Meeting of the American Political Science Association, Washington, D.C., 1979.

Fuchs, Ester K., and Robert Y. Shapiro. "Government Performance as a Basis of Machine Support." New York: Columbia Univ. Memo, June 1981.

Gibson, James L., Cornelius P. Cotter, John F. Bibby, and Robert J. Huckshorn. "Assessing Party Organizational Strength." *American Journal of Political Science* 27 (May 1983), 193–222.

_____. "Whither the Local Parties?: A Cross-Sectional and Longitudinal Analysis of the Strength of Party Organizations." *American Journal of Political Science* 29 (Feb. 1985), 139–60.

Gibson, James L., John P. Frendreis, and Laura L. Vertz. "Party Dynamics in the 1980s: Changes in County Party Organizational Strength, 1980–1984." Paper prepared for Annual Meeting of the Midwest Political Science Association, Chicago, April 1985.

Gibson, James L., and Gregg W. Smith. "Local Party Organizations and Electoral Outcomes: Linkages Between Parties and Elections." Paper prepared for Annual Meeting of the American Political Science Association, Washington, D.C., Sept. 1984.

Gilbert, Charles. "Some Aspects of Nonpartisan Elections in Large Cities." *Midwest Journal of Political Science* 6 (Nov. 1962), 346–54.

Gilbert, Charles, and Christopher Clague. "Electoral Competition and Electoral Systems in Large Cities." *Journal of Politics* 24 (May 1962).

Golembiewski, Robert T., William Welsh, and William Crotty. *A Methodological Primer for Political Scientists.* Chicago: Rand McNally, 1969.

Gosnell, Harold F. *Machine Politics: Chicago Model.* Chicago: Univ. of Chicago Press, 1937, rpt. 1968.

Gottfried, Alex. *Boss Cermak of Chicago.* Seattle: Univ. of Washington Press, 1962.

Gove, Samuel K., and Louis H. Masotti, eds. *After Daley: Chicago Politics in Transition.* Urbana: Univ. of Illinois Press, 1982.

Grimshaw, William J. *Black Politics in Chicago: The Quest for Leadership, 1929–1979.* Chicago: Loyola Univ. Center for Urban Policy, 1980.

_____. "The Daley Legacy: A Declining Politics of Party, Race, and Public Unions." In *After Daley,* ed. Samuel K. Gove and Louis H. Masotti, pp. 57–87. Urbana: Univ. of Illinois Press, 1982.

_____. *Union Rule in the Schools: Big-City Politics in Transformation.* Lexington, Mass.: Lexington Books/D.C. Heath, 1979.

Guterbock, Thomas M. "Community Attachment and Machine Politics: Voting Patterns in Chicago Wards." *Social Science Quarterly* 60 (1979), 185–202.

_____. *Machine Politics in Transition.* Chicago: Univ. of Chicago Press, 1980.

Harder, Marvin, and Thomas Ungs. "Notes Toward a Functional Analysis of Local Party Organizations." Paper prepared for Annual Meeting of the Midwest Political Science Association, Chicago, April 1963.

Harmel, Robert, and Kenneth Janda. *Parties and Their Environments: Limits to Reform?* New York: Longman, 1982.

Hawley, Willis D. *Non-Partisan Elections and the Case for Party Politics.* New York: Wiley, 1973.

Hennessey, Bernard. "On the Study of Party Organization." In *Approaches to the*

*Study of Party Organization*, ed. W. Crotty, pp. 1–44. Boston: Allyn and Bacon, 1968.

Hershkowitz, Leo. *Tweed's New York: Another Look*. Garden City, N.Y.: Anchor Books, 1978.

Hirschfield, Robert S., Bert E. Swanson, and Blanche D. Blank. "A Profile of Political Activists in Manhattan." *Western Political Quarterly* 15 (Sept. 1962), 489–506.

Hofstetter, C. Richard. "The Amateur Politician: A Problem in Construct Validation." *Midwest Journal of Political Science* 15 (Feb. 1971), 34–50.

————. "Organizational Activists: The Basis of Participation in Amateur and Professional Groups." *American Politics Quarterly* 1 (1973), 244–76.

Holli, Melvin, and Paul Green, eds. *The Making of a Mayor*. Grand Rapids, Mich.: Eerdmans, 1984.

Huckshorn, Robert J. *Party Leadership in the States*. Amherst: Univ. of Massachusetts Press, 1976.

Ippolito, Dennis. "Motivational Reorientation and Change Among Party Activists." *Journal of Politics* 31 (Nov. 1969), 126–39.

Jackson, John S., III. "The Party's Not Over: It Has Just Moved to a New Place." Paper prepared for Annual Meeting of the Southern Political Science Association, Savannah, 1984.

————. "Political Party Leaders and the Mass Public: 1980–1984." Paper prepared for Annual Meeting of the Midwest Political Science Association, Chicago, April 1985.

Jackson, John S., III, and Robert Hitlin. "A Comparison of Party Elites." *American Politics Quarterly* 4 (Oct. 1976), 441–81.

Janda, Kenneth. *Political Parties: A Cross-National Survey*. New York: Free Press, 1980.

Jewell, Malcolm E., and David M. Olson. *American State Political Parties*, 2d ed. Homewood, Ill.: Dorsey, 1982.

Joseph, Laurence. "Neoconservatism in Contemporary Political Science: Democratic Theory and the Party System." *Journal of Politics* 44 (1982), 955–82.

Katz, Daniel, and Samuel E. Eldersveld. "The Impact of Local Party Activity Upon the Electorate." *Public Opinion Quarterly* 25 (Spring 1961), 1–24.

Kennedy, Eugene E. *Himself: The Life and Times of Richard J. Daley*. New York: Viking, 1978.

Kent, Frank R. *The Great Game of Politics*. Garden City, N.Y.: Doubleday, 1928.

Key, V.O., Jr. *Politics, Parties, and Pressure Groups*, 5th ed. New York: Thomas Y. Crowell, 1964.

————. *Southern Politics in State and Nation*. 1949; rpt. Knoxville: Univ. of Tennessee Press, 1984.

Kirkpatrick, Jeane J. *Dismantling the Parties*. Washington, D.C.: American Enterprise Institute, 1978.

Kleppner, Paul. *Chicago Divided: The Making of a Black Mayor*. DeKalb: Northern Illinois Univ. Press, 1985.

Kramer, Gerald H. "The Effects of Precinct-Level Canvassing on Voter Behavior." *Public Opinion Quarterly* 34 (1970), 560–72.

Kurtzman, David H. *Methods of Controlling Votes in Philadelphia.* Philadelphia: Univ. of Pennsylvania Press, 1935.

Lawson, Kay, ed. *Linkage and Political Parties.* New Haven: Yale Univ. Press, 1979.

Lee, Eugene C. *The Politics of Nonpartisanship.* Berkeley: Univ. of California Press, 1960.

Leiserson, Avery. *Parties and Politics.* New York: Knopf, 1958.

Longley, Charles H. "National Party Renewal." In *Party Renewal in America*, ed. Gerald M. Pomper, pp. 69–86. New York: Praeger, 1980.

———. "Party Nationalization in America." In *Paths to Political Reform*, ed. William Crotty, pp. 167–205. Lexington, Mass.: Lexington Books/ D.C. Heath, 1980.

———. "Party Reform and Party Nationalization: The Case of the Democrats." In *The Party Symbol*, ed. William Crotty, pp. 359–78. San Francisco: W.H. Freeman, 1980.

Lowi, Theodore. "Toward Functionalism in Political Science: The Case of Innovation in Party Systems." *American Political Science Review* 57 (Sept. 1963), 570–83.

Mandelbaum, Seymour J. *Boss Tweed's New York.* New York: Wiley, 1965.

Marvick, Dwaine. "Continuities in Recruitment Theory and Research: Toward a New Model." In *Elite Recruitment in Democratic Politics*, ed. H. Eulau and M. Czudnowski, pp. 29–44. Beverly Hills: Sage, 1976.

———. "Ideological Thinking Among Party Activists: Findings from India, Germany, and America." *International Political Science Quarterly* 4 (1983), 94–106.

———. "Introduction: Political Decision-Makers in Contrasting Milieus." In *Political Decision-Makers*, ed. D. Marvick, pp. 13–28. New York: Free Press, 1961.

———. "The Middlemen of Politics." In *Approaches to the Study of Party Organization*, ed. William Crotty, pp. 341–74. Boston: Allyn and Bacon, 1968.

———. "Party Activists in Los Angeles, 1963–1978: How Well-Matched Rivals Shape Election Options." In *Political Elites and Social Change*, ed. Moshe Czudnowski, pp. 64–101. DeKalb: Northern Illinois Univ. Press, 1983.

———. "Party Organizational Personnel and Electoral Democracy in Los Angeles, 1963–1972." In *The Party Symbol*, ed. William Crotty, pp. 63–86. San Francisco: W.H. Freeman, 1980.

———. "Political Linkage Functions of Rival Party Activists in the United States: Los Angeles, 1969–1974." In *Linkage and Political Parties*, ed. Kay Lawson, pp. 100–28. New Haven: Yale Univ. Press, 1979.

———. "Political Recruitment and Careers." In *International Encyclopedia of the Social Sciences*, 12: 273–82. New York: Macmillan, 1968.

———. "Recruitment Patterns of Campaign Activists in India: Legislative Candidates, Public Notables, and the Organizational Personnel of Rival Parties." In

*Elite Recruitment in Democratic Polities,* ed. Heinz Eulau and Moshe Czudnowski, pp. 133–162. Beverly Hills: Sage, 1976.

Marvick, Dwaine, and Samuel J. Eldersveld, eds. "Party Activists in Comparative Perspective." Symposium in *International Political Science Review* 4:1 (1983), pp. 11–12.

Marvick, Dwaine, and Charles Nixon. "Recruitment Contrasts in Rival Campaign Groups." In *Political Decision-Makers,* ed. D. Marvick, pp. 193–217. New York: Free Press, 1961.

Matthews, Donald R. *The Social Background of Political Decision-Makers.* Garden City, N.Y.: Doubleday, 1954.

Merton, Robert K. *Social Theory and Social Structure.* New York: Free Press, 1957.

Meyerson, Martin, and Edward C. Banfield. *Politics, Planning, and the Public Interest.* Glencoe, Ill.: Free Press, 1955.

Michels, Robert. *Political Parties.* 1915; rpt. New York: Dover Publications, 1959.

Miller, Zane L. *Boss Cox's Cincinnati.* Cambridge: Oxford Univ. Press, 1968.

Mladenka, Kenneth R. "The Urban Bureaucracy and the Chicago Political Machine: Who Gets What and Limits to Political Control." In *After Daley,* ed. Samuel K. Gove and Louis H. Masotti, pp. 146–58. Urbana: Univ. of Illinois Press.

Mosca, Gaetano. *The Ruling Class.* Ed. A. Livingston and trans. H.D. Kahn. New York: McGraw-Hill, 1939.

Mosher, William E. "Party and Government Control at the Grass Roots." *National Municipal Review* 24 (Jan. 1935), 15–18.

O'Connor, Len. *Clout: Mayor Daley and His City.* Chicago: Henry Regnery, 1975.
————. *Requiem: The Decline and Demise of Mayor Daley and His Era.* Chicago: Contemporary Books, 1977.

Olson, Mancur. *The Logic of Collective Action.* Cambridge: Harvard Univ. Press, 1965, 1971.

Ostrogorski, M. *Democracy and the Organization of Political Parties, Volume II: The United States.* Ed. and abridged by S.M. Lipset. New York: Anchor Books, 1964.

Ostrom, Elinor. "An Agenda for the Study of Institutions." Paper prepared for Annual Meeting of the Midwest Political Science Association, Chicago, 1984.

Pareto, Vilfred. *The Mind and Society.* Ed. and trans. A. Livingston. New York: Harcourt, Brace, 1935.

Patterson, Samuel C. "Characteristics of Party Leaders." *Western Political Quarterly* 16 (June 1963), 332–52.

Peel, Roy V. *The Political Clubs of New York City.* New York: Putnam, 1935.

Pomper, Gerald M. "The Decline of Party in American Elections." *Political Science Quarterly* 92 (1977), 21–42.
————, ed. *Party Renewal in America.* New York: Praeger, 1980.

Putnam, Robert D. *The Comparative Study of Political Elites.* Englewood Cliffs, N.J.: Prentice-Hall, 1976.

Rakove, Milton. *Don't Make No Waves . . . Don't Back No Losers*. Bloomington: Indiana Univ. Press, 1975.

————. *We Don't Want Nobody Nobody Sent*. Bloomington: Indiana Univ. Press, 1979.

Reif, Karlheinz, and Roland Cayrol, eds. *European Elections Study: European Political Parties' Middle-Level Elites Project*. Mannheim: Institut fur Sozialwissenschaften und Europa-Institut, Universitat Mannheim, Aug. 1981.

Riordan, William L. *Plunkitt of Tammany Hall*. New York: Dutton, 1963.

Salisbury, Robert A. "The Urban Party Organization Member." *Public Opinion Quarterly* 29 (Winter 1965–66), 550–64.

Saloma, John S., III, and Frederick H. Sontag. *Parties: The Real Opportunity for Effective Citizen Politics*. New York: Knopf, 1972.

Salter, J.T. *Boss Rule*. New York: McGraw-Hill, 1935.

Sartori, Giovanni. *Parties and Party Systems: A Framework for Analysis*. New York: Oxford Univ. Press, 1976.

Scarrow, Howard A. "Have Primary Elections Caused Party Decline?: The Evidence From New York." Paper prepared for Annual Meeting of the Midwest Political Science Association, Chicago, April 1984.

————. "The Function of Political Parties: A Critique of the Literature and Approach." *Journal of Politics* 29 (Nov. 1967), 770–90.

Schattschneider, E.E. *Party Government*. New York: Rinehart, 1942.

Schlesinger, Joseph. *Ambition and Politics*. Chicago: Rand McNally, 1966.

————. "On the Theory of Party Organization." *Journal of Politics* 46 (1983), 369–400.

————. "Party Units." In *International Encyclopedia of the Social Sciences*, pp. 428–36. New York: Macmillan, 1968.

————. "Political Party Organization." In *Handbook of Organizations*, ed. James G. March, pp.764–801. Chicago: Rand McNally, 1965.

Schumpeter, Joseph A. *Capitalism, Socialism and Democracy*, 3d ed. New York: Harper, 1950.

Shefter, Martin. "The Emergence of the Political Machine: An Alternative View." In *Theoretical Perspectives on Urban Politics*, ed. Willis Hawley, pp.14–44. Englewood Cliffs, N.J.: Prentice-Hall, 1976.

Sorauf, Frank J. *Party Politics in America*, 5th ed. Boston: Little, Brown, 1984.

Stone, Clarence N. "Elite Theory and Political Evaluation: Is Elite Theory Worth Reclaiming?" Paper prepared for Annual Meeting of the Midwest Political Science Association, Chicago, April 1985.

Tarr, Joel Arthur. *A Study in Boss Politics: William Lorimer of Chicago*. Urbana: Univ. of Illinois Press, 1971.

Tsebelis, George. "Parties as Two-Step Collective Action Problems." Paper prepared for Annual Meeting of the Midwest Political Science Association, Chicago, 1985.

Ware, Alan. *The Breakdown of Democratic Party Organization, 1960–1980*. New York: Oxford Univ. Press, 1985.

Wattenberg, Martin P. *The Decline of American Political Parties, 1952-1980.* Cambridge: Harvard Univ. Press, 1984.

Weaver, Leon. "Some Soundings in the Party System: Rural Precinct Committeemen." *American Political Science Review* 34 (Feb. 1940), 76-84.

Weber, Max. *The Theory of Social and Economic Organization.* New York: Oxford Univ. Press, 1947.

Weber, Ronald E. "Competitive and Organizational Dimensions of American State Party Systems." Paper delivered at Annual Meeting of the Northeastern Political Science Association, Boston, 1969.

Weber, Ronald E., and T. Wayne Parent. "National Versus State Effects on State and Local Elections." Paper prepared for Annual Meeting of the Midwest Political Science Association, Chicago, April 1985.

Weinberg, Lee S. "Stability and Change Among Pittsburgh Precinct Politicians, 1954-1970." *Social Science* 50 (1975), 10-16.

Weinberg, Lee S., Michael Margolis, and David F. Ranck. "Local Party Organization: From Disaggregation to Disintegration." Paper prepared for Annual Meeting of the American Political Science Association, Washington, D.C., Sept. 1980.

Wendt, Lloyd and Herman Kogan. *Bosses in Lusty Chicago.* Bloomington: Indiana Univ. Press, 1971.

Wilson, James Q. *The Amateur Democrat.* Chicago: Univ. of Chicago Press, 1962.

————, ed. *City Politics and Public Policy.* New York: Wiley, 1968.

————. *Negro Politics: The Search for Leadership.* New York: Free Press, 1960.

————. *Political Organizations.* New York: Basic Books, 1974.

Wolfinger, Raymond E. "The Influence of Precinct Work on Voting Behavior." *Public Opinion Quarterly* 27 (Fall 1963), 387-98.

————. "Why Political Machines Have Not Withered Away and Other Revisionist Thoughts." *Journal of Politics* 34 (1972), 365-98.

Wood, Robert C. *Suburbia.* Boston: Houghton Mifflin, 1958.

Zink, Harold. *City Bosses in the United States.* Durham, N.C.: Duke Univ. Press, 1930.

# About the Authors

*William Crotty* is professor of political science and research associate, Center for Urban Affairs and Policy Research, Northwestern University. His books include *The Party Game*, *Party Reform*, and *Decision for the Democrats*. He has written on political party organization and operation and on comparative electoral behavior.

*Samuel J. Eldersveld* is author of *Political Parties: A Behavioral Analysis*, *Citizens and Politics: Mass Political Behavior in India* (with Bashiruddin Ahmed), and *Elite Images of Dutch Politics: Accommodations and Conflict* (with Jan Kooiman and Theo van der Tak). He has been professor of political science at the University of Michigan since 1946, specializing in political parties and comparative elite and mass political behavior.

*Anne H. Hopkins* is assistant provost and professor of political science at the University of Tennessee, Knoxville. She has served as assistant to the chancellor. She is author of *Work and Job Satisfaction in the Public Sector* and *Issues in the Tennessee Constitution*, and co-author of *Individuals, Unionization, the Work Situation and Job Satisfaction: A Five State Comparative Analysis* and *Tennessee Votes: 1796–1976*; as well, she has made numerous contributions to journals and symposia. She is a member of the editorial boards of the *Journal of Politics*, *American Politics Quarterly*, and *Administration and Society*. Her teaching and research interests include state politics, political parties, elections, and intergovernmental relations.

*Dwaine Marvick* has been professor of political science at the University of California at Los Angeles since 1954. He is author of *Competitive Pressures and Democratic Consent* (with Morris Janowitz) and *Career Perspectives in a Bureaucratic Setting*, and editor of *Political Decision Makers: Recruitment and Performance* and *Harold D. Lasswell On Political Sociology*; as well, he has numerous articles and contributions to journals and compendiums. He is secretary for the Research Committee on Political Elites of the International Political Science Association, and he has served on committees of the National Academy of Sciences and the National Science Foundation. His research interests include the comparative and longitudinal study of political parties; elite ideological values, motivations, and recruitment patterns; and the political behavior of mass electorates.

*Richard W. Murray* is professor of political science at the University of Houston. He is co-author of *Texas Politics* and operates a political consulting business. His areas of concern include political parties, elections, state politics, campaigning, and methodology.

*Kent L. Tedin* is professor of political science at the University of Houston. He is co-author of *American Public Opinion* and has published over twenty articles, chapter contributions, and reports in such journals as the *American Political Science Review, American Journal of Political Science, Journal of Politics, Public Opinion Quarterly*, and *American Politics Quarterly*. His academic specializations include public opinion, elections, and research methods.

# Index

activists. *See* party activists

affectual exchange model of party behavior, 13

Arvey, Jake, 168, 170, 171

Baker, Howard, 66

Beck, Paul A., 3

billboards and posters, 49, 185–86

Blank, Blanch D., 9

Bone, Hugh A., 9

Bowman, Lewis, 9

Boynton, G.R., 9

Bibby, John F., 3

Burke, Edmund, 60

Burke, Edward M., 168, 171, 172

Burnham, Walter Dean, 2

Byrne, Jane, 193

campaign activities, 29–30; *see also* Chicago; Detroit; Houston; Los Angeles; Nashville

campaign literature, 49, 76, 179, 185

candidate-centered organizations, 2, 5, 79

canvassing, 48–49, 76, 108–9, 144, 185–86, 189

CBS/New York *Times* poll, 56

Center for Political Studies, 3

Center for Public Policy, 40, 57, 59

Chicago, local party operations

—brokerage function of precinct captains, 13

—campaign activities, 179–81

—characteristics of party activists, 158–63, 188–89

—decision-making patterns, 176–82

—effects of new campaign technology, 181–82

—as example of local party adjustment, 5

—high level of organization development, 25

—machine politicians over time, 169–72

—machine strength, 14, 191–93

—motivation for political involvement, 172–75

—organizational involvement by activists, 166–69

—party operations, 189–91

—party structure, 176–77

—party tasks, 185–86

—political background of activists, 164–68, 188–89

—political in-breeding, 173

—profile of, 23–25

—services offered by ward organizations, 14, 182–83

108, 145, 187, 189; *see also* Chicago;
Detroit; Houston; Los Angeles;
Nashville
ethnicity, impact on voting behavior,
24; *see also* Chicago; Detroit;
Houston; Los Angeles; Nashville
Epton, Bernard, 193
Equal Rights Amendment, 56

federal funding of races, 2
Feigert, Frank B., 9
"floating" vote, 149
Florida, party clashes in, 60
Forthal, Sonya, 9
Frost, Richard T. 13
frost belt 5, 23; *see also* Detroit
fundraising, 49, 76, 86, 109, 144, 187

get-out-the-vote activities. *See* election
day get-out-the-vote
Gibson, James L., 3
Goldwater, Barry, 60
Gosnell, 2, 8, 9, 12–13, 164
Guterbock, Thomas M., 13, 14

Harris County. *See* Houston
Heard, Jack, 59
help for the poor, as an issue to
activists in Los Angeles, 141
Hirchfield, Robert S., 9
Hopkins, Anne H., 24; Nashville study,
65–88
house to house canvassing. *See*
canvassing
Houston, local party operations
—campaign activities in 1980, 47–48
—commitment to party, 53–54
—demographic characteristics,
40–41
—emerging Republican strength, 5
—evaluation of party operations by
party leaders, 51–54

—fundraising, Republican advantage in, 48
—ideology and issue positions,
54–58
—interpretation of party change,
56–60
—level of campaign activity, 48–50
—motivation for political involvement, 50–51
—party activists, characteristics of,
43–46
—party activists, political background of, 46–47
—party organization, 40
—party tasks, 48–49
—Republican gains, 42, 48
—voting patterns, 41–43
Huckshorn, Robert J., 3

ideology: political issues and Chicago
activists, 168–69, 173–75, 191;
positions of activists in Houston,
54–60; positions of activists in Los
Angeles, 123, 127–34; reasons for
party activism in Detroit, 105, 107
issue alignment perspectives: in
Chicago, 168; of activists in Los
Angeles, 138–44
issue positions. *See* ideology

Jackson, John S., 2–3
Johnson, Lyndon, 42

Kent, Frank R., 9
Key, V.O. Jr., 2, 40
Kurtzman, David H., 9

labor organizations, 28, 187
Leiserson, Avery, 2
"liberal" self-characterization, 127–32
local parties
—activity of, over time, 3–4
—adaptiveness of, 90